The Word that Kindles

The cover depicts an ancient Aztec ceremony. The Aztecs believed every 52 years the sun died. They extinguished all fires. The people waited in fear and darkness, offering human sacrifices. As the new sun arose, fire was kindled, and runners with torches rekindled the hearth fires, bringing light and life to each home. The mural depicts a man sitting dejectedly while his wife lifts her head and listens with wonder. It is the dawn of a new day and the kindling of new hope. The painting is taken from a 16 by 49 foot mural designed by K. Voigtlander, adorning the S.I.L. administrative center in Mexico City. Cover art by Alice Erath.

The Word that Kindles

GEORGE M. COWAN

P.O. Box 2727
Huntington Beach, CA 92647

Acknowledgments

This book would never have been possible if my colleagues had not shared so generously with me in so many ways reports of what God was doing in their lives and in the lives of the ethnic peoples among whom they live and labor.

My thanks to Valarie Sluss who typed the final copy, to Rosemary Chase who also helped, and especially to my wife, Florence, who not only lived with the book but typed all the preliminary drafts, proofread the final one and cheered me on.

Picture Credits

Cornell Capa: Nos. 1, 7, 8, 10, 16
Don Hesse: Nos. 4, 9, 13, 14, 17, 18
Bob Hills: No. 11
Don Horneman: No. 12
Ed Johnson: Nos. 2, 20
Paul Smith: No. 5
Hugh Steven: No. 24

Library of Congress Cataloging in Publication Data

Cowan, George M
  The word that kindles.
  1. Bible—Translating.   2. Linguistics.
3. Illiteracy.   4. Wycliffe Bible Translators.
5. Summer Institute of Linguistics.
BS449.C68   266'.023   78-64837
ISBN 0-915684-47-0

First Edition
CHRISTIAN HERALD BOOKS, 40 Overlook Drive,
Chappaqua, New York 10514
Printed in the United States of America

Contents

PART THREE: RELATIONSHIPS

Foreword

"Love God with all your ... mind. ..." That is not in Christ's last command but his *first—along with* heart and soul. Evangelicalism has been in danger here. And the work of the Summer Institute of Linguistics alongside that of the Wycliffe Bible Translators has helped to reinstitute the command in act and heart.

Translation theory is one variety of linguistics. Effective translation into languages not ours by birth needs the help which the science of linguistics can give. By "reverse lend-lease" the struggle to translate forces scholars to examine some principles of linguistics not clear to that academic community to whom we are so greatly indebted for teaching us earlier linguistics principles—from the Sanscrit grammarians of 500 B.C. and the Greeks to the moderns.

But why should Christians bother to translate the Scriptures? Why, indeed, except that we are to have in us the mind of Christ, who being in the form of God stooped to incarnate himself in a human body and a *human local dialect—* that of the fishermen of Galilee.

And we are to follow the pattern of the Holy Spirit who gave us the words of Christ in translation—in Greek, not the Aramaic of Galilee (except for a few phrases, such as the poignant heart throb of *"Eloi, Eloi, lama sabachthani?"*)

And we are to follow the pattern of the Father who speaks to our conscience in *our* vernacular.

But there are "human" considerations as well. Man's personal identity comes to fullness through expressing himself freely in his mother tongue. It is a *burden* for the poor and the uneducated to struggle with *any* other tongue. Should we deliberately force them to struggle to learn about Christ in our language simply because it is hard for *us* to learn their language? We are supposed to carry their burden—not make them carry ours. *This* was the mind of Christ.

In this book my friend and co-worker, George Cowan, describes the outworking of this view.

Kenneth L. Pike
President
Summer Institute of Linguistics

Preface

This book seeks to provide an answer to two basic questions. How can the Christian share his "Good News" in an effective way with people of other cultures without belittling them or making them dependent? And how can ethnic minorities be helped to survive the impact of encroaching civilization without loss of dignity or identity? Practical answers to these two questions have emerged from the program developed by the Summer Institute of Linguistics and the Wycliffe Bible Translators. It is a program based on linguistic research and the use of the mother tongue, a program emphasizing Bible translation, literacy, bilingual education and community development.

As of March 1984, over 5,057 members of the Wycliffe Bible Translators and the Summer Institute of Linguistics from 32 countries are at work in more than 728 minority languages of the world. Most of these languages had never been analyzed or written. Already more than 9,500 linguistic and literacy publications have appeared in or about 650 of these languages. Portions of the Bible have been published in about 725 of them, New Testaments in 207 more.

This book is an attempt to capture the dynamic and expound the policies and practices of the people involved in this worldwide movement. It is written to tell you, the reader, why we do what we do the way we do.

After reviewing the past and present of the movement, the book will describe three of its major activities: Bible translation, linguistic research and literacy. It will express three basic attitudes of the movement: service to all, dependence upon God and commitment to pioneering. And finally it will give the reader a picture of two types of relationship, the organizational and the interpersonal.

The book should help students and teachers of missionary methods, people involved in cross-cultural contacts with ethnic minorities, church people devoted to giving the Bible to all, those seeking a place of service with a group whose vision they share and whose policies they endorse, and everyone interested in what God is doing today through his Word in the lesser-known languages of the world.

A Mazatec widow wavered between spending her last few pennies for corn for herself and her hungry children or for a fresh portion of God's Word in her language. She had read portions of the Bible before. She knew it met a need in her own and her children's lives that corn tortillas did not. She chose the Book. She esteemed God's Word more than her (and her children's) necessary food.

That incident reaffirmed the conviction that we and minority peoples alike live by bread, but not by bread alone. For the author, that made the years of pioneer living as a member of the team that translated the New Testament for the Mazatec people of Mexico worthwhile.

1
In the Fullness of Time

BIBLE TRANSLATION is one index to the spread and establishment of the Christian faith. As the Christian message crosses language frontiers, translations of the Bible are needed. As Christian communities grow and become established, revisions and new translations need to be made. If a group of people have no translation of even a portion of the Bible, it is unlikely the Christian faith has made much if any impact.

Historical Perspective

The history of Bible translation can be divided into three periods. First, the Bible was translated into the languages of the ancient world, beginning with the Greek translation of the Old Testament in the third century B.C. Following the close of the New Testament canon, as Christianity spread, Syriac, Georgian, Coptic, Gothic, Slavic and Latin translations appeared. By the first half of the fifteenth century the Scriptures had been translated into thirty-three languages.

The second period began with the Renaissance and the Reformation and was marked by the translation of the Bible into the principal languages of Europe: English, German, French, Spanish, Portuguese, Czech and Hungarian. The invention of movable type, with its immediate application to the publication of Scripture, made the Bible more directly accessible to the common man as the final authority in matters of faith and practice. By the end of the eighteenth century the Bible had been translated into thirty-four more languages.

11

The third period began with the modern missionary era, following in the wake of the European explorers who opened up communications with the Americas, Asia and Africa. Missionaries made translations into scores of languages. They not only had to learn to speak hitherto unwritten languages but also to devise alphabets for them.

This period began with the monumental achievement of William Carey and the Serampore trio, who were instrumental in translating and publishing Scripture portions in thirty-four of the languages of India. The Bible society movement also arose at this time to reinforce the worldwide missionary effort by publishing and distributing the Scriptures. In the last 175 years the Bible has been translated into over 1,500 more languages, a third of them in the last twenty-five years.[1] Currently Scripture is being published in new languages for the first time on an average of one every fourteen days.

A significant factor in the impetus to Bible translation during the past thirty-five years has been the application of linguistic science to various aspects of the missionary task. As members of the Wycliffe Bible Translators and the Summer Institute of Linguistics, we have played a leading role in this development by making linguistics a part of missionary and translation training and focusing attention on those languages still needing translation. The United Bible Societies also have introduced linguistic insights to those translating and revising Scripture under their guidance.

The Contemporary Scene

Today Bible translation work is emphasizing the revision of existing translations, special translations to reach social and regional dialects, common language translations that bridge the range of social dialects, and pioneer translations for those in whose languages the Scripture is not available in any form. This last category comprises over 3,000 languages spoken by groups ranging in size from those that can be counted on the fingers to those numbering hundreds of thousands.[2] Together they represent only a small percentage of the world's population, but their need for the Bible is just as great as that of the others. The fact they speak a different language, usually still unwritten, and that many of them live in remote areas should not mean they cannot have the Book given for all mankind. Our efforts are being directed to helping provide the Bible for those who have never had it in their own language.

The need to translate the Bible into the remaining languages of the world is there. The ethnic minorities who speak these languages are being increasingly recognized, and their languages recorded and studied. What will they read? Nationalism has awakened their desire to have what others possess, but in a form that is indigenous, not foreign. This desire has led to requests for Bible translations. The acceptance of literateness as a cultural value has stimulated local authorship, encouraged higher education, and increased the number of those able to translate into their own language.

The growth of indigenous churches and the need to train leaders for these churches makes it imperative that they have the Scriptures in their own language. The renewed call in evangelical circles and congresses for the worldwide proclamation of the Gospel underlines the importance of the mother tongue for effective communication and the need for the Scriptures to declare the Good News fully and accurately. In the ideological battle for the minds and allegiance of people today, the Christian point of view needs the authority and demonstrated power of the Bible in the mother tongue.

Advances in linguistic methodology make it possible as never before to speed up and improve translation. Technological advances—aircraft and radio that make every ethnic group accessible, computers that greatly reduce the time involved in text editing and typesetting, and transistorized equipment that make recorded readings of Scripture available even to the illiterate—make previous excuses no longer valid and further delay inexcusable.

We are, of course, just as concerned as anyone about the rights of the ethnic minorities. Their languages are important not only to them but to the world. We are ready to train nationals in the skills we possess. The indigenous principle recognizes the right and ability of people to make their own decisions. Our policies and practices were established before some of these attitudes and points of view became popular. They may even, in fact, have contributed to their acceptance and diffusion.

William Cameron Townsend

While historically there are precedents for almost every aspect of the program, our policies and practices were not consciously patterned after them. They were developed when one man saw a need and met that need—and have been refined by others who caught the vision.

Breaking away from traditional missionary practices, William Cameron Townsend, our founder, saw a job that needed to be done and a way it could be done. Moving ahead vigorously and persistently, he translated for one language himself, then started two organizations to do the same for hundreds of others. Those of us who became associated with him in the work learned much from him and became increasingly convinced of the soundness of his approach. The work has far outgrown the direct influence of Townsend's personal presence and leadership, but the imprint of his convictions and way of doing things is everywhere apparent.

Townsend's career began in 1917 as a distributor of Spanish Bibles in Guatemala. Confronted with the need of the Cakchiquel people, the majority of whom could not read or understand Spanish, and impressed by their response to his Cakchiquel traveling companion who spoke to them in their own language, he was soon convinced that he would do far better by learning the Cakchiquel language and translating the Bible into it. Without special training, experienced teachers or written aids, he learned to speak Cakchiquel by living with the people and repeating words after them. Cakchiquel grammar baffled him, since it did not follow the pattern of English or Spanish. On the suggestion of an archeologist who told him each language has its own pattern, Townsend proceeded to describe Cakchiquel simply as he found it. He

14

developed his own method of teaching people to read their own language. Convinced that both the Bible and education were essential to the emancipation of the Indians from the virtual slavery in which they lived, he promoted schools, clinics and other practical community projects. Turning these projects over to others, he pushed ahead with the translation of the Bible. When unavoidable interruptions and involvement in local church and community activities brought his translation work to a standstill, he and his wife took two language helpers to the States and finished the New Testament there.

1. *W. Cameron Townsend speaking at Bible Translation Day ceremony, established by the U.S. Congress in 1967 for recognition each September 30.*

As a colporteur, Townsend found it important to get permission from the local authorities before distributing the Scriptures. This gave him an opportunity to witness to them, too. When an international congress of government officials met in a city close to the Indian community, the believers, at his suggestion, put on a special program for them. When the Cakchiquel New Testament was completed, he arranged a special presentation ceremony of the first copy to the president of Guatemala. In this way he gained the attention and approval of the government for the Cakchiquel work.

Deeply moved by the needs of tribespeople throughout Latin America and believing that the Cakchiquel, now with the Scriptures, could get along without him, Townsend decided to pioneer again. He considered Mexico as his next field of endeavor, but Mexico was closed to missionaries. After he made an exploratory trip in 1933, the way opened to enter Mexico as "a student of Indian languages." Writing articles to inform the American people of Mexico's aspirations and progress in rural education, he began a "Summer Training Camp for Prospective Bible Translators" on a small farm in Arkansas.

After the second summer session in 1935, the first contingent of workers went to Mexico. Soon after arrival, in keeping with their goal of linguistic research, the group participated in the Seventh Inter-American Scientific Congress. The following year Townsend submitted a report of his work to the American ambassador, who thought it would be of interest to the Mexican government. Before long a copy in Spanish was passed on to President Cardenas by the Secretary of Labor. Cardenas immediately made arrangements to visit the Townsends in the Aztec village where they were living. Impressed by their language work, the psycho-phonemic primers they had developed to teach the Aztecs to read, a vegetable garden to improve the people's diet, and the Townsends' desire to translate the Bible and serve the people in a non-sectarian, non-ecclesiastical way, the President assured them of his support and encouraged them to bring more workers to initiate similar projects in other tribes.

When in the same year, 1936, Townsend was asked to write a recommendation for a student who wished to go to Guatemala, he did it in the name of the "Summer Institute of Linguistics." Until this time, and indeed for some time after, he and his associates were commonly known in Mexico simply as "the Townsend group." The courses in the States, because of the rustic, rural setting, were referred to as "Camp Wycliffe." In 1937 Townsend asked Kenneth Pike, a promising phonetic student with a degree in theology, who had gone to Mexico but was back to teach in the summer courses, to take further linguistic studies at the University of Michigan.

In 1942 the summer course was invited to the University of Oklahoma campus. That fall, in order to facilitate arrangements with the university and the government of Mexico, Cameron Townsend, Kenneth Pike, Eugene A. Nida (who had joined the work in 1936 and now co-directed the courses with Pike) and William G. Nyman (a businessman who agreed to serve as secretary-treasurer) incorporated as the Summer Institute of Linguistics. At the same time they established another organization, the Wycliffe Bible Translators, Inc., to handle the receipting and transmission of funds, the recruiting of candidates, and relationships with supporting churches and the home constituency.

In 1943 Pike went to Peru at the request of the American Bible Society to help resolve alphabet problems in a translation it was publishing. Since Pike was now teaching part of each year at the University of Michigan, he was invited to give lectures at a university in Lima, through which he came in contact with government personnel concerned with Indian affairs. The result was an invitation from the government of Peru to Townsend to survey their jungle areas with a view to establishing a program similar to the one in Mexico. This resulted in a signed agreement in 1945 between the Summer Institute of Linguistics and the Ministry of Education in Peru, establishing a linguistic and translation program for Peru's ethnic groups east of the Andes. To prepare workers for the rigors of life in Amazonia, a jungle training camp was started in southern Mexico. In 1946, twenty-five jungle-trained S.I.L. field workers arrived in Peru and a center of operations was established in the eastern Peruvian jungle.

For workers to be able to live with their families in remote jungle villages, aircraft and radio services were imperative. When Townsend and his family were injured in a commercial plane accident as they flew out of Mexico's jungle camp, he realized the organization must have its own dedicated pilots and well-maintained equipment to provide safe and adequate transportation. This Jungle Aviation and Radio Service would also serve the government and all others working in the jungle. As a means of building international goodwill, Townsend suggested in 1951 that the government and people of Mexico donate a Catalina PBY to Peru. They did. The plane was designated for use in Peru's eastern jungles. Townsend offered the services of the Institute's pilots and mechanics to operate it for the Peruvian government.

To teach the Indians to read both their own and the national language and to train them as teachers and leaders for their own communities, Townsend in 1952 worked out with the Peruvian Minister of Education a system of bilingual education and community development. He offered the Institute's facilities in the jungle for the training course for Indian teachers. Members of the Institute served as tutors in the Indian languages under the Spanish-speaking Peruvian administrators and professors. A committee of high ranking Peruvians was formed to sponsor the work of the Institute in the country and to help make it known to the people in general. The government accepted the Institute's offer to serve. The formal agreements which resulted led to the importation of equipment and made office space at the ministry building available. In 1953, the government provided land in Lima on which the Institute built a group house. The understanding was that when the work was done the Institute would leave and the house would be turned over to the government.

The whole range of precedents set by Townsend became a familiar pattern as doors opened to other countries in the

18

Americas, Asia, the South Pacific and Africa. Interest spread and recruits and support came from the Christian constituencies in countries around the world. Additional Summer Institute of Linguistic courses were developed to train the workers. Jungle Aviation and Radio Service operations were also expanded to meet the need. In the chapters to follow we will consider the people and principles which, beginning with Townsend, have given and continue to give the work its distinctive character.[3]

PART ONE
ACTIVITIES

Bible translation (Chapters 2,3), linguistics (4,5) and literacy (6,7) are the three major activities of the program of the Wycliffe Bible Translators and the Summer Institute of Linguistics. They go together and are essential to each other.

2

Bible Translation

"HAVE YOU read your Bible today?" ran the poster in front of the church in an African village. For eighty percent of the members the answer had to be "No." Not because they did not want to read it, but because there was no Bible in their language and they did not understand any other. For the other twenty percent the only Bible they knew was in a trade language they used for business with outsiders, seldom if ever for communication with one another, and never in matters of the heart.

In spite of all that has been done and is being done by others, many culturally distinct groups of people still do not have the Scriptures in their own language. We are convinced that pioneer translation of the Bible constitutes a need of the highest priority. Members of the Wycliffe Bible Translators and the Summer Institute of Linguistics seek to forward in every way possible the translation of the Bible into all the languages of the world where it is needed. This is our deepest and most pervasive motivation.

With the exception of those accepted as support personnel, members are assigned to learn and analyze specific languages, with a view to translating the Bible. To avoid duplication or overlapping of effort, translators are not sent where usable translations of the Scripture already exist or where others are translating or planning to translate. We are not involved in the revision of the translation of others, except when invited to help. We also encourage and help others translate the Bible, including some who are translating it into their own mother tongue.

Why the Emphasis on the Bible?

We emphasize the Bible for three reasons: because it is God's Word, because it meets the needs of people, and because it is implicit in Christ's Great Commission.

First, the Bible is God's Word to mankind, not merely people's ideas about God. God has revealed his power and glory by his workmanship in nature, his providence and justice in his acts in history, and his essential being and character in the person of Jesus Christ. The Bible is God's record and explanation of these things. Without the Bible, the revelation of God in nature and history is inadequate and may be misunderstood. Apart from the Bible there is no reliable source of information concerning the person and purpose of Jesus Christ. But God, by the operation of his Spirit in the writers of the Old and New Testaments, said what he wanted us to know. What they wrote has the viewpoint of revelation, the authority of inspiration, and the reliability of inerrant omniscience. The Bible is God's statement of truth, to be believed; his message to all mankind, to be delivered; and his standard of conduct, to be lived.

Although given through specific people at specific times in specific languages in terms of specific cultures, the Bible is by its own statement God's truth for all people everywhere through all time and of every culture (Matt. 28:19; Mark 16:15, Matt. 24:35). Since the Bible is God's message to all mankind, every person has a right to access to this source of knowledge about God. Regardless of what other sources of knowledge he may have, each person on this globe ought at least to have the opportunity to know what God has said to him and what God requires of him. He needs to know that his own being, dignity and destiny derive from God.

"If your God is so great, how is it that he doesn't speak my language?" These words from a Guatemalan Indian made a Bible translator out of Cameron Townsend. A Bible colporteur in West Africa, quoted by David Barrett, was shaken by the question, "Why do you hate my people? You have books for others but none for me." Barrett goes on to state that the refusal of missionaries to translate into the vernacular has been construed as an attempt to withhold the Word of God and keep the people dependent and in ignorance.[1] If God has spoken and his Word is for all mankind, Bible translation is not a luxury. It is a necessity and must have top priority. We have no right to withhold it.

Second, the Bible can meet the spiritual needs of people everywhere. As the Word of God it is powerful and works in the lives of those responding to it (Heb. 4:12; Isa. 55:10, 11). Those who accept its statements concerning the person of whom it speaks find their lives transformed.

The wife of the translator's language helper among the Cotabato Manobo*was demon possessed. Her eyes were full of hate and terror. Her body jerked and betel nut juice dribbled down her chin. She gnawed at the cloth covering her tortured body. The day she broke into the translators' home it took seven men to capture and tie her down. Her language was foul, her laughter loud and mirthless. One day the translator's wife asked, "What can I do for her, Lord?"

A strong impression came to mind, "Read her the Scriptures."

"Just *read* to her? What good will that do?" she thought.

But armed with the Gospel of Luke, she obeyed and went to the woman's hut next door. "Would you like me to read you God's Word?" she asked. The woman nodded. On two other occasions she read to her. The response each time was a belligerent stare.

After four months away, the translators returned to discover the woman was telling everyone that Jesus had healed her. The translator's wife asked her, "When did you begin to be healed?"

"When you began to read God's Word to me," she answered.

One of the commonest reasons given by our members for why we want to give others the Bible is "because of what it did in my own life." As beneficiaries ourselves we seek to share (often in the face of opposition from much in our culture) what has met our need with others with similar needs in other cultures.

A translation team had been working among the 3,000 Satare for fifteen years when finally the Gospel of Mark was published. Nearly everyone who read that book became a believer—over one hundred in three years. They were not wishy-washy believers either. They stood up against immorality and idol worship and were Christians to the core. Then one of the leading believers struck his wife. She went home to her mother and he took off downstream. With a heavy heart the translator typed out the parts of Titus which tell of the qualities expected of a Christian leader and wrote the husband. "You couldn't be expected to know these things," he said. "But you can't live this way any more."

When the man read the letter, he wept, then returned to his wife. Together they asked the local church to forgive them.

Not that the Bible is a panacea with ready-made solutions for all problems. But it does offer a solution to every person's basic spiritual need which, once met, gives a moral basis and spiritual resources for tackling personal and social problems.

"Man does not live on bread alone, but on every word that comes from the mouth of the Lord" (Deut. 8:3 NIV). Any program that fails to provide for a person's spiritual need falls short of providing for the whole person and can at best have only limited results. The "new man" is not the end product but the prerequisite for Christian living, the foundation on which all else is built. The Bible is the *only* book we know of that shows how this is brought about—by coming into a personal relationship with God through Jesus Christ. For this reason we emphasize the translation of the Bible as an integral part of our total program. We feel that the Bible is absolutely basic to its success.

Third, Christ's command to his followers to make disciples of all nations included "teaching them to obey everything I have commanded you" (Matt. 28:20). The Bible alone preserves what Christ commanded his disciples. He pointed them to the Old Testament Scriptures (Luke 24:25, 26) and pre-authenticated the New Testament Scriptures (John 14:26, 15:26, 27; 16:13-15). The Apostles, in their proclamation of the Good News, made clear that becoming a follower of Jesus Christ involved a commitment to obey the Scriptures (Romans 16:26). Implicit is the assumption that the biblical text would be available. Translation of the Bible is part of our obedience to his command.

When some of the members of the Society in Scotland for Propagating Christian Knowledge opposed the idea of translating the Scriptures into Gaelic, Dr. Samuel Johnson wrote indignantly: "If obedience to the will of God be necessary to happiness, and knowledge of his will be necessary to obedience, I know not how he that withholds this knowledge, or delays it, can be said to love his neighbor ... To omit for a year, or for a day, the most efficacious method of advancing Christianity ... is a crime. ..."[2]

Why Just the Bible?

Jesus Christ sharply distinguished between the Old Testament documents and the teaching of men in elaboration and explanation of them, whether oral or written. The traditions of the elders were "traditions of men" and all too often "broke" or "nullified" the Word of God (Mark 7:6-8; Matt. 15:3, 6, 9). They were by no means to be equated with Scripture. At the same time Christ "placed his own teaching alongside the Word of God as an authoritative commentary, which he handed down to his disciples"[3] (Matt. 5:22, 28). As the Messiah, he spoke with divine authority and not as the scribes (Matt. 7:28, 29). His contemporaries recognized this. His followers also distinguished human tradition and the teaching of Christ (Col. 2:8). "Apostolic tradition" (which included eye-witness as well as revealed truth) "was at one time oral, but for us it is crystallized in the apostolic writings containing the Spirit-guided witness to the Christ of God."[4] The written documents of the New Testament, even before the close of the canon, were recognized as the inspired, authoritative Word of God alongside the Old Testament documents and distinct from other human traditions.

This is why we of the Wycliffe Bible Translators have chosen to put the highest priority on the translation of the Bible and not on books about the Bible. In certain situations we do provide non-interpretive materials on the cultural background of the Bible. But we agree with Lane that "other teaching, while it may be instructive and useful and worthy of serious consideration, cannot claim to be placed alongside

27

the Old and New Testaments as authoritative without manifesting the same defects as condemned Jewish tradition in the eyes of the Lord."[5] And the twentieth-century Christian has shown no less tendency to impose interpretations on the Scriptures than the ancient scribes and elders. Where possible, people should read the Bible itself, first, then other books about the Bible as may prove helpful.

We do not subscribe to the view that the spiritual truths of the Bible are beyond the capacity of uneducated people to understand. Cultural differences and lack of general biblical background may limit or delay full understanding of some parts of the Bible. But faith in Christ and a commitment to know and do his will as enabled by the Holy Spirit, based on the reading of the Bible for oneself, will produce more spiritual insight, growth and stability than any amount of supplementary materials. This is not to deny or belittle the general need for education or the value of theological training, so long as these do not take the place of Bible reading itself.

Limiting ourselves to translation of the Bible also helps us avoid promoting individual or sectarian points of view and minimizes foreign interpretations and applications. Readers are encouraged to learn from the Word of God itself, and to trust the same Holy Spirit who inspired the Scriptures to guide them in applying it to their own way of life. The decisions made should be their own, based on what God said and not on what other people, including the translator, say or do. Their faith and life should be based on the Word of God, not on man-made restatements or summaries of it.

Why the Emphasis on the Written Documents?

Our Christian faith is based on a Savior described in written documents. The writings of the Old and New Testaments place great emphasis upon their written state. The fact they were written and the reasons why they were written are still valid grounds for giving people the Bible today in written form.

Writing was the medium God chose for preserving and transmitting the truth revealed by and concerning himself.

28

He generally spoke but at least once he wrote (Exod. 31:18). However, he often commanded those to whom he spoke to write what he said to them (Exod. 17:14). By his Spirit he personally participated in the writing process so that the result was not simply their words but his (2 Tim. 3:16; 2 Pet. 1:21). The written word was not only considered a record of what God had said but was considered to be God still speaking (Matt. 22:31). To present the message of Jesus Christ without the documents on which it is based is to leave the hearer one step removed from the ultimate basis of faith, dependent upon the messenger's integrity and accuracy, and without direct access to the intermediary's sources. It is the difference between "God says . . ." and "So-and-so says that God said . . . ." Faith in God should be based on God's integrity, not on any person's reliability.

Reasons are given in the Bible why it was *written*. These are not peculiar to the Bible but apply to writing in general.

Writing Gives Permanence

Writing gives a message permanence far beyond the spoken word and the human capacity to recall. Moses wrote the book of the covenant and delivered the written copy to the priests and elders in order that it might be preserved, read to all the people every seven years at least, and used to teach each succeeding generation of children (Deut. 31:9-13). "For transmission of anything important to posterity the Ancient Orient insistently resorted to written rather than oral transmission."[6] God's command to Moses to write the law was not an innovation. It was the custom of the time for all important documents. Even though the written documents were lost and forgotten for a time, when rediscovered and reexamined, as in Isaiah's day (2 Kings 22:8ff.), they carried the same message and served to reestablish the truth in practice.

When Jesus prayed for those who would believe in him through the word of his disciples, he may well have been referring to the New Testament documents they would write which would preserve and make available to generations still to come the record of his life, death, resurrection and teaching (John 17:20). Nothing of what God said, of what the prophets and apostles said, or of what Christ said remains today, except what was written.

Because the Bible was written it is still available today and speaks with the same authority to all who will listen. John Wycliffe (1319-1384) wrote: "Worde and wyne and mannes mynde is ful schort, but letter writen dwelleth." Or, as one Mazatec of Mexico said, "One doesn't forget when it is written." We are simply passing it on as we have received it, in written form, so our generation and generations still to come will have it, too.

Writing Facilitates Distribution

Writing makes possible the multiplication and distribution of the message. The mass of cuneiform tablets, ostraca and papyri already found show the prominent place the written document had through the Ancient Near East (Eccl. 12:12). Copying of written documents was common, both for private use and for multiple distribution, even in Old Testament times (Deut. 17:18; 2 Chron. 30:1-6). The wide distribution of the written Scriptures in the history of the church since the first century is well-attested by the number still existing. The invention of movable type made more copies available faster, more accurately, and at greatly reduced cost per copy. Even limited editions for small groups are not prohibitive. The Bible in written form has reached and continues to reach many who have no opportunity to hear by word of mouth.

On the other hand, a single written copy, read aloud, gives further distribution of the written message to those who do not possess a copy themselves or are unable to read. In Bible times distribution of the Scriptures was limited, due to the fact that copies were handmade and expensive.[7] Public reading to listening audiences was common and commanded by God (Deut. 31:11; 1 Tim. 4:13; Rev. 1:3). Churches were to exchange and share copies (Col. 4:16). Today the Bible can be read to widely dispersed listeners by way of radio, television and cassette players.

From the beginning God has used both spoken and written media, but once the message was written, the spoken word was to be based on it. Oral proclamation is thus to be an extension of the written, not a substitute for it. When Marshall McLuhan announced that we had moved out of the age of Gutenberg into the age of television "he had to write a book to declare (it) and thereby ruined his point."[8] Christ based his oral ministry on the Old Testament documents and the church did likewise. It also included the New Testament documents as they were written.

Writing Demands Accuracy

Writing demands an accuracy and reliability that the spoken word may lack. What is written can be tested for accuracy and truthfulness. Writing makes one vulnerable in a way that speaking does not.

This is especially true when the speaker predicts future events, as the prophets frequently did. One of the proofs that a prophet was a true prophet and spoke from God was the fulfillment of his predictions (Deut. 18:21, 22). Some predicted events took place while the prophet and hearers were still around to bear witness to the fulfillment. In some cases God even ordered such prophecies written, made a matter of public record with witnesses, so that the fulfillment would be incontrovertible when it occured (Isa. 8:1-4).

But where a prophet's message was for a longer time, it was doubly important that it be written. Its moral and spiritual message could thus be passed to succeeding generations. And the prophet's truthfulness, divine authority and reliability could be established by the fulfillment of the predictions, even after the prophet and his contemporaries were dead (Isa. 30:8; Jer. 30:2; Hab. 2:2, 3). Verification would have to be made by those who witnessed the fulfillment (Dan. 9:2). Meanwhile its implications for the prophet's own generation would have to be taken by faith. But for those who witnessed the fulfillment and for succeeding generations it would establish beyond any shadow of doubt the veracity and reliability of the prophet's word. In order that the

31

original prediction would be on hand to compare with the fulfillment it must be written. The historical, self-authenticating character of divine revelation and of the Bible as the Word of God is made possible by the fact that we have it in written form.

Jesus Christ and the New Testament writers underscored the reliability of the Old Testament documents in their frequent reference to and quotations from them. The statement that "this fulfilled that" (over 30 times) gave eloquent testimony that true prophecy and historic fulfillment were both from God. Thus the New Testament writers in their turn recorded the statements of prophecy and the historic fulfillment concerning Jesus Christ, "that you may believe that Jesus is the Christ, the Son of God, and that by believing you may have life in his name" (John 20:31).

At the beginning of his Gospel, Luke states that the reason he wrote was so that Theophilus might know the reliability of the things he had already been taught by word of mouth (Luke 1:1-4). Many had previously undertaken to set forth an orderly statement of the things believed by Christians, based on the testimony of eyewitnesses. Luke was aware of these accounts but he also knew that writing preserves facts more faithfully than oral tradition. If the writing is based on careful investigation and research, and the accuracy and adequacy of the statements made are carefully weighed and checked against all the evidence, as Luke states he had done, then what may already have been learned by word of mouth has an added reliability and certainty that only such a document can give. In addition, the document itself remains, its statements open to further verification or challenge as further information comes to light. Luke's writings and his reliability as a historian have only been enhanced by every attempt to disprove them.

It is not enough that people be told the Bible is reliable. They must have it for themselves to get the full impact of its self-authentication as the Word of God. It is for this reason we are committed to providing the Bible in written form for all who do not have it.

In addition, the reliability of any translation can be checked against the Hebrew or Greek texts.

The accuracy of the spoken message can be tested by the written statements of Scripture. A true prophet's message had to agree with previously revealed and recorded truth. "To the law and to the testimony! If they do not speak according to this word, they have no light of dawn" (Isa. 8:20). The New Testament writers emphatically state that the written record provides the content of teaching, the basis for correction and reproof of error, and is not to be added to nor taken from (2 Tim. 3:14-4:2; Rev. 22:18, 19). Written while there were still many eyewitnesses alive to vouch for or deny the facts, the New Testament canon was recognized by the early church to be what it claimed to be, the inspired Word of God, reliable and of equal authority with the Old Testament.

There are many voices vying for the attention of people today, and the ethnic minorities cannot possibly remain for long unaffected. Providing them with the written text of Scripture is of the highest priority. It will give them a basis for deciding whether what they hear or read is true to the Word of God. This they must be able to do for themselves, and not be dependent on any other man's judgment, based as it may be on his slanted interpretation of the Word of God.[9]

Writing Adds Importance

Committing a message to writing adds importance to what is said. The translators asked one of the Walmatjari of Western Australia several times to make some boomerangs for them. But he never seemd to get around to doing it. Finally one of them, absent in the city of Darwin, wrote him in his Walmatjari language, repeating the request. Immediately, with bag slung over his shoulder and axe in hand, he set off to chop the wood for the boomerangs. A request in writing somehow demanded action that a mere verbal request did not. Those squiggles on paper in the Walmatjari language were not only meaningful but important.

The very fact that God commanded his words to be written indicates that they are important, and not to be forgotten or neglected. When the tablets of the law were broken, they were ordered rewritten (Exod. 34:1); when

Jeremiah's prophecy was burned, God commanded it to be written again (Jer. 36:27, 28). The importance of a written document was also enhanced by the rank and authority of those issuing or agreeing to the statements by signature or seal (Neh. 9:38; 10:1 ff.); the material on which it was written (Exod. 31:18; but see John 8:6, 8); the location and visibility given the writing (Josh. 8:30-32; John 19:19, 20); and the care with which the document was to be preserved (Deut. 10:5). Orders and warnings given verbally, then put in writing, were to be taken seriously (Isa. 30:8-11). A written, verbatim copy powerfully reenforced a verbal summary (Esth. 4:7, 8). People could be held responsible for how they read what was written in the same way and to the same degree as those to whom it was originally spoken (Luke 10:26).

We believe the message of the Bible is the most important message any people can possess. Putting it in writing helps give it the importance it merits. It also helps the people realize they are important to the One who gave the message. It contributes to their own self-esteem. For those whose language has not been written before, it is convincing proof that their language can be written, is adequate to convey such concepts and is not inferior to other languages which already have books. For those who accept it as a way of life, it provides a tangible and lasting basis for their faith and obedience. They have the full text of the message as originally given, not just parts or someone else's digest of it. They can read it for themselves and make their own decisions and applications.

Writing and Progressive Revelation

The fact that God's Word was written contributed considerably to the progressive character of revelation. God's revelation was given over centuries of time and to widely separated generations of people. Instead of starting over again with each new generation, God built on what was already written and added to it. Revelation was progressive, not through falsehood to truth, but from a less to a more complete unfolding of truth. The latter transcended the former as fulfillment does promise. What God said through Moses was added to in what he said through the prophets. What he said through both was fulfilled and surpassed in Christ (Heb. 1:1, 2). The church as one body including both Jews and Gentiles was a revelation "not made known to men in other generations as it has now been revealed by the Spirit to God's holy apostles and prophets" (Eph. 3:5).

Christ on "It is Written"

The highest indication of the importance of the Scriptures however is Christ's constant reference to, and personal subordination to what was written. He accorded the Old Testament Scriptures the full authority of God himself. The Apostles and New Testament writers likewise emphasized the importance of what was written.

Christ considered the writings of Moses and the Prophets as more important than miracles. "If they do not listen to Moses and the Prophets, they will not be convinced even if someone rises from the dead" (Luke 16:31). Christ thus taught that the writings are sufficient. The person who will not be convinced by Scripture will not be persuaded by a miracle. Christ's raising of Lazarus and Christ's own resurrection did not convince those who opposed the Old Testament's teaching. Miracles are easily misinterpreted unless Scripture shows that they are a purposeful part of the revelation and activity of God. Christ himself said the Bible is more important to people than "signs" and "miracles."

Christ considered the testimony of Scripture more basic than eyewitness experience. After his resurrection Christ showed the disciples his hands and feet, and invited them to touch him and see for themselves, but "they still did not believe . . . because of joy and amazement" (Luke 24:41). He gave still more evidence, eating fish before them. Finally, "he opened their minds so they could understand the Scriptures" (v. 45). Seen in the light of the written, prophetic word, experience made sense and had validity. Peter got the point, for preaching later to the ones who had delivered

Christ to death, he did not base his witness of Christ's resurrection as much on his own eyewitness experience as on the testimony of Old Testament Scripture (Acts 2:24-32). Later, he wrote that the Prophets foretold the sufferings and glory of Christ for the specific benefit of the Apostles' generation, which then bore testimony to the events it had seen fulfilled (1 Pet. 1:12; 5:1). The writings, thus made "more certain," were to be heeded, including the New Testament books already in existence (2 Pet. 1:16-21; 3:15, 16). The authority and accuracy of the New Testament documents were not based on the reliability of the eyewitness character of the sources but on the operation of the promised Holy Spirit, who reminded the writers of everything Christ had said and done (John 14:26). The documents were written to be the solid basis of faith (John 20:31; 21:24), and such faith, Christ reminded Thomas, was in no way less well founded than seeing with one's own eyes (John 20:29).

A person's faith in Jesus Christ should be based on the biblical record rather than solely on one's own or another's experience, whenever possible.

Christ, in fact, considered the writings of the Old Testament a basis for his own credibility. Christ's witness concerning himself, the miracles he performed, John the Baptist's testimony concerning him, all had been refused by the Jews. Finally, he turned to the Old Testament writings. Christ equated what Moses wrote with what God had said. The Jews said they also did. They prided themselves on being followers of Moses. But Moses wrote of Christ and now they were refusing to accept him as the one Moses wrote about. He said to them, "If you believed Moses, you would believe me, for he wrote about me. But since you do not believe what he wrote, how are you going to believe what I say?" (John 5:46, 47). Their attitude to the Scriptures had predetermined their attitude toward Christ. If they did not believe what Moses wrote about him (which they could check for themselves), then they certainly would not believe his statements about himself, which they must accept on his word alone.

Christ said his incarnation was not self-explanatory. God gave him words of explanation as to who he was and why he came, and he in turn gave them to his disciples (John 17:8). The New Testament writers incorporated these words into the written record under the guidance of the Holy Spirit. Faith in Christ today, as much if not more than then, needs this written explanation of who Christ really is (John 20:31). Since Christ accepted the Scriptures as God's Word and accorded them the place of ultimate authority concerning himself, we believe all people ought to have the opportunity to know and trust him on the basis of the biblical record itself.

The Holy Spirit and the Scriptures

Instrumental in the writing of both the Old and the New Testament, the Holy Spirit witnesses now primarily in and through the Scriptures. The Scriptures, in turn, are the basis of testing what are true and what are spurious manifestations and experiences attributed to the Holy Spirit.

The ministries ascribed to the Holy Spirit are often said to be the ministries of the written Word. In the Old Testament the law of the Lord is described as "reviving the soul," "making wise the simple," "giving joy to the heart," and "giving light to the eyes" (Psalm 19:7, 8). According to the New Testament the Scriptures testify and bear witness to Christ (John 5:39), "make . . . wise for salvation through faith in Christ Jesus" and are "useful for teaching, rebuking, correcting and training in righteousness, so that the man of God may be thoroughly equipped for every good work" (2 Tim. 3:15-17). They are the basis for testing the truthfulness of what is read or heard (Luke 1:4; Acts 17:11). They are our defense against error and Satan's lies, and are the corrective for the misuse of Scripture (Matt. 22:29; Matt. 4:1-4; Acts 20:29, 32). The Scriptures warn and admonish (1 Cor. 10:11) and encourage and comfort (Rom. 15:4; 1 Thess. 4:18).

These are also ministries of the Holy Spirit. The Spirit and the Scriptures work together. The witness of the disciples in the power of the Holy Spirit (Acts 1:8) was to be the witness of Scripture.

The work of the Holy Spirit in and through the people for whom we translate, while not limited to the written Word, is more effective when the Scriptures are available and used.

Rita, a Balangao believer, decided to quit reading the Scriptures. She said that every time she read the Word, it showed some defect or sin in her life. When she discovered that the Scriptures, like a mirror, showed her these things so she could get rid of them, she resumed her reading. Now the light of the Word of God was medicine, not condemnation.

To free men and women from evil spirits and distinguish between false and true manifestations of the Holy Spirit, the written Word of God is important. Witnessing and preaching in the power of the Spirit have an added authority, truthfulness and fullness when based upon the Scriptures.

3

Lack and Lag

SOMETIMES WE forget that the Bible has been around for 2,000 years. We've grown accustomed to having it. Ethnic peoples that hear about it for the first time are not so blasé. A Casiguran Dumagat language helper, after hearing the story of Christ's life, asked, "How long ago was it that Jesus was crucified?" When the translator told him it happened almost 2,000 years ago he said, "And not until this year are we hearing about it!"

As of the end of December 1983 at least a portion of the Bible has been translated into 1,785 languages. Millions of people speak these languages. Many of them possess and can read portions of the Word of God when they choose. Some have many versions, but many are seldom if ever read.

But at least 3,000 other languages spoken in our world today still lack any part of the Scriptures. In some of these language groups believers and churches exist, but without any Scripture in their own language. Translation of the Bible lags far behind the proclamation of the Gospel.

Using interpreters William Wade Harris preached and baptized 100,000 people along the coast of West Africa. When they asked him how they would be instructed after he was gone, he replied, "Wait for the white man who will bring you the Bible and teach you how to read it." That was in 1913. Most of those groups which accepted his teaching are still without the Word in their own language.

Some of those who have only recently tasted of the knowledge of God in the Bible remind us of the need and the urgency to provide it for still others. A Piro believer wrote, "My brothers in Jesus, I greet you. I also have received Jesus and have translated the New Testament. I think of my father who is dead. He kept searching for God's Word. He went where there was a vine called *ayahuasca,* which was said to cause one to see God. He pressed out its juice and drank it, because he wanted to see God.

"Can it be that you think that the people of this land know God? They do not know him. Some of them make any kind of a thing their God.

"I am sad because of those who live around me, those who speak other languages, those who need to hear about Jesus. They cry in their souls. There are many who do not understand the Spanish language.

"You who first and for a long time have had the message of God, help us."

Why is there this lack of translations of the Bible? Why is there a lag in translating it? Sometimes it is because of our attitudes toward the Bible and the communication of spiritual truth. Certainly those with a low view of the Bible are not going to give its translation priority. Even those with a high view of Scripture often place their emphasis on preaching to the neglect of translation, evangelism to the neglect of nurture, training an elite leadership rather than a literate membership, denominationally oriented literature about the Bible rather than the text of the Bible itself.

Language problems have kept others from translating. Trade languages are often used by expatriates in preference to the mother tongue of the people to whom they minister. Learning additional languages without any of the usual helps is not easy. If the Bible is already in the trade language, it is often assumed that those who can read it understand what they read. Often this is not the case. Lack of training and technical know-how to determine an alphabet for a previously unwritten language have deterred many. Difficulties in finding equivalent words for important biblical concepts have led some to believe the languages were deficient and not adequate for a translation of the Bible. The possibility of educated speakers of a mother tongue being freed from

40

other duties to get the training and do the translation has all too often never been seriously considered.

Most astonishing of all is the silence of missionary literature in general and text books on missions in particular about the need for Bible translation. Missionaries were expected to teach the Bible, but the question of its availability in the language of the people taught was seldom raised. Bible translation, if mentioned at all, was not emphasized in recruitment, training or assignment of mission personnel. Missions themselves were not structured to promote it. A highly motivated missionary might request permission to translate, but had to do it in addition to other duties. For many missionaries, Bible translation came only at the end of their missionary career when retirement gave them time, if at all.

By focusing attention on this one basic aspect of the church's witness to the world, we seek to stimulate a new sense of responsibility and priority in Christians everywhere—to provide the Scriptures for those who have never had them. By providing training and a field methodology geared specifically to this one task, we hope to encourage many more to become involved in doing it, including citizens of the Third World who are members of the younger churches in their own countries. By concentrating on the languages having nothing in writing, and in which no one else is translating, we seek to supplement the work of others until the initial Bible translation is done for all the languages of the world.

Once it was known that a group of people specializing in Bible translation was offering training for the task and sending out workers to give this top priority, many responded by applying to work with us. Some missions requested help or sent their own personnel for training. Ethnic groups, hearing of Bible translation possibilities, requested someone be sent to translate for them or to help them translate. Governments, seeing in the program a positive contribution to their literacy and community development efforts on behalf of their ethnic minorities, extended invitations or welcomed our offers of service.

2. *Dedication of the Hixkaryana New Testament, Brazil.*

The Bible is the greatest contribution we can make to any people or culture. We give it top priority. Our goal is a translation of at least the New Testament "as soon as practically and technically possible." Once our language analysis is well under way, an alphabet tested and approved, and our speaking proficiency in the language adequate for discussion of the problems involved, we begin translating. First attempts are very tentative, but one learns to translate by translating. Putting the emphasis from the beginning on the Bible and on having it available as soon as possible has many advantages.

Advantages to Early Translation of the Bible

The Bible is recognized as a literary and religious classic. It transcends nationalism, denominationalism, ethnocentrism; it is of general interest. Even non-Christian leaders may allow translation of the Bible because they recognize it as a book of high moral value and cultural interest.

Translation of the Bible is more impersonal and noncoercive than other religious activity. The individual to whom it is offered decides whether or not he will read it and follow its precepts. It can be read privately or publicly, and at any convenient time and pace. It is much less threatening to the timid or fearful.

By emphasizing the Bible as the Word of God, the translator can make it clear from the beginning that he is only a temporary go-between. Early availability of translated Scripture makes it possible for faith to be based on God's Word, not just the translator's word. This lessens the likelihood of the translator becoming the authority figure. And since the God of the Bible is the God of all men, he is not just "the foreigner's God." Candoshi chief Tariri considered the Gospel "just women's words" and to be retold as such. When he learned it came from a book which was God's Word he began to take it seriously, obey it and pass it on to others as authoritative.

By making the text of Scripture the object of study, the reader or listener has the thrill of personal discovery of spiritual truth under the guidance of the Holy Spirit, independent of the translator. Finding it himself makes it mean much more and stick much longer than having it spoonfed by someone else. Another person's summary of the messages of Moses, David, Isaiah, Paul or Christ is often helpful to those lacking biblical background but still second best to reading them directly for oneself.

The full gamut of spiritual truth in each passage is available in a translation. The reader may get insights that the translator himself never responded to, and may see implications for his own culture that the translator would never sense and applications he would never make.

If the Scriptures are available early enough, individual young believers and the local group may be taught to feed themselves and make their own decisions concerning forms of worship and conduct appropriate to Christians in their culture. Otherwise they may end up mimicking the foreigner's form of worship and adopting his standards of conduct.

As the people are directed to the Scriptures to find answers to questions that arise and principles for making decisions, those of spiritual discernment and maturity become

43

apparent and leadership develops. One reason for the scarcity of spiritually gifted people for church leadership may be the lack of translated Scriptures as the soil in which such ministries grow. Qualifications for leadership in any given culture are often quite different from those given in the Bible. Since the Bible states the qualifications for spiritual leaders, the local believers, once they have the Bible, are in a position to recognize and can be encouraged to choose as their spiritual leaders those who meet the biblical standards.

3. *"When your words came, I ate them; they were my joy and my heart's delight." Jer. 15:16*

The local leaders' ability to assess the character of their own people became apparent among the Tzeltal, when a large number presented themselves for baptism. The leaders of the church invited an ordained Mexican pastor from the nearest town to perform the ceremony. But before he proceeded, the leaders of the church examined each candidate carefully. Out of over a hundred candidates, about one-third were asked to wait until they had further instruction and the elders were satisfied they understood fully what the ordinance signified.

A genuinely indigenous church must have the Bible. The Holy Spirit and the Scriptures were all the early church had and needed. The imposition of already highly developed Christian forms and standards from foreign communities or more developed cultures is not necessary or wise. Once the church has developed its own leadership and patterns of Christian life and worship, leaders who have proved themselves, are recommended by the church, and feel the need of further training should get it. If such training is only available abroad, the fact that they already have the Bible in their own language and have already developed their own forms of worship will help them distinguish what is foreign and what is biblical in their training abroad.

Another advantage of having the Bible is that it provides its own motivation for outreach to others. The command of Christ to go into all the world and preach the Gospel, when read in one's own Bible, has compelling power. This sense of being called and sent by God, rather than acting in obedience to some person, and especially a foreigner, even the one who may have led you to Christ, is convincing evidence that the translation of the Bible is crucial to the completion of the Great Commission.

One day a translator in the Philippines met a group of believers on the trail and asked them where they were going. They replied that they were going to witness in a distant village. "Who sent you?" he asked. "Why does someone have to send us? Doesn't God's Word say that we are to go and preach the Gospel to every creature?" was their reply.

Bible translation is also a common ground on which Christians of different denominations and views can fellowship and work together. We ourselves come from widely different church backgrounds. Our common life in Jesus Christ, our common commitment to the Bible as the Word of God, and our common calling to share it with others in its written form unite us in a genuine fellowship as well as in a Bible translating task force. On the field, missions and churches in the same language area that have not previously worked together often do so on a project to provide the Scriptures.

An emphasis on early translation gives the testimony of the translators and the local believers an authority and authenticity it would not otherwise have. The translator is himself a recipient of the grace of God, not its dispenser.

Futhermore, listeners can check in their own Bibles to see if what the translator says is true (Acts 17:11). The translator must submit his own spoken witness and teaching to the test of vernacular Scripture. He can no longer appeal to an authority unavailable to his hearers.

Translators can also fall into bad habits in speaking the language. These can subtly affect the translation if not discovered. People usually react more to inaccurate, inappropriate, stylistically poor use of words in the written translation than they will to the same errors when the translator is speaking and present. Mistakes and unclear translations can thus be caught, and often in discussion with readers more acceptable ways of saying the same thing will be found.

Since the Bible touches on every aspect of life, translating broadens the translator's working vocabulary. It forces him to discuss in depth many aspects of the local culture he would seldom if ever otherwise talk about. The text of Scripture determines the topic of conversation and what must be said about it. The result is a much better understanding of the culture and how the Gospel applies to it.

At the translation desk terms used for key theological concepts can be tested for adequacy before becoming "set in concrete" through popular use. National preachers profit greatly by translating beforehand into their own language the passage of Scripture they expect to speak on. This opportunity to think through a passage unhurriedly often clarifies what may have been only partially understood, especially if the preacher's training was in a foreign language. He can explore and carefully test alternative ways of expressing scriptural truth rather than drifting into the habit of using the first thing that comes to mind while speaking (translating) on his feet. In fact, the exercise of making one's own translation of a passage will do more for any preacher, in any language, than any other single thing he can do by way of preparation.

Translating greatly extends the translator's ministry. Once the book is available, he can train the people to consult it. This relieves him of having to handle all the questions and queries himself. Using the text of Scripture as the basis of teaching, he can train others to explain it and preach it. These in turn can train others. The teaching thus continues whether the translator is temporarily absent or permanently gone (2 Tim. 2:2).

Translating the Bible permits the translator to share his faith in places and with people where other more aggressive types of missionary activity are restricted or impossible. As part of the literature produced for new readers, as a book contributing to the development of high moral character and the eradication of evil, and as a book offering an alternative way of life to all, it is read or listened to with respect, gains a hearing, and is often permitted if not promoted by those in authority.

Our emphasis on the Bible and the convictions underlying it has had a profound effect on our overall program, the day-to-day activities and the administrative decisions of our leaders at all levels, as the answers to the following questions will show.

For Whom Do We Translate the Bible?

The Bible is God's Word for all people, not just for Christians. It is useful for proclamation to those hearing for the first time as well as for the instruction of those already followers of Christ. We therefore translate for ethnic peoples among whom there are no Christians as well as those with Christians. The basic criterion is whether a usable translation exists in the language they speak.

Population size is not a basic consideration when deciding whether a certain group should have a translation. God did not make numbers the criterion but emphasized the worth of the individual and the importance of smaller social units

(Deut. 7:7; Luke 15:4; Mark 16:15; 1 Tim. 2:4; 2 Pet. 3:9; Matt. 16:26; Acts 8:26). "Large" and "small" are relative terms. Any cutoff point is purely arbitrary. A person's need of the Scripture is the same whether he is one of a hundred or one of a million.

Who Should Get a Translation First?

If there were sufficient workers to enter all language groups at once, we wouldn't need to ask the question. Shortage of translators, however, forces us to make assignments on a basis of priorities. Factors considered and often favoring a specific language group include: doors open but threatening to close to translators, government programs, a language strategically related to other languages also needing Scripture, a substantial percentage of the people speaking only or by preference their mother tongue, a number of churches without mother tongue Scriptures, and potential for recruiting and training translators. Groups in imminent danger of dying off may even be given priority attention because of our Christian convictions, humanitarian concern or linguistic commitments. The most important consideration is often the translator's conviction of God's providential guidance and the administration's confirmation of this, arrived at in consultation and prayer.

How Soon Should Bible Translation Be Started?

Bible translation should be started as soon as possible. Our pre-field courses include training in the principles of translation. The goal of early translation makes language learning more productive and keeps the worker from involvements that could hinder. Early attempts at translating passages of Scripture give valuable insights into the difficulties ahead, show up inadequacies and uncertainties in one's knowledge of the language, which in turn direct and speed up language acquisition. Early translation makes it possible to have the language competence and exegetical accuracy of the worker checked by a consultant before bad habits become fixed.

Once the basic linguistic analysis and testing of a practical orthography are far enough along, limited-edition trial publication follows. It is not uncommon for a whole Gospel to be published during the worker's first term on the field.

Early translation depends also on the availability of local speakers of the language to work with the translator and the translator's ability to train and motivate them to carry an increasing share of the translation load. Language helpers who grasp the principles involved may become co-translators, preparing initial drafts and polishing the completed translation, thus contributing significantly to earlier publication. In the case of nationals translating into their own or closely related languages, even earlier publication may be possible, since there is no language learning delay. For those who already speak the language as their mother tongue, however, training in translation principles and some linguistic analysis of their own language will greatly improve their work. Our members with linguistic and translation experience but limited proficiency in the language can often help them produce better translations sooner.

What Part of the Bible Is Translated First?

We translate the New Testament first, but not to the exclusion of Old Testament portions. We do not believe it is necessary to repeat the historical sequence by starting with the Old Testament which was anticipatory of Christ, when the historic facts about him, in all his fullness and finality, can be known directly through the New Testament Scriptures (cf. 1 Cor. 13:9-12). This in no way makes the Old Testament unimportant. The Old Testament is equally inspired of God, part of his total revelation and necessary to the fullest understanding of the New Testament record. For this reason translators often prepare parts of the Old Testament in translation or in summary form before the New Testament is completed. In cultures where the Old Testament patriarchs are held in high esteem, translation of Old Testament portions may serve as a logical preparation for the New Testament and come early in the translation program.

Among the New Testament books, most translators begin with one of the Gospels—usually the Gospel of Mark. Mark's Gospel is easier to translate because it has more descriptive vocabulary, less abstract preaching, fewer figures of speech and a simpler narrative style. Mark gets into the story of Christ more quickly and directly. He makes fewer references to the Old Testament. The Gospel of Mark is the shortest of the four Gospels. Because it is so often translated first, more translation helps are available for it than for the other Gospels.

There is considerable diversity in sequence of translation of the remaining books of the New Testament, depending often on the needs of local believers. A first Gospel is most often followed by Acts or one of the Epistles.

How Much of the Bible Should Be Translated?

The writer knows of no defensible reason for stopping short of a whole Bible for every person. Both Old and New Testaments are the Word of God and bear testimony to Jesus Christ. If anyone needs all of it, then everyone needs all of it. Progressive revelation, while giving higher practical recognition to the New Testament, does not render the Old Testament obsolete or unnecessary. Christ, while raising the demands of the Law, did not do away with the Law but rather established the Law. Much of New Testament teaching based on the lives of Noah, Abraham, David and others assumes a knowledge of the Old Testament record. In fact New Testament exhortations concerning the Scriptures refer in most cases to the Old Testament. Less frequently they refer to some of the earlier New Testament books.

In view of the shortage of personnel and resources and the large number of languages still needing translation, should a whole Bible be provided for some as soon as possible while others remain without any portion, or should some part at least be provided for all first and the whole Bible completed when possible? Our practical answer to this dilemma is to assign members to translate at least the New Testament, with liberty to do varying amounts of the Old Testament. Once the New Testament is done, however, workers are encouraged to move on to translate for others still without any portion of the Bible at all.

This has certain advantages. Believers left with only the New Testament may use it more intensively, with resulting spiritual profit. Too much may result in spiritual indigestion, with knowledge rather than obedience the result, to their own spiritual loss. Experienced translators going on to second or even third languages normally take less time to complete a Testament for each new language, especially if the new language is related to the previous one. Thus more people receive something of the Bible for the first time sooner and with it the opportunity to know Christ and grow in him.

Disadvantages of moving on after completing the New Testament are that the momentum gained in doing the New Testament may be lost, the experienced translator may not be available to help with the Old Testament and the people may be left a long time without the rest of the Bible. This is only partially compensated for in some situations by the fact that Christians, whose appetites for the Word of God have been whetted by the New Testament, will often be more willing to make a greater effort to use the Old Testament in some other language or dialect which they at least partially understand.

Most translation teams do some Old Testament passages or at least an outline summary of the Old Testament. In the Chol language one team continued until the whole Bible was published. In other situations workers with other organizations in the area have continued with Old Testament translation. In the case of the Navajo, the New Testament was completed in 1956. It quickly went through eight editions, with more than 15,000 copies sold. During this time, the principal Navajo members of the translation team, working with missionaries, completed a first draft of the Old Testament and revised the New Testament. Special "read-ins" to check the final translation were held. At one, 26 different Navajos came, some traveling 300 miles, to lend an ear and give their approval. From 35 congregations, only one or two with Navajo pastors in 1950, there are now 343 Navajo churches with over 12,000 in regular attendance. Two hundred and three churches have Navajo pastors and "the quality of Christians has risen beyond belief."[1] The use of the New Testament and the involvement of the Navajo community in the revision and further translation has played an important part in both numerical and quality growth as well as in the increase in the number of Navajo pastors. The final reading through of the Old Testament was a six-month project, during which the Navajo also "proofsang" through their 360-page Navajo hymnbook.

What are the Qualifications of a Translator?

Translators do not come ready made. Certain minimum requirements of health, motivation, perseverance, teachability and Bible knowledge must be met. People with an average or better academic background are encouraged to take introductory linguistic courses to determine if they have the ability to analyze and use a language under pioneer field conditions. Once we are satisfied on these points, motivated, maturing Christians can learn to produce acceptable translations of the Bible in our type of field operation. One learns to translate by translating, in frequent consultation with others, using the helps and facilities provided. Teamwork, with each member of the team contributing different expertise, means that no one member has to qualify as an expert in all fields that have a bearing on the quality of the finished translation. Each, however, to warrant a place on the team, must satisfy the candidate committee of his or her ability to make a positive contribution that will more than offset limitations, deficiencies and negative factors.

Members are involved in an ongoing program of linguistic and translation seminars, workshops, advanced studies, consultant apprenticeships and teaching assignments, that keep them moving ahead in their own assignment, upgrading their own skills, and contributing to the work of others. Recently minimum academic and cross cultural adaptability requirements have been raised to meet changing field situations, demands of host countries, and the limitations on the amount of help the organization can give those needing it most.

At What Standard of Translation Do We Aim?

We seek to produce translations that are faithful to the original and idiomatic in the language of the readers. Using standard commentaries and lexicons and special helps provided by our own translation department, the translator is expected to stay within the mainstream of conservative scholarship in interpreting the text. Translations are carefully checked by consultants and the interpretation and rendering of difficult or problematic passages discussed. Intelligibility and naturalness of style are tested with native speakers of the language. Translators continue to improve their own work on the basis of feedback from its use with the people. Usually one or more books have been published and thoroughly reworked before the entire New Testament is completed. The New Testament thus may have the quality of a revision when first published.[2]

How Can Translation Be Speeded Up and Quality Maintained?

Several measures help translators save time where it will not affect quality. Linguistic training enables them to learn a language more quickly than they otherwise would. Field orientation courses reduce the time it takes to live efficiently under less than ideal conditions. Early translation gets one started sooner and early consultation helps one correct bad habits before a lot of time and effort are wasted. Translation centers, where the translator and language helper can get away from the distractions of village living and where library facilities and consultants are available, speed up translation progress. Workshops and seminars, where several translators may be working on the same passage, or where common problems may be helped by discussion and the solutions others have found, are scheduled frequently. Commentary compilations and other exegetical helps, prepared with pioneer translation needs in mind, save the worker much of the time spent hunting through commentaries. Back translations into the translator's language show up distinctive language and cultural patterns in the language of translation. They also serve as a type of commentary to help orient new translators much more quickly to what they may find or need in their work on some other language in the same cultural area or language family. Multiple translations in related languages, where the translator, knowledgeable in at least one of the languages, works with several nationals, each translating in his own language, move the work ahead in several languages simultaneously. The use of computers in text editing and typesetting reduces the time involved in final preparation of the manuscript and getting it on the press. Training of national helpers in linguistic and translation principles enables them to contribute much more, either as co-translators or as translators in their own right.

Who Publishes the Translations?

Aside from the very earliest trial editions for limited circulation, translations are submitted for publication through various outside agencies. In the early years of the work the principal publisher was the American Bible Society and other national societies of the United Bible Societies. For the last several years the vast majority have been published by the World Home Bible League and the New York International Bible Society.

4

Which Language?

THE ACCUMULATIVE results of language surveys and linguistic research have made us aware of the immensity and complexity of the language situation in the world today. Of the languages spoken in the world today perhaps one-third are written. Fewer have been adequately studied or described. The opportunity and need for linguistic research simply boggles the mind. While all languages have some basic things in common, every new language studied has its own unique differences. Each has something to contribute to our understanding of language in general. Languages which serve as the mother tongue for some community of people have the capacity to express and preserve the total experience of those who speak it. They can also find ways of talking about any innovation either within or from outside the culture.

This world language situation has implications for those committed to Bible translation. Our own most recent count of the number of languages spoken today is 5,445.[1] Of these living languages 1,634 have a complete Bible, a Testament, or at least one book of the Bible already published. This leaves people speaking 3,811 languages with no mother tongue translation. Of these languages, 176 are almost extinct and 242 may be able to use Scriptures in some other language because the majority of the people are bilingual. Preliminary surveys have already clearly established the Bible translation need of 723 of the remaining groups. Experience to date would indicate that as high as six out of every seven of the remaining 2,670 languages (i.e. over 2,000) also will need a translation. While languages without Scripture are principally those spoken by minority peoples, in the aggregate they probably total at least 200,000,000 people. Language communities without the Bible range in number of speakers from millions on down to tens and twenties.[2]

The multiplicity of languages has caused some to propose radical solutions, such as teaching everyone to speak and read one language. But which one? Each community votes for its own and we are back where we started.

Solutions which promote bilingualism and the acquisition of a national or official language for the common needs of a larger political community are more realistic. Bilingualism is seen by many as an asset, even where not a necessity. But the acquisition of a second language must be promoted by persuasion, not imposed by force.

The immensity of the task, in terms of numbers of distinct languages still unwritten and the relative numbers of people speaking them, has caused many to despair of using each language as a vehicle for literature and teaching. The fact that in our own experience over 600 such languages in the short space of forty years have been so used for the introduction of basic education, for a vernacular literature, as well as a base for the acquisition of other languages, shows it can be done. We are not alone in this emphasis. Several governments in recent years have enacted laws and developed programs for the use of vernacular languages in fundamental education.

Needed are hundreds, even thousands of linguistically trained personnel, both expatriate and national,[3] to implement such programs. For the expatriate, to live and work for many years under field conditions where these languages are spoken requires unusual motivation. The national must also have a genuine sense of call to tackle the task. For both, Bible translation provides such motivation. But motivation is not enough. Tools and training are also necessary. Linguistics provides these and helps us accomplish the task. It enables us to be more realistic in our approach and brings the solution much nearer.

To understand our emphasis on linguistics, one must realize the important role language plays in human affairs.

The Importance of Language

Language is mankind's unique communicative faculty. By it one person makes contact with the mental world of another. He influences the other person and is influenced by him. He receives, retains, reproduces and transmits prior communication. He categorizes, invents or adapts terms for every kind of reality. And he thinks creatively. The ability to speak, hear and reason in the conventional symbols of language is part of God's unique endowment of mankind (Gen. 2:19, 20).

Language is the key to culture. Language interpenetrates all experience. Every ethnic community interacts, talks about, codifies, stores and transmits its common experience, knowledge, and values by means of language. Language is the chief means by which a culture identifies, relates, manipulates, evaluates, and incorporates all persons, artifacts, processes, states and systems, both old and new, into one comprehensive, integrated whole. Man in his social and spiritual dimension cannot function without language. Since language is so inextricably a part of our social and spiritual existence, linguistics, the study of human speech in all its aspects, is a most rewarding field of study, not only for Bible translation but for understanding ourselves and our fellow man.

Language was also the medium God used to give his special revelation to mankind through the Prophets, the Apostles, and his Son, Jesus Christ. He used language to record and explain his general revelation in creation and history, and to describe the rationality of his own being and activity (Gen. 1:3, 5, 26, 29; 3:22; John 1:1, 14; Heb. 1:1-3).

Jesus Christ, God's ultimate self-revelation in still another mode, that of our humanity, was called "the Word" (John 1:1), "a prophet, powerful in word and deed" (Luke 24:19). He constantly emphasized language as God's and his own medium of communication (John 14:24). He claimed his words, spoken in the language of his day and culture, were adequate for the transmission of God's thoughts to men (John 17:8), instrumental to salvation (John 5:24), the basis of judgment (John 12:48), and more permanent than creation itself (Matt. 24:15). By the Holy Spirit's inspiration of Scripture, Christ's words were made available in a trustworthy record for all generations to come (John 14:26).

Language is our most basic means of communication with God. By means of language more than any other medium, our thoughts, motives and choices are expressed. God holds us morally responsible for our use, disuse, or misuse of words (Matt. 11:15; 12:35-37; Luke 19:40; Rom. 10:9; Phil. 2:11; Heb. 13:15; James 3:8-10; Hosea 14:2). These are the factors that make languages and linguistics of such great concern to the Christian.

But for any given person or language community, it is not language in general but a specific language that is important and of immediate and practical significance. We now need to clarify the meaning of certain terms we will be using concerning language and languages, the people who use them, and the situations in which they are used.

Terminology[4]

The following statements concerning the terms used in this book are given to help those unfamiliar with linguistic jargon or who may use the terms in a different sense. They are not intended to be strictly technical definitions.

By *mother tongue* (or *native language,* without any pejorative sense) we mean the language spoken from infancy. This language is the first, and perhaps the only one spoken. It seems natural to a person and is adequate to talk about all of life's situations. The term *vernacular* refers to the standard and commonly used spoken form of a language or dialect native to a region or people. It will be used as synonymous with mother tongue, particularly when contrasted with classical or foreign languages.

Many people learn to speak more than one language. A person who speaks two languages habitually and with a control like that of a native speaker is a *bilingual.* A person who understands and speaks several languages is *multilingual*. A person who understands and speaks only one is *monolingual*. Communities may be wholly or partially monolingual, bilingual or multilingual. Language situations are far from uniform and seldom simple to describe. Even two languages learned from birth may not be true alternates but be used by the same person under different circumstances, with different people, and with quite different emotional significance. Any language spoken from birth, however, evokes quite a different depth of response than one *acquired* as an adult.

A person who leaves or loses contact with his original speech community may even lose proficiency or forget his mother tongue. For all intents and purposes the new language replaces the mother tongue as the language of his greatest competence and group identity. Psychologically the new takes on characteristics of a mother tongue; it is the one he feels most at home in and uses regularly in his private life. In what follows, statements about the mother tongue apply to it also.

In contrast to one's own language and people, all other language communities are seen as different or *foreign*. If the speakers of a given language are conscious of differences in the speech of the other, but the differences are not sufficient to render communication impossible, we say they speak different *dialects* of the same language. If they cannot communicate at all, they certainly speak different languages. To the one who does not understand or speak a given language, it is *foreign*; to the one who has learned to speak it, it is *acquired*; to the one who speaks it without conscious effort, from birth, or in place of the first or childhood language, it is for our purposes here, the mother tongue.

In addition to serving one cultural community as its mother tongue, a language may have additional roles and serve a broader community. As a means of communication among speakers of different languages, for trade and other purposes, it is called a *trade language* or *lingua franca*. Recognized by a government for political and educational purposes, it may be referred to as an *official* or school language.

An official language may be a *national language*, (that is, the mother tongue of some segment of the population) or a *colonial language*. In Nigeria, for example, English is the official but not a national (Nigerian) language. A language used for international purposes by people of a number of countries may be referred to as an *international language*. Trade, national, official, and international languages are mother tongue languages to those who speak them from birth, and what is said of the mother tongue applies. They are acquired languages to all others who use them. They are foreign languages to those who do not speak or understand them, even though they're spoken in the same country. Thus to many speakers of minority languages, other minority languages as well as trade, national and international languages spoken in their country or local area may equally be foreign languages. Even where a trade, official or international language is spoken, for the vast majority of the people the mother tongue holds a special place. This is true not only for those who speak no other language but also for many who also speak or understand other languages.

The Mother Tongue

Perhaps the most important factor relating a person to the world in which he lives, is his mother tongue. For most people the mother tongue remains the preferred language for effective communication even where other languages are used.

Use of the mother tongue gets and holds the attention of the people who speak it (cf. Acts 21:40; 22:2). When someone is addressed in a language he does not understand at all or only poorly, he is likely to feel ill at ease and even inferior. In self-defense he may tune the speaker out or be unwilling to make the effort required to understand. In our hearing a Mazatec-speaking guide commented to his uncle, "If they were speaking Spanish, we wouldn't be listening." Elderly Cree Indians, nodding with sleep in the back row during an English language meeting, snapped wide awake when I injected a sentence in Cree into my talk. Even a few words in the mother tongue invite participation and response. An educated gypsy who knew several languages and was speaking with me in English, exploded with excitement when handed a booklet in his Kalderash language—"Why this is my language!" Nothing would deter him from reading it to the end.

How does one determine a bilingual community's language preference? If workers investigating the language habits of a particular community speak only the trade language, only those who know the trade language will speak to them. They may draw the erroneous conclusion (as some have) that everyone speaks the trade language when actually very few do. Once they have learned the vernacular they will discover how few had spoken to them in the trade language. All the rest had avoided them, embarrassed by their ignorance of the trade language. Even most of those who had spoken to them preferred to use their own language, once they knew the field workers spoke it.

Use of the vernacular speeds up identification with and acceptance by the people. So long as workers speak only the trade language, they tend to be identified with the trade language people, which may brand them as outsiders, and even, if the trade language people are disliked, enemies.

One day I encountered a contingent of Mexican soldiers on a remote trail in Mazatec country. The officer in charge checked my identification, seemed satisfied, then noted with surprise that I carried no gun. Because of past enmity between the Mazatec and Spanish-speaking outsiders, visitors usually carried a loaded pistol. Even the mail came in twice a week to our village with four armed guards. Before I could explain to him why I never carried a gun, the Mazatec in whose home he was having breakfast at the moment answered for me. "He doesn't need a gun," he said. "He speaks our language." We also noticed that people in the market gave us the local price "because we spoke their language." Without question the most effective means of identifying with the people and being accepted by them was the fact we had learned their language.

The mother tongue communicates best, is not limited to

certain topics or vocabulary, relates matters more directly to life and makes it easier to clear up misunderstanding. Doctors and teachers are often shocked to discover how little people understand when instructions are given in the official tongue. This is true even when the patient or student said he understood the instructions and even quoted them back verbatim. Only when they asked him to explain the instructions in his own language did it become evident he had not understood. For effective communication and understanding, the mother tongue is best.

The mother tongue is also the most satisfactory medium for mental and spiritual development. Struggling to understand and apply new concepts in a language other than one's own is much less effective. A Guarayu woman was ill at ease, fearful of using the few words of Spanish she knew. During the Bible study she understood the teacher to tell her to leave the room. With great difficulty she was convinced she had misundertood and was persuaded to rejoin the class. Such misunderstandings create a situation that wouldn't occur in the mother tongue. Where the learner handles the language with ease, he can give full attention to the concepts involved. For this reason, biblical truth is more easily understood and related to life when the Bible is in the mother tongue.

Native language workshops have demonstrated that the mother tongue is the best medium for creative self-expression and the development of latent gifts and abilities.

When a person speaks in his mother tongue, it isn't just his intellect that is involved, but his whole self, including his emotions and will. An individual may master another language adequately for all practical purposes—but its emotional connotations will not be the same. A Guatemalan Indian said he preferred to hear preaching in Spanish, rather than in his own language. He frankly admitted the reason: "In Spanish it sounds so pretty and I don't have to do anything about it, but in my own language I have to do something about it."

Each mother tongue serves as a "contrastive-identificational" marker for the culturally defined in-group that speaks it (see Judges 12:6; Neh. 13:24). It identifies the speaker as a member of one group in contrast to all others. This gives continuity to life, linking the present generation with past generations from whom the language was learned and with future generations now acquiring it. A translation of the Bible and native-authored writings in the mother tongue enter the stream of the group's cultural heritage.

The mother tongue is an integral part of one's personality and sense of personhood. Aspersions cast on one's way of speaking may be taken as attacks on one's person. Dr. Kenneth L. Pike relates two conversations which illustrate this:

> A Welshman once said to me, when I asked him about his mother tongue, "A man who loses his own language loses his *soul*." (He was a principal of a Baptist seminary, and I assume he was speaking in metaphorical terms!)
>
> Some years ago I was talking with one of the greatest linguists that Denmark has produced. I said, "Why doesn't your country drop Danish and just use English—since you are teaching it nine years in your schools?" He drew himself up to his full tall height and said, "It's a good thing you asked a *friend* that question!"
>
> Then I said to him, "Look, I'm not trying to be crude. I have given twenty-five years of my life to minority language groups, and some people say its ridiculous. I've got to know why I'm right. Why *am* I right? Why haven't I wasted twenty-five years? You are a sophisticated, educated man and a member of a small language group. Tell me why."
>
> He was speechless for a few moments (his initial reaction was in his integrating computer—and it took a while to bring it up to the conscious computer). Finally he said, in perfect English, "Well, you know, Pike, you lose your language and you've lost your moral substance. You've learned this at your mother's knee through stories in your own language, and it's—*you*."[5]

The use of the mother tongue by the translator and the translation of God's Word into the vernacular often give the speaker of that language a new sense of personal worth and cultural pride. This is especially true of minority groups whose language and way of life has been belittled and who may even have lost the will to live. That someone should esteem their language worth learning and their people worth knowing is hard enough to understand. But to know God has a message for them in their language and is not just the God of the national or foreign language people rekindles hope and purpose in life. When they point to their language as written like other languages, read literature they themselves have written, listen to their language on the radio and have God's Word in their own language, minority peoples lift their heads, straighten their shoulders, and see themselves as people God loves and others appreciate. They are on their way to taking their place in their nation and world with dignity.

The mother tongue gives the greatest potential for any group to handle its own affairs. A sense of insecurity, inferiority and dependence often characterizes minority leaders when they must deal with outsiders and innovators in a foreign language. When the Navajo first received the New Testament, one tribe member was heard to comment, "Now we can conduct our own church service." Churches with the Bible in the language of the people have direct access to their message and source of authority. They may voluntarily interact with other churches but are not dependent upon them.

The legitimate role of each mother tongue should be recognized and the basic rights and dignity of each language community and individual protected. Why should anyone who never expects to participate outside his own community be forced to learn another language? And when did learning a second language require that one cease to speak his first? The native speakers of a language are the ones to decide when they will cease to speak it. Meanwhile we show respect for them and their language by learning it and using it.

Not only pragmatic considerations, but biblical precedents and principles emphasize the importance of the mother tongue.

Biblical Languages

The original languages in which we have the biblical documents throw considerable light on the importance of the mother tongue. The Scriptures were written in the vernacular of their day. The particular language used was the language of those to whom the message was given. Moses was highly educated and an orator in Egyptian (Acts 7:22). His lack of fluency in speaking Hebrew embarrassed him when he was asked to go before the elders of his people (Exod. 4:10-16). But he gave God's Word to them in their own Hebrew language. Daniel wrote in Aramaic matters of special interest to the Aramaic-speaking Gentiles of Babylon (Dan. 2:4-7:28). Passages of special Jewish interest he wrote in Hebrew (Dan. 1 and 8-12). Ezra recorded the official correspondence between the local governments of Palestine and the Persian court in Aramaic (Ezra 4:8-6:18; 7:12-26) but the edict of Ezra 1 is in the Hebrew language, doubtless representing the actual wording as it was delivered to the Jews themselves.[6] We know Ahasuerus translated royal decrees for the Jews of his realm (Esther 8:9).

After the return from captivity, Aramaic was the vernacular language of the common people of Palestine. Hebrew continued to be studied and spoken by the learned class, but the oral translation of the Hebrew text of the Old Testament was common in the synagogue services (Neh. 8:8). Not until the first century A.D. were these Aramaic translations written down.

Meanwhile, with the spread of Greek language and culture, a Greek translation of the Old Testament was made for Jews in Egypt who spoke Greek but not Hebrew. This translation was used by Christ, the apostles and the early Christian church. By the time the New Testament documents were written the church had moved from a Jewish to a Gentile base. The bilingual writers of the New Testament documents, even when they were recording the teaching of Christ, in all probability given in Aramaic, wrote in Greek for the Greek-speaking world. They were sensitive to the needs of the Greek-speaking readers who did not know Aramaic, and interpreted Aramaic terms and names for their benefit (e.g. John 19:13, 17; Mark 5:41; 15:34).

Thus the precedent was clearly established that the preferred language for God's message to men was the language of the people to whom it was given. And the style of the language was that of everyday life.

Precedents in the Bible

Other facts recorded in the biblical narrative also support an emphasis on the mother tongue.

Long before the time of Christ the strategic role of the mother tongue for effective communication, even in multilingual situations, was recognized. In a moment of deepest emotion Joseph dismissed his interpreter and switched from Egyptian to his mother tongue. The Egyptian language had proved an effective barrier to hide his identity from his brothers but was inadequate for his reconciliation with them (Gen. 42:7, 23; 45:1, 12). Rabshakeh, Ezra, Ahasuerus and Nebuchadnezzar used the mother tongues of people as the most effective way to achieve their goals (2 Kings 18:26-28; Neh. 8:7, 8; Esther 1:22; 3:12; 8:9).

The world into which Christ commanded his disciples to go and preach the Gospel was a world of many local and regional languages.[7] At Pentecost (Acts 2) devout Jews from both east and west assembled in Jerusalem. Two great lingua francas were used—Greek by those from the Western and Mediterranean world and Aramaic by those from the Eastern Mesopotamian world. But the initial proclamation of the "wonders of God" on the inaugural day for the worldwide mission of the church was not restricted to these two trade languages that ostensibly would reach all there. Each heard "in his own language in which he was born." This was not the "reversal of Babel." The Holy Spirit was using the very diversity of Babel for maximum intelligibility and personal impact on the listeners.

The disciples needed Pentecost's lesson in strategy for the

long-range task ahead. As Galileans they were probably bilingual in Aramaic and Greek and hence able to get along in either trade language. Only by a special concession of the Jewish authorities were non-Hebrew-speaking pilgrims allowed to use their own local languages to worship in the temple area at Pentecost. Hearing the wonderful works of God described in their local languages, the visitors were not only amazed but enthusiastic in their response.

Some time later the multilingual Saul of Tarsus had a personal encounter with Christ on the road to Damascus. Christ did not speak to him in Latin (although Paul was proud of his Roman citizenship) nor in Greek (although Paul was a highly educated man and spoke it fluently), but in Aramaic, Paul's mother tongue, which he had learned as a child in his Jewish home. Twenty-six years later Paul still regarded the use of his mother tongue as a significant factor in his conversion experience (Acts 26:14).

Paul knew that his "ability to speak the ancient languages (Hebrew and Aramaic) was a mark of faithfulness to the old culture."[8] The fact that Aramaic was his mother tongue identified him with his Jewish people (Phil. 3:5, 6; "a Hebrew of the Hebrews" means an Aramaic-speaking Jew). When charged by the Jews with desecrating the temple because he had a Greek as his companion, he deliberately responded in Aramaic, their common mother tongue. Paul apparently had spoken to the officer in Greek but switched to Aramaic with the Jewish mob, probably leaving the Roman officer wondering what he was saying. In doing so he ran the risk of being misunderstood and even considered discourteous by the Roman officer who had rescued him. But the language he used was the mother tongue of the Jews, and Paul knew what he was doing. The strategy worked and he got the crowd's attention. Lest we miss the point, Luke adds the explanation that the silence of the crowd was accentuated by the fact that Paul spoke in their Aramaic mother tongue (Acts 22:2).

The Bible's teaching also emphasizes maximum intelligibility as the normal communicative role of language. In 1 Cor. 14 Paul considers the public proclamation of the truth in a known language more important and more beneficial than any amount of speaking in an unknown tongue. Five words understood are preferred to 10,000 words not understood (v. 19). To be spoken to in an unknown tongue or unintelligible language is to be shut off from the truth and rejected (1 Cor. 14:21-25). If foreign languages are spoken there must be interpretation, otherwise they should not be used in public (v. 28). The implication is clear: maximum intelligibility in the language of the hearer is the goal.

Mission History

The history of missions since Christ bears testimony to the importance of translating the Bible into the mother tongue. G. Campbell Morgan wrote, "The story of missions the whole wide world over shows that the success or failure of . . . missions has always been dependent on whether those brought to Christ had the Scriptures in their own language or not."[9] Stewart of Lovedale said, ". . . no record exists, as far as I know, of any mission, whatever be its methods or history, making much real progress and becoming permanent among any people, if the Bible had not been given to them in their own vernacular." William Carey, who was instrumental in making 34 translations of all or part of the Bible in the languages of India and Asia, was "reproached for wasting valuable strength on subordinate dialects of India, but he . . . often remembered and made mention of the experience of Great Britain, which had required the Scriptures, not just in the tongue of the predominant partner, but also in Welsh, Gaelic, Irish, Cornish, and Manx. Indeed till the Book was thus wrought into these fireside dialects it remained aloof and barren and unloved. These were the considerations which persuaded Carey to this output of his strength."[10] Indeed "history records no single example of a sound, long-lived, indigenous church without vernacular Scriptures."[11]

5
Linguistics

LINGUISTICS, THE science of language, provides a theoretical framework, guiding principles and practical methods for learning, analyzing and describing languages. It also furnishes insights into the principles and problems of communication and translation.

In the process of learning Cakchiquel, Townsend became convinced that linguistic training was essential if Christians hoped to translate the Bible into the remaining languages of the world. When he began, Cakchiquel had never been written or systematically studied. He learned to pronounce the four different *k* sounds by trial and error, mimicking the people. Some sounds of the language were made with air going in, others with air coming out. Several had a strange popping sound as the Adam's apple moved up or down like the plunger of a pump. The grammar was unlike anything he had heard of, let alone studied. Verbs had several thousand potential forms. He ended up simply describing what he found, not trying to fit it into any foreign language mold.

By the time he had finished the New Testament in Cakchiquel he knew that translation required more than a good knowledge of the Bible. Linguistic training for learning such languages under field conditions must be obtained or provided for all who would go. This would greatly speed the task. The experience of those who learned such languages must be made available for others before they went. Information about such languages would be of interest to linguists. It would provide a basis for serving the governments and universities of the countries where the work was carried

69

on. Linguistic research and publication thus became a major commitment from the very beginning. From first to last, our work has been related to language, language communities, language-related tasks and organizations interested in linguistics.[1]

The Role of Linguistics

Linguistics provides a way of serving governments, educational and scientific communities and the minority people whose languages we study. The service offered includes the formation of alphabets for unwritten languages, the publication of dictionaries and grammars of the languages studied, the preparation of literacy materials and the stimulation of native-authored literature.

Countries differ in the amount of linguistic training available and the number of people doing linguistic research. Depending on the situation, we may teach introductory courses or our more competent staff may lecture to graduate students.

Our field work in several countries has also included a program of apprenticeship training for local university students. As part of their university work, students of linguistics in national universities live with and work alongside our personnel for a period of months in an ethnic language community. By invitation of the national universities, a number of our field workers lecture, conduct linguistic seminars, or serve on committees of advanced study programs. Our members have thus contributed to the training of independent national linguists, as well as encouraged the formation and activities of national linguistic societies and the publication of local linguistic journals.

Our hope is that Christian students in these countries will see the need of Bible translation and take the training offered to qualify for such work. A translation team in Upper Volta was praying for a good language helper. Imagine their surprise when they learned that a student who had taken linguistics was a speaker of the very language they were studying and was willing to help!

Such linguistic services help in obtaining visas and authorization for our members to work in otherwise restricted areas. They also enable us to transcend the limitations of religious comity agreements. Some of those we train end up in government departments also carrying on programs where we are working, which makes for congenial and mutually helpful relations.

Linguistic surveys identify language communities, their centers and approximate boundaries. For each language area survey, teams gather information concerning the social status of the dialects of the language, other languages also used, and the ability of people to understand any languages already having Scripture. On the basis of this and other information and with the agreement of the national and local authorities, linguistic-translation teams are assigned.

Linguistic training prepares us to learn and use the local language from the very beginning of contact with an ethnic group. This opens up communication, establishes rapport and awakens local interest. Early mastery of the language expedites development of interpersonal relationships, acceptance by the people and identification with them as a distinct language community. This is essential to the initiation and completion of linguistic projects, translation of the Scriptures, and training of mother tongue speakers of the language.

Linguistics provides methods and models that enable us to make available to linguists, teachers and the public what we have learned of the languages we study. Our members have contributed considerably to a knowledge of the lesser-known languages of the world and their relationships as well as to linguistic, literacy and translation theory, practice and training. In the process we validate our credentials and upgrade our own competence for these tasks.

Linguistics and Translation

Linguistic training and research contribute to Bible translation. Translation, restating in one language what was first said in another, requires competence in at least two languages. The task calls for a proper understanding of what the original document says, an adequate knowledge of the range of possibilities for saying it in the second language, plus criteria for determining what constitutes the most adequate equivalence between the two. The resultant translation should faithfully say what the original said but in a way that is natural and understandable in terms of the second language and culture. Linguistic principles are involved in every part of this process.

Grammars, lexicons, commentaries, historical and cultural background materials and courses in seminaries and Bible schools help the translator understand the biblical text. A knowledge of the original languages, Greek and Hebrew, while not indispensable, helps the translator use resource materials to better advantage and also provides a basis for judgment where these materials differ or do not resolve the problems encountered. Current linguistic research on Greek and Hebrew paragraph and discourse structures, is providing new exegetical insights where traditional helps often are lacking.

But no amount of biblical knowledge or spirituality will compensate for inadequate control of the language into which the translation is made. This is where linguistics probably makes its greatest contribution—helping the translator master and use effectively the vocabulary and grammatical devices of the target language. In the process of translation, in turn, much more is learned about the language, especially the subtler nuances of meaning and usage that become apparent in the struggle to say what needs to be said in the most natural way.

Workers among the Canela discovered the language had past, present and future verb tenses. In addition it had what seemed a distant past tense as well. The two kinds of past tense were marked by particles, *te* for recent past, *pe* for distant past. Over a period of time they prepared booklets for the Canela to read, observing this distinction. One thing bothered them, however. When the people told stories, even in distant past time, they often threw in a string of recent past *te*s. Finally, at a workshop, they went through a number

72

4. *Polopa translation team.*

of stories the Canela had told them, marking the *pe*s with an orange pencil, the *te*s with a blue pencil. To their amazement every one of the stories began in orange, turned blue in the middle and then went back to orange at the end. As they examined the stories further they noted that the orange parts were background information, bits of explanation, description of settings. The blue parts were the important part of the story, the main action and the climax. Their first quick observation had been wrong. Only when they applied rigorous linguistic procedures did they discover how these two particles really worked. As a result their translation of the Scriptures now will be much more accurate, and read much more intelligibly to the Canela people.

The involvement of mother tongue speakers of the language, either as helpers or as co-translators, is essential if the finished product is to speak naturally and be culturally acceptable. The final assessment of the correctness and intelligibility of any translation must be made by such speakers of the language. But mother tongue translators profit greatly

73

5. *Amuzgo translator in Mexico rests after a long and difficult translation session.*

from linguistic training, even those called and otherwise qualified to translate in their own right. Already competent in speaking their own language, they usually have difficulty deciding how to write it. Many are not consciously aware of the full range of devices that make for explicitness, style and creativity in their own language. Linguistic insights help them understand what is involved in maintaining faithfulness to the original without sacrificing naturalness and intelligibility in their own language. This is especially true in handling cross-cultural differences with respect to explicit and implicit information and figures of speech. Expatriate translators maximize the contribution of mother tongue speakers by giving them some linguistic training too.

Thus while translation theory and practice have profited greatly from linguistic training, it in turn has contributed much to the interest in, and development and application of, linguistic theory and training. This in turn has stimulated the spread and availability of training courses in linguistics not only for our own workers but for others interested, both at home and in the countries where we work.

Linguistic Training and Teaching

All who do language-related work with us are required to have our training in linguistics.[2] By agreement with certain universities in the United States, we provide the teaching faculty and staff, the university provides facilities and students receive regular university credit for the courses taken. At the Universities of Oklahoma, North Dakota and Washington (Seattle) the courses are offered during summer school. During the fall and spring semesters similar courses are given at our Dallas center, with credit from the University of Texas. Similar training is also given in England, Germany, Australia, Brazil, France, Japan and the Philippines.

These university level courses

teach the skills necessary for learning, writing, and describing unwritten languages: recording and reproduction of non-English speech sounds, alphabet formation, dictionary preparation, description of grammar and sound systems, primer preparation, and translation.

The courses deal with the general principles basic to all languages. These principles are illustrated by materials from Eurasia, Africa, Oceania, and the Americas so that the qualified graduate is prepared to face any language he may meet even though there is no literature written in or about it. The courses are especially designed for those who are preparing to serve preliterate people, to do some specific linguistic task such as Bible translation, or to study languages for which written linguistic materials are inadequate.

Modern techniques of language analysis make it possible to train students in advance for languages, which have never been studied. Underlying every language is a set of simple principles. The most intricate of sound systems is produced by a combination of a few moving parts in the mouth and throat. The analysis of the most extensive verb or sentence structure similarly reduces to a few basic principles. Modern linguistics makes it possible to summarize for the student the general kinds of structures which he is likely to meet and to give him in advance a methodology for solving the difficulties which face him.[3]

The introductory courses are oriented to the practical aspects of learning and analyzing a language, a how-to approach. Further courses give a broader introduction to current linguistic theory and research and include principles of translation, cultural anthropology, literacy and community development.[4]

6. *Training in linguistics is provided in special Summer Institute of Linguistics courses, such as this class at the University of Oklahoma.*

On this foundation the member begins his language assignment as a practicing linguist. Our contractual obligations with the universities where we teach and the government of the countries where we work, plus the personal motivation to maintain the quality of our linguistic and translation work keep us in an on-going program of linguistics. On the field, language analysis and writeups are frequently discussed with consultants. Attendance at periodic linguistic seminars and workshops is required. The member is encouraged to publish significant linguistic findings and to attend linguistic conferences. Members often take refresher and advanced courses on furlough. In some cases workers are urged to obtain an advanced degree in linguistics which will make them more independent in their own work and better able to help others.

We not only study and practice linguistics, we also are often called on to teach linguistics. This requires that many of our members do graduate work in linguistics to keep ahead of those they will be teaching, both at home and abroad. With increasing emphasis on the training of nationals, the introductory linguistic courses are increasingly acquainting members with ways of sharing their linguistic skills with mother tongue speakers of the languages they will study. Members with teaching gifts staff more formal field courses offered nationals in their own countries and universities.

Many of our members are asked to return to teach in the university courses in their homeland which they themselves attended. While this means time from their field and translation programs, it keeps them current in linguistics and upgrades their skills as linguists. This in turn results in greater productivity and usefulness in the total linguistic and Bible translation program. Since workers under many mission boards serving in many parts of the world also attend our courses, we share in Bible translation on an even broader basis than our own work.

Linguistics is a genuine and integral part of our total service. Universities recognize the high caliber of the training given in the courses offered on their campuses. The scholarly, scientific world has expressed appreciation for the data provided as well as the theoretical articles and books written or co-authored by our members.[5] In 1948 the Linguistic Society of America passed a resolution strongly recommending our work, terming it, "One of the most promising developments in applied linguistics in this country." While only a few of our members would qualify as scholars, all of those assigned to language-related tasks are properly known as practicing linguists or linguistic technicians.

For all our language-assigned members linguistics must be taken seriously. It absorbs a major part of their time during their years on the field. For those asked to serve as consultants to others with their analysis and writeups, or as instructors at the linguistic training courses, linguistic activities and studies occupy a much larger proportion of their total service. Members serving in other than language-related tasks are required to take a series of introductory lectures in linguistics, language learning methods, cross-cultural communication and cultural anthropology. They are expected to be knowledgeable about the linguistic work and emphasis of the group.

Our linguistic orientation and involvement come through clearly as we relate to various audiences. In academic and government circles, linguistics and membership in the Summer Institute of Linguistics are the foundation of our relationships and service. In these circles the spiritual emphasis in our lives and our Bible translation goals mark us as something more than linguists. The respect gained and maintained by the genuineness and caliber of our linguistic service has provided opportunity for and reinforces our Christian witness in such circles.

With Christian and church-related groups we report on and ask prayer for our linguistic activities. We ask prayer for alphabets, dictionaries, primers, technical linguistic articles, linguistic conferences and teaching linguistics at universities. The primary interest of such groups is in Bible translation, transformed lives, indigenous churches and the spiritual needs of our families and those for whom we are translating. But they never fail to show keen interest in many aspects of the linguistic work. Translation problems and demonstrations of how we go about learning an unwritten language never fail to arouse interest. This blend of linguistics and Bible translation, of the academic and the spiritual, is tremendously stimulating and opens up an aspect of Christian responsibility and effort all too often taken for granted.[6] Similarly, furloughs spent in getting further training in linguistics or in teaching linguistics to other prospective workers make sense to our supporting friends when it is seen in the light of the total program and our distinctive approach.

Field Practice

Our linguistic policies and practices reflect our convictions concerning the role of language, the importance of the mother tongue, and what we believe God has called us to do.

Each member accepted and trained for language-related work is assigned to a specific minority language. Two single men or women, or a married couple, are a minimum linguistic-translation team. Their goal is to become experts in that specific language as soon as possible. For maximum exposure to the language they live in a community where the language is spoken. Where this is not possible the language may be learned from mother tongue speakers living elsewhere. But this is only a temporary, second-best expedient until residence is possible in a community where it is used constantly.

Some ethnic groups are violently opposed to intruders of any kind. In the case of the Aucas of Ecuador, five men were killed trying to establish peaceful contact. The sister of one of them learned to speak the language from Dayuma, an Auca woman working on a ranch outside the tribal area. Dayuma later returned to her people and told her mother about the woman who had befriended her and now spoke their language. On invitation from Dayuma's mother to live with her she entered Auca territory for the first time. The fact that she was able to speak to the people in their language went a long way to easing tensions and gaining their confidence.[7]

Learning a language from books or recordings is never acceptable for the achievement of our goals. Since language is primarily for communication of ideas, every effort is made to learn to speak the language from the very beginning in the full range of real life situations with those who speak it as their mother tongue.

The use of interpreters is discouraged even on a short-term basis. One learns a language by doing his own talking, not by having someone else do it for him. One never knows

79

what the interpreter is saying. After he became a follower of Christ, the Navajo who had translated for the missionary confessed that he had ended his translation each time with a phrase that meant "That's what he said but I don't believe it."

While learning to speak the language, we also write down expressions we hear, and linguistic analysis begins. Spoken forms in current use by members of the ethnic community are the data to be learned and analyzed. Analysis is based on what is actually heard or written spontaneously by a mother tongue speaker or declared to be natural and acceptable by a native speaker of the language. The analysis reflects the language as it is actually spoken, not as any individual or group, mother tongue or foreigner, thinks it ought to be spoken. All materials prepared for use with the people must be checked with and have the approval of native speakers of the language. Such approval may be very informal. Where the community leaders are actively involved, however, approval of the alphabet to be used and literature to be published may be much more formal.

All members of a team are expected to learn to speak the language. Preferably each member chooses a different aspect of the language analysis. One may work on the sounds, the other on the grammar. Later they may specialize in literacy or translation. Where both translate they may do different books and thus supplement each other and not compete. Mothers have reduced assignments according to time available.

On their field of service, members are expected to live in a community where the language is spoken and the materials produced can be tested. Residence in isolated and remote areas is interrupted when necessary for health, rest, family, or group assignment reasons, or to attend workshops.

At strategic points in their analysis, members attend field workshops. Such workshops may last three or four months. They are usually held at a center where facilities are provided. This reduces the time spent in living and maximizes the time for study. Accomodations are also provided for language helpers who accompany them. Once proficiency in the language is attained, members may spend more extended

7. *Workshop brings translators in several languages together with experienced consultants to check work done and seek solutions to problems.*

periods at such centers, away from the distractions and interruptions of village life. This hastens the completion of major linguistic, literacy or translation projects. Language materials prepared away from the village are normally rechecked in the ethnic community before final publication.

While top priority is given to the ethnic languages, the linguists as well as other support staff are expected to learn enough of the national or trade language for necessary everyday purposes and for public relations with national and local officials. Members whose principal assignment involves constant contact with speakers of the official language are expected to be more proficient in that language.

Members often work with bilinguals, using the national language to get started in learning the mother tongue. They are expected, however, to discipline themselves in its use in the ethnic community lest it become a crutch and hinder their learning and use of the mother tongue. In locations where members become so identified and involved with the trade or national language speaking people in the community that their learning of the ethnic language is seriously

81

hindered, they may be asked to move to a new community and start over again speaking only the local mother tongue. In situations where the people are highly monolingual, or where the linguist wishes to avoid the use of any other language, language learning proceeds by gesture and mimicry, without the use of any intermediate language.

In one ethnic community, for example, a few of the leading people knew Spanish. One member of the team assigned knew Spanish. The other did not. The first learned the language through Spanish, the second by pointing at objects. Even when the first used the vernacular the few in the village who knew Spanish insisted on speaking Spanish with him but would immediately repeat what they had said in the vernacular for the second. The end result was that the second was totally immersed in the vernacular, the first in spite of knowing the vernacular had to spend much time listening to the local brand of limited Spanish.

The linguist-translator who specializes in an ethnic language must sooner or later give serious attention to the official language. While technical articles for international journals may be written in English, they are much more useful locally by scholars and educators when published in the national language. Dictionaries, native-authored texts and Scripture translations are often published in diglot, that is, in both the mother tongue and the official language. This makes them usable both by national language speakers and by ethnic language speakers. Sometimes the latter find them a help in learning the national language. Since we are not specialists in the national language, the national language part of all such materials must be carefully checked and edited by a competent speaker of that language.

We do not analyze or teach the national language as such. We believe that should be done by national language linguists and educators. We do prepare bilingual bridge materials to help ethnic language speakers master the pronunciation and differing grammatical patterns of the national language.

Mazatec speakers distinguish only four vowels. Spanish uses five. Mazatecs do not hear or make the difference between *u* and *o* as Spanish do in *luna* ("moon") and *lona* ("canvas"). Mazatecs can learn to hear and make the difference. Special drills in which the two are contrasted help. Spanish teachers often grow impatient with their Mazatec pupils, attributing the difficulty to "stupidity" rather than to a clash of language systems.

Because of our ability to speak the language and linguistic insights into the structure of the language, we are able to prepare pilot literacy materials built to fit the natural structure of the language. We then proceed to teach the people to read and write their own language, to author literature themselves and to teach others these skills.

The people are fascinated when we point out to them things about their language which they have never thought about before. After I drew the town president's attention to the four contrasting levels of voice he used to distinguish Mazatec words, he embarrassed me by telling a visiting official that I spoke his language "better than he did." This was not true and he knew it. But it was his attempt to give credit for the insights I was able to give him into the subtleties of his own language.

As a scientific organization we are committed to making the results of our training and research available. Members are expected to publish technical articles concerning the languages studied. These are written in field workshops, some on advanced study programs. Members present papers at linguistic conferences. Some are assigned to teach in our own training institutes. Some lecture in university courses on the field or in the home country.

Members are encouraged not only to use mother tongue language helpers as a source of information about the language but also to train them in the same skills so they may increasingly contribute in their own right to the linguistic analysis and translation work. The contribution of those so trained is recognized by co-authorship of articles and books. Some become authors in their own right.

Academic Excellence

Both our linguistic commitments and our Bible translation goals require us to strive for constant self-improvement and academic excellence. As already pointed out, introductory linguistic training is required of all members. Those with linguistic assignments are required to take advanced linguistic training, to attend periodic workshops, and to make the results of their linguistic research available in written form. Some are encouraged to work toward linguistic degrees, to present papers at linguistic conferences, to write books and articles for publication in linguistic journals, and to give a major portion of their time to training and helping others.

All of this gives to the work a distinct academic emphasis. Whether as students, teachers or field workers in linguistics, literacy and translation, we move freely in academic and professional circles. We are indebted to many professional linguists and have benefited greatly from their teaching and writings. We are grateful that in turn we can contribute to knowledge of the languages of the world, the development of linguistic science and the advance of translation theory.

Motivation

Too few well-trained linguists are available to go into the out-of-the-way areas where most of the languages concerned are spoken. Not only must a translator undergo hardships and isolation but he must also devote years of his time to learn a language, analyze the grammar, write the books describing it, teach the people to read, and provide a literature for them. As a result, of all the languages spoken in the world, we still know little or nothing about half of them. So while linguistics provides the necessary skills to do the job, of itself it seldom provides the motivation that will see it through. For us, Bible translation supplies the motivation that makes the conditions bearable, the time well spent, and the linguistics worthwhile and worth doing well. Our members are people of serious Christian convictions and motivation. They desire to make the Bible, the Book that has transformed their own lives, available to all people in their mother tongues. Since translation of the Bible is a linguistic task and calls for linguistic competence, they find no conflict of interest in a dual commitment to both Bible translation and linguistics. Bible translation is simply one, and for us a major, application of linguistics. Linguistics is the tool that helps us do it well (2 Tim. 2:15).

But Bible translation is by no means the only reason we devote ourselves to linguistics. The first and greatest commandment includes loving God with all our mind (Matt. 22:37). The intellectual discipline of linguistics gives ample opportunity for obedience to this part of the command. Some find academic pursuits more congenial than others. Learning another language, striving to understand another culture, and writing up for publication what we have discovered are agonizing and humbling processes. But they are tremendously rewarding in the achievement.

The field of linguistics offers open-ended possibilities of limitless proportions to those with a yen for research. To push the frontiers of knowledge further, to find solutions to language problems that have baffled mankind for years, to contribute to the understanding and effectiveness of communication in general and cross-cultural communication in particular—these are genuine motivational factors for some of our members.

For those members who are people-oriented and for all of us who seek to know how other people think and live, the program requires much time with those who speak the language. We interact with them in every type of situation, come to appreciate them as people and relate to them as friends. Linguistic commitments requiring time at the desk away from the people is a price well worth paying, however, since it results in a better understanding of the language and greater fluency in using it.

In addition to all the personal and utilitarian reasons for involvement in linguistics, the fact remains that language in general and languages in particular have an intrinsic fascination. Languages identify, separate, and yet relate communities of people. The comparison of languages throws light on the historical origins and movements of the peoples who speak them. Differences between languages, factors common to all languages, and the variability and creativity within each language tell us something about our own humanity. The fact that over 5,000 mutually unintelligible languages are spoken in the world today, each one capable of handling in its own unique way all of life's situations, including the space age, means that each language is important and has something to contribute to our understanding of language in general.

Finally, as creatures made in the image of our Creator, our own capacity to use language and to learn and use other languages surely tells us something about the character of the one who made us so.

Thus our study of languages (linguistics) adds to our understanding of ourselves, of all who speak a different language, and of the God we serve. It adds a new perspective to interpersonal relationships, cross-cultural communication, and the divine-human encounter.

From the standpoints of Christian conviction, academic interest and humanitarian concern, every language of the world merits serious study and the people who speak it deserve our respect and help in realizing their full potential.

To bring the combined resources of all the languages of the world, each with its own eloquence, to the task of declaring God's greatness and goodness as recorded in the Bible is not wasted effort. It turns Babel's curse into heaven's greatest glory (Rev. 5:9; 7:9).

6

Motivation for Literacy

"WHEN I learned to read I became a new person," said an Amis tribesman of Taiwan. "I still cannot understand how only twenty-one marks put together on a piece of paper can have so much power."

"Before I could read, I would go to the church, but it didn't mean anything to me. Now that I can read I have learned the meaning of the Gospel. Now I have peace," testified another.[1]

Literacy, the ability to read and write, is something we seek to develop among the people whose languages we study. In the formation of the alphabet and preparation of teaching materials our linguistic analysis of the mother tongue finds immediate application. The ability of people to read their own language is crucial to the use of our translation of the Bible.

The goal of literacy is written communication. To express oneself, one writes. To comprehend, one reads what is written. We do not equate reading with merely pronouncing words written on a page, nor writing with simply tracing symbols on a sheet of paper. To be literate, a person must understand what he reads and be understood when he writes. This is why literacy in the mother tongue is such a powerful and at the same time pleasurable skill.

In the context of our work we use the terms "literacy" and "literate" in contrast to "illiteracy" and "illiterate," not with reference to people of considerable education or learning. We are involved primarily with preliterate peoples whose languages have not been previously written. Since they have never been written down, no one has ever read them. Some of those who speak them may have learned to read or write in a school language. Only occasionally do we help with literacy programs in more advanced situations and national languages.

Linguistics and Literacy

Linguistic analysis helps determine the number of sounds that contrast and need to be represented in the alphabet. The choice of characters to represent these sounds is heavily influenced by the way other languages in the area are written, especially the official school language. The sequence and combinations in which letters of the alphabet are introduced in the primers vary according to the structure of each language. Culturally related materials in the common grammatical and discourse styles of the language provide motivation for those learning to read.

The linguistic analysis in turn profits. Where mother tongue speakers stumble or hesitate in reading or deviate in writing, the linguistic analysis underlying the writing system may need to be revised. Literate mother tongue co-workers, after they learn to type, can provide quantities of stories, both traditional and original, for the linguist to study. These materials become the basis for further analysis of the language, from the smallest particles to the most inclusive discourse. People writing original literature in their own language develop a feel for how their language should be written. They make significant contributions to final decisions on correct spelling of their language. Literate speakers of the language may contribute to the preparation of grammars and the compilation of dictionaries of their languages.

A speaker of Creole in Australia's Northern Territory learned to read and write his language, even though a spelling system was not fully developed. He soon became a writer of original Creole stories. In one year he wrote fifty. Some were published in booklet form, some in the local newspaper. Then the School of Australian Linguistics sponsored a Creole Writers Course. One goal was to help Creole writers decide how to write their own language. Because of his experience as a writer and editor, this man made a valuable contribution toward the final solution.

Bible Translation and Literacy

The availability of literature provides an incentive for people to learn to read. A Bible translation provides a veritable library of reading material. A graded series of carefully selected portions of Scripture can be used to perfect reading skills. The transformation of character which the Bible brings about plays an important part in providing readers who are motivated to teach others. Whether paid or not, some are eager to share their newly learned skill with others in their community. These in turn become potential readers of the Scriptures.

The Managalasi New Testament created a phenomenal enthusiasm to learn to read. Within a year and a half 850 out of a population of 5,000 were reading. Two teachers each taught ten students for five months. When these finished the reading courses they wanted to buy Testaments. Then four more classes were started. Pleas came for people to teach the Bible. Volunteer trainees were given a one-week course. The only requirement was that they be fluent readers. Out of nineteen trainees, all but one accepted Christ before the end of the course. Soon each was leading a Bible study in his own village.

While Bible translation provides motivation and materials for literacy programs, people who know how to read and write can contribute a great deal to the Bible translation program.

The people whose languages we study use different styles in different social contexts. Once people learn to read their language and then begin to write spontaneous materials, a distinctive writing style begins to develop. Individual authors, writing creatively and naturally, will each develop a style of his or her own. Once aware of what makes for clarity and pleasing style, such mother tongue co-translators contribute a great deal more to the quality of the finished translation. For example, Amuesha writers show clearer organization, greater chronological and logical ordering of events, and more explicit paragraphing when writing than when speaking. What intonation or gestures makes clear in speaking, Amuesha indicate by extra words when writing. Writers identify who they are writing about more often by repeating nouns instead of using pronouns as in speaking.[2] Attention to these details in the Amuesha translation makes it read much more smoothly and clearly.

When Scripture is used as reading material, translators testing the comprehension of readers discover where the translation is ambiguous or misleading. Disinterest or difficulty in reading on the part of good readers may indicate that the translation is unnecessarily pedantic or unnatural. Literate mother tongue speakers who read the Scriptures for personal profit or in their public ministry often suggest ways in which the translation can be improved. They themselves may be the ones to make the revisions.

Some readers become translators in their own right. A Huambisa believer, able to read the New Testament in Aguaruna, a related language, proceeded with some guidance from a consultant to make a translation for his own people. Fifteen literate Quechuas, using Scripture already available in one of their dialects, are making translations for the millions of speakers of other dialects of that language.

Literacy and Community Development

The lifestyle of those who want to learn the new skills of reading and writing changes. A nomadic way of life may become more sedentary, focused seasonally at least around the school. Morris Watkins has pointed out that "literacy can influence development in a number of ways. It is an essential aid in the improvement of agriculture and public health, in the development of skills for industry, in an intelligent adjustment to changing society, in responsible participation in political affairs, and in the enrichment of cultural and spiritual life."[3]

90

Illiteracy on the other hand can be a deterrent to these kinds of development, leaving a community backward and open to exploitation. In all too many cases illiteracy coincides with poverty and famine conditions, greater incidence of disease and shorter life expectancy.

Once people begin writing their own language, they can record their own history and verbal literature not only for their own posterity, but through translations for the outside world. One Mazatec has already published a biography of a noted shaman and a description of the local mushroom ceremonies. Literacy opens the door to education, to the learning of other languages, and to the world beyond ethnic borders. It enables people to contribute to as well as learn from other cultures.

For the Christian, literacy can present a whole new way of life and service. Advanced education, including biblical studies, linguistics, even Greek and Hebrew, are now not impossible. Those who help on the first pioneer translation, after getting more training, may go on to complete the whole Bible for their own people in their own language. For some we hope it will ultimately mean ethnic groups with the Scriptures will be sending some of their own as pioneer translators to still other languages without the Bible.

Motivation for Literacy

We still occasionally find people so isolated from the rest of the world that they are unfamiliar with writing and reading. A translator, building his home, picked up a chip and wrote on it a message to his wife. The man who delivered it was amazed when the wife looked at the chip then went into the house, got some money, and paid him exactly what her husband had agreed to pay him.

"But how did you know?" he asked.

"Oh, the wood told me," she replied.

"You mean wood can talk!" Somehow he had never realized that squiggly marks on a chip or any other flat surface could have some connection to the noises we make when we talk.

For such, writing is a type of magic. Just think, by writing one's name on a piece of paper one can get great sums of money! Some people are highly motivated to learn to write their name and that is all. But literacy for communication is neither understood or desired.

8. *The first step in the making of an ethnic language author.*

Sometimes we are motivated to teach people before they are motivated to learn. An unscrupulous merchant sold an illiterate Mazatec who had a stomach ache a can of sewing machine oil at several times its value. The labeled can had the government regulated price stamped on it. But the Mazatec could not read. To provide him a means of protecting himself against such exploitation, I'm ready to teach him to read. Once he learns how he's being exploited, he's motivated too!

Many ethnic minority people want to learn to read. People who know how to read and write often get better jobs and make more money. Since important people often know how to read, the desire for power and prestige motivates some to learn. Some have a genuine curiosity and realize that books are a source of ideas and information about many things. The creative urge to communicate something burning in one's bones moves some to write. Others learn because the community expects them to learn, provides facilities and teachers and encourages attendance in classes.

Some communities may see in literacy a means of keeping abreast of the world around them and communicating with government offices and personnel. The older generation may see it as a way of recording and preserving their culture, or as necessary for their children to get ahead and earn a living. Literacy has often had a special value to the Christian portion of a community, once the Scriptures were available.

But what makes people indifferent or even antagonistic to literacy? Several factors. The Tunebos have a strong taboo against paper with writing on it. It was not given them by their gods, they say, and is dangerous and may cause disease. A letter from the central government to the local authority defending the rights of the Tunebo sat several months undelivered because the Tunebo man who brought it believed it had made him sick and he did not want to expose anyone else to it. One day after the translator explained writing to him as one person talking to another, the man ventured to have him write a letter on his behalf to a friend in another village. He had bought a dog from the friend. The dog had disappeared and he assumed it had gone home. Would his friend please send the dog back? Unfortunately the friend never answered and the dog never showed up. The Tunebo was far from convinced. So when the translator later proposed literacy classes and a school the authorities were strongly opposed. Away from their village some Tunebos would help with language and translation work and some even learned to read. Enroute home, however, they always "forgot" or "lost" their books.

Leaders who maintain control by keeping people in ignorance may actively oppose literacy programs. In one village the entire consignment of government primers was burned by a leader who opposed the campaign. Prominent people often fear embarrassment if they should try and fail. Some minority people have been told for so long they lack ability that they seem to believe it and refuse to try. Others know people who do not know how to read or write and who are making out all right, so why bother? Some tried once but never reached the proficiency where they could read for enjoyment and are discouraged. Many others lack anything to read.

Some communities resist the idea of literacy because it threatens to disrupt their established views and creates tension between the generations of those who do not read and those who do. New patterns of conduct, such as sitting in school or at home doing nothing but reading instead of working in the fields and participating in community activities, are considered disruptive. Obviously they have no immediate, practical community value, such as providing food. The teacher is a threat to the authority of those who make the decisions for the community, especially if they were not consulted or made partners to the decision to promote a literacy campaign in their community in the first place.

Motivation is crucial in any literacy effort. Highly motivated people have learned to read in spite of faulty alphabets, poorly designed materials, poor methods and insufficient teachers. On the other hand, given a good alphabet, the best of materials and methods and dedicated teachers, a literacy program may still flounder if people lack motivation.

In one African country a five-week conference was planned for fellowship and the instruction of thirty-four Christian leaders. The leader of the association wrote beforehand, "These men must learn to read the Gospel for themselves in their own language if we are to see significant progress."

The men however replied, "We are farmers and hunters from the jungle. Reading is for those who have been in the city for many years or for those who have been to school. We have passed the age of learning. Surely, reading is not possible for most of us." In spite of the enthusiasm of their leader and of the literacy teachers, this attitudinal albatross made each lesson a chore for both teachers and students.

Finally one group finished the second primer and moved on to read a book of selected Bible verses. To their amazement they read straight through it in ten minutes. They reread it to get a better understanding of what the verses said. Then they turned to the Gospel of Mark and began to read in unison. Break time came and went and they continued reading, stopping only for an occasional discussion of the context. The group was dramatically transformed. Their teachers gained new courage and vision as the men read nonstop through the remaining hour and for another twenty minutes after it was time to close. One of the older learners came to the teacher and said, "Before today we didn't understand reading business. Now we understand and we thank you."[4]

Among the Otomi pastors, interest in the use of Otomi Scriptures was slow in coming. Most of them had learned to read Spanish and were accustomed to using the Spanish Scriptures. In a special class to introduce the Otomi Scriptures, the Otomi leader had the pastors read passages from the Otomi Scriptures for their devotional time together at the beginning of each day. With a greater understanding of what the passage was saying in their mother tongue than they had ever had in Spanish, the discussion became animated and the spiritual profit was evident to all. By the end of the week they were much more motivated not only to use the Otomi Scriptures for themselves, but also to recommend them to their people. For the Christian, and often for others too, the very availability of the Word of God in the mother tongue often results in a greater motivation to learn to read.

Literature of known reputation that offers a solution to a felt need or is written by known people on subjects of current interest is the most important element in stirring people to want to learn. A continuing supply of fresh literature helps develop the reading habit. An ongoing program calls for the training of indigenous authors and literacy teachers as well as the development of publication and distribution channels.

The availability of the Scriptures does not of itself guarantee that people will learn to read, or that they will read the

Bible after they learn. But the most irrefutable reasons why people do not read the Scriptures are: first, no translation has been made in their language; second, if translated, they do not possess a copy; and third, if copies are available, they have never been taught to read.

The writer participated in a meeting of the Bible Society in Mexico with representatives of the churches working among the minority language groups of that country. The meeting had been called to discuss why the Scriptures in the minority languages were not being promoted by the churches. One after another arose to say that his church had no program of distribution because the people could not read the translations. The accumulated impact of report after report of this nature finally brought the meeting to a seemingly unanimous impasse. Finally one representative, a very humble Maya, arose and quietly asked: "Why don't we talk about the real question?" Everyone looked at him, startled. "How many of your churches have any program to teach the people how to read?" Not a single one represented in the meeting had any such program! Sometimes the vision and motivation is lacking in those who should teach the people.

Our Christian conscience demands that others have the same opportunity to possess and read a copy of the Scriptures in their own language as we have. While all may not exercise the option, none should be deprived of the opportunity. Our goal for each illiterate ethnic community is an ongoing literacy program that will teach a growing number of each generation to read. The Bible was written, and we translate it, to be read.

Literacy in the Bible

Our commitment to literacy finds strong support in the Bible. The Bible is not only literature for the literate. It puts a high value on the ability to read and underlines some of the most basic principles involved.

God did not assume that because his Word was written it would be read. On many occasions he commanded that it should be read and gave instructions on how it should be read (Joshua 1:8; Deut. 17:19; 6:7). Providing the Bible for people in written form in their mother tongue includes in the very nature of the case translating for them the divine injunction to read and use it responsibly and to teach others to do the same.

The Bible affirms that reading and writing are as legitimate and genuine a form of communication as speaking and hearing. God spoke, men heard and wrote what God said, that people today might read what they wrote and again hear God speak (Deut. 31:9-13). God speaks through the written Word just as surely as he did through the original spoken word. Christ equated what Moses wrote with what God said (Mark 7:9, 10, 13; 12:26). He also equated reading what Moses and the Prophets wrote with hearing them speak (Luke 16:29-31).

The Bible never considers reading a mere oral exercise, although Scripture was always read aloud, whether the one reading was alone or in a group. Philip's question to the Ethiopian: "Do you understand what you are reading?" (Acts 8:30) was not an impertinent query to an educated man, but went right to the heart of the matter. Reading was useless unless it was accompanied by understanding. The account of Ezra's reading of the Book of the Law of Moses to the children of Israel emphasized this. "Ezra . . . brought the Law before the assembly, which was made up of men and women and all who were able to understand. . . . The Levites . . . read from the Book of the Law of God, making it clear and giving the meaning so that the people could understand what was being read" (Nehemiah 8:2, 7, 8). So we read that the people celebrated with great joy "because they now understood the words that had been made known to them" (v. 12). Reading for understanding is the biblical example and goal.

But the reading of Scripture makes those who read it, and those who hear it read, responsible for what they have read and heard. Christ rebuked the chief priests, the elders and the scribes with the words: "Have you never read in the Scriptures?" (Mt. 21:16, 42). Indeed they had read it, many times, but they had not committed themselves to the truth

97

read, either to believe it or obey it. Christ's words to the lawyer who asked him, "Teacher what must I do to inherit eternal life?" were "What is written in the Law? How do you read it?" And he answered, "Love the Lord your God with all your heart and with all your soul and with all your strength and with all your mind;" and, "Love your neighbor as yourself" (Luke 10:25-28). He not only read well, but understood what he read well enough to be able to reproduce it, apparently, from memory. But reading for Christ implied more than verbalization of the words and more than understanding what was read, for he continued: "You have answered correctly. Do this, and you will live." John writing by the Spirit in Revelation 1:3 said: "Blessed is the one who reads the words of this prophecy, and blessed are those who hear it and take to heart what is written in it."

Where the illiterate may regard writing as magic and the Bible as a fetish because "sacred", the literate person is faced with the moral demands of obedience to the truth read and understood. A Navajo said, "I used to think I was a pretty good Christian until I began to read the Bible in my own language!"

The ability to read brings moral responsibility to choose, to discern and to obey what is right, both to the one reading and to those hearing what is read. It is no light thing to teach a person to read and put a copy of the Scripture in his hand. But where ignorance means eternal loss, reading with under-standing opens the door to eternal life.

The ability to read gives every believer the potential for a ministry based on the Word of God. The Bible makes it clear that reading the Scriptures aloud is itself an essential ministry and basic to all other oral ministries. Our cultural practice of teaching people to read in silence, rapidly and efficiently, has largely closed our eyes to this method and resulted in a de-emphasis on the reading of Scripture aloud in church services. The result is an emphasis more on what the speaker is going to say *about* the Word of God than listening to the Word of God itself. In every context of Scripture, unless clearly indicated otherwise, the reading referred to is aloud.[5] Twenty-one of the twenty-seven New Testament books were written to be read aloud in Christian services (1 Thess. 5:27; Col. 4:16). The rest were also so used.

9. Preaching from the Piro New Testament.

To Timothy Paul wrote: ". . . devote yourself to the public reading of Scripture, to preaching and to teaching" (1 Tim. 4:13). The Christian church took over the familiar pattern of the synagogue service: first a reading of Scripture aloud, then exhortation based upon it (preaching), then a question-and-answer catechizing of the people on the great doctrines of the faith found in it (teaching). In this passage Paul was telling Timothy to prepare himself well in advance in private for the public reading of Scripture. This was especially necessary because Greek was written as continuous text without word divisions. He is to improve his skill for the sake of his own reputation. Despite his youth, oral reading of the Scripture was something in which he could excel.

99

Paul urged Timothy to seek not man's but God's approval by straightforward reading and explanation of the text of Scripture and the proper application of the word of truth to the issues involved (see 2 Tim. 2:15). This was especially important in view of the error and false doctrine others were teaching. The Scripture and the church leader's ability to read it were his equipment for every situation, especially for teaching, reproving, correcting, and training the believers under him for their respective ministries. All these ministries were to be based on the Scriptures, both for authority and for content (2 Tim. 3:16-4:5). For this reason Timothy should devote himself to the private study and public reading of the Scriptures. This would assure a fruitful ministry for him as well as spiritual welfare for his flock (1 Tim. 4:15, 16).

Everyone should be encouraged, as soon as he is literate, to read the Scriptures aloud to others. It is the easiest type of service to perform, yet it can have far-reaching results. According to Romans 10:17, faith comes by hearing. In the biblical context this includes hearing both the oral reading of Scripture and the preaching based on it.

Literacy through the Ages

Literacy was widespread in the periods of Egyptian, Babylonian, Hebrew, Greek and Roman greatness. Long before Abraham, highly developed ideographic and phonetic writing was in use. Millions of cuneiform documents in Babylonia and papyri, leather and skin documents in Egypt in Abraham's time presuppose people who could write and read, since all documents were written individually by hand. Books were common from Babylonia to Asia Minor to Egypt. Kings, priests, military officers, scribes, schools of writers and many private individuals were able both to read and write in Old Testament times. The prevalence of writing in this period "may be compared perhaps to the ratio of college graduates in modern life."[6]

Prior to and at the time of Christ, literacy was common from Italy to Egypt to Palestine. The remarkable school system in the synagogues of the Jews—public schools in almost every town of Palestine, and compulsory education from the age of six or seven—has caused some to believe literacy had reached a level it would not reach again for 1800 years.[7] Certainly in the world of Christ's day business-men, fishermen and even a carpenter's son could read and write not only Hebrew but Greek.

During the period of the New Testament and the first five centuries of church history many Christians could read and write. They authored many books, in which they quoted or made frequent mention of Scripture. Some of the early Church Fathers were prolific writers. They also made many copies of the biblical documents by hand. Over 4,000 Greek manuscripts of the New Testament in whole or in part, the earliest dating from the second century, exist. No other book was so copied. Christians were indeed "the people of the Book." Watkins points out that "where the Church was strong, we find great writers. Where the Church was weak and corrupt, we find few writers or none at all. It is difficult to determine which was cause and which was effect."[8] Literacy of itself did not guarantee doctrinal purity, for many scholarly men who read the Bible promoted heresy. But "there is no record of the Church in any land becoming strong spiritually where the leadership was illiterate or where laymen were not encouraged to read the Bible."[9]

During the Middle Ages literacy dropped to what may have been an all time low. Even kings, nobles, lawyers and some clergy were illiterate. Formal education was in the hands of the church, but in Latin, a foreign language. Bible reading by the laity was not encouraged. "There is no record of any mission work by illiterate people, although it is quite possible that many illiterate laymen did witness for Christ with some success."[10] The expansion of the Church during this period came as a result of Bible-reading and Bible-preaching missionaries who made good use of the freedom and favorable climate provided by mass political conversions through the edict of a ruler who proclaimed himself and his subjects Christians.

During the latter half of the fourteenth century references

to literate laymen in England began to appear. Then came the Renaissance, the Reformation, the printing press, a literate middle class, and an emphasis again on laymen reading the Bible for themselves.

Beginning around A.D. 1800 the Gospel spread around the world in the wake of the explorations and colonizing activity of the European nations. Missionaries translated the Bible and began schools which trained the leaders of the church and the nations. Education was usually in a European language and not for the masses. Trade language Scriptures served educated preachers but not, in many cases, those to whom they ministered. Vernacular translations served both pastors and people, but widespread illiteracy (which continues to this day in many countries) limited the illiterate to what they heard, even where the written Scriptures were available. In summing up, Watkins states, "We know of no permanent indigenous church that did not have the Scriptures in its own language and at least one church leader who was able to read those Scriptures or who had committed to memory a large amount of Scripture."[11] But surely this is a bare minimum and a far, far cry from the New Testament church situation!

While vernacular Scriptures and a literate membership may not guarantee doctrinal purity, personal maturity or church growth, they combine to produce a lot more of all three than the absence of them does. History also tells us that for a strong, growing, outgoing ministry Christians need to express their faith in writing for the edification of the believers and the winning of the lost. Only then will it match the vitality and make the lasting contribution of the early Church.

Literacy and the Indigenous Principle

To be fully indigenous, the basis of authority and the decision-making must be within the culture itself, not in some foreign system, person or document. This is why Bible translation is so essential to the establishment, growth, discipline, independence, doctrinal soundness and outreach of indigenous churches. Literacy in the mother tongue gives direct access to the basic document of the Christian faith. Some have even felt literacy should be required for church membership. It is undoubtedly necessary for the teaching leadership.

Reading God's Word for oneself makes the message more personal and relevant. A young believer, despite a missionary's assurance that the verse "Casting all your care upon him, for he careth for you" was for her, went away quite unconsoled.

The next day she returned, radiant, and read the same verse to the missionary.

The missionary replied, "But that is what I told you yesterday."

"Oh! But now I've found it myself," was the ecstatic reply.

Literacy makes possible a healthy independence from what people say and a healthy dependence on what God has said. A former headhunter chuckled as he said, "Even when you are not here, we can read it for ourselves."

The literate Christian reading the Scriptures aloud to others speaks with authority. A Mazatec with a sixth-grade education, reading a copy of the Mazatec New Testament to hundreds of his people over the radio, speaks with the authority of the written Word of God. A former medicine-man among the Navajo won many as followers of Christ by reading the Scripture to them. One humble, barefoot widow who had never been to school but who knew how to read her own language taught other Mazatec men, women and children verses of Scripture until they could quote them by memory to others in their homes. Then they in turn could say, "God says."

Literacy is an appropriate area of social action. The Christian, whether of the national majority or ethnic minority, or a foreigner, can help those who want to learn to read. The extended contact with non-Christians in a helpful atmosphere builds friendship and gives opportunity to share one's faith. An ongoing literature program that includes biblical stories, local believers' testimonies and the translated Scriptures gives new literates a broader and unhurried exposure to the implications of accepting Christ.

A literacy program tied to the teaching of the Word by literate believers can be a vehicle for church growth. Equipped with primers, the first and most mature Amuesha believer began a Bible school, teaching young believers from several villages to read, then training them in the Scriptures. These in turn gathered their neighbors together and retaught what they had learned, using the Scriptures they could now read. The result was several new churches. A translator commenting on the growth of the church among the Aguaruna wrote: "From my point of view at least, the translation would not have done it apart from the literacy

10. *Literacy supervisor watches as an indigenous teacher goes over a lesson with a student.*

program, especially where we were able to train key men and the church developed through them."

In the Huixteco church, literacy made a tremendous difference in the administering of discipline. Whenever the leaders discussed and rebuked others without actually reading the relevant Scripture, it only led to further trouble. But when they read the specific Scriptures with the person and then disciplined him on the basis of what they had read, it was observed that the discipline was much better accepted.

A Piro couple, both of whom could read, found searching Scripture for God's standards of conduct stabilized their relationship. On one occasion the husband reported: "When I do something I shouldn't, she says to me, 'Moran, doesn't God's Word say thus and so?' So then I go and read it and by God's help I don't do that any more."

A Bimoba language helper of Ghana was sobered one day when he read in Luke 16:18 the words: "Any one who divorces his wife and marries another woman commits adultery." He and his wife had been going through a very severe domestic crisis for almost a year. Literacy and the availability of the Scripture made it possible for him to know how God looked upon the very matter that had been threatening his home.

Literacy is no replacement for godliness nor a panacea for all ills, of course. One indigenous church in Mexico, in order to cooperate with a literacy campaign in the national language and refute false charges of being against progress and the government, decided to hold all meetings in Spanish rather than in their mother tongue. The result was chaotic. Neither the church leaders nor the people knew enough Spanish to conduct the meetings or pray in Spanish. Less obvious but more subtly disastrous was the substitution of language learning for worship and Bible study as the object of their gatherings. Finally, a happy compromise was found. The believers scheduled weekly classes specifically for Spanish and literacy, thus fulfilling their obligations as patriotic citizens. Meanwhile worship and prayer meetings continued in the mother tongue, so their spiritual needs were met too.

Bible translation tied to literacy makes it possible for

churches to be indigenous from the very beginning. The first believers are given the Scriptures in their own language, taught to read and search the Scriptures for themselves and make their own decisions on the basis of what they find there. The translator provides the book, trains them to obey it and trusts the Holy Spirit to guide them in applying it in ways that fit their culture. But the ultimate source of author-

11. Huixteco family Bible study, Mexico.

ity is the Bible, directly accessible in the language of the pulpit and pew.

In the early days of the Tzeltal church few could read. Those who could read helped successive classes of illiterate believers memorize extended passages of Scripture. Week after week each person returned to the same class and the same lesson until he knew it word-perfectly *and* was living it according to the testimony of his neighbors. Then and then only did the Tzeltals consider him ready to move on to a new lesson. How different from our insistence on a new lesson or sermon each week before we have done anything about applying the last one!

The already highly developed and very effective oral-aural

patterns of teaching and learning in some preliterate cultures should not be abandoned, however. Literacy in such a culture should not replace these but be the added element that links these patterns of learning to the Scriptures and feeds the Scripture into such channels of teaching.

Is Literacy for Everyone?

Not everyone learned to read in Bible times, although reading was more general than we usually acknowledge. Not everyone today possesses a copy of the Scriptures—although the potential for putting a copy in every literate's hand is greater now than ever before. But everyone should have the opportunity to hear the text of Scripture read in the language he understands. "Blessed is the one who reads the words of this prophecy, and blessed are those who hear it and take to heart what is written in it" (Rev. 1:3).

The importance of reading the Scriptures aloud has taken on new significance with the use of cassettes. Scriptures read aloud onto cassettes are making it possible for many more to hear the translated Word of God. Those who cannot read, including many who may never learn, as well as those who can read, are listening to the Scriptures read aloud. Entire Gospels and Epistles have thus been made available in some languages. As a result of frequent repetition, many are memorizing the extended passages.

When our workers were forced to leave Viet Nam, Scripture translation projects in seventeen languages were incomplete. Our members transferred to the Philippines and continued translating there. The Far East Broadcasting Company in Manila made time available to broadcast to these language groups of Viet Nam. The available Scripture in each language is read in fifteen minute segments. Segments from two languages are aired each day. All language groups in turn have the possibility of hearing God's Word in their mother tongue by radio. The result will be ever so much greater, however, if literate listeners write down what they hear and read and reread it or if, as is hoped, the printed text can also somehow be gotten to them.

People are being taught to read by lessons on cassette. Among the Kamano many learned to read in classes, but few men could be persuaded to attend, perhaps through fear of failure and ridicule. A special primer was prepared with all the instructions taped just as taught to a class, including time for the learner to read and the instructor's voice to come in for reinforcement or correction. The primer was divided into sections corresponding to each tape. The tape, the edges of the pages and the corresponding set of flashcards were marked with the same color for easy identification by those still unable to read. By starting each day from the beginning of one side of the cassette and a given color, the learner could review as well a find the right place each day. In addition to the reading lesson, Scripture verses and songs were included with each lesson. These helped keep up interest. Face-to-face lessons at intervals with an itinerant teacher present supplemented the tape lessons. Later, literate teachers were trained to use cassettes and to act as traveling supervisors to visit classes and test the students.

Television, transistor radios and cassettes do not replace the printed page, but they do supplement it. True, some addicted to them read less, but book sales on the whole are up, not down. Media ministries are highly dependent on producers who can and do read. Effective followup is largely limited to the literate among the listening audience, even in technological societies.

Whether everyone should be literate and to what level of literacy they should be educated may depend on the motive for wanting to learn to read. Many literate people who are technically trained think only of themselves and their families, and of financial and personal gain. If there are not sufficient job opportunities to absorb them all, teaching everyone to read may only lead to disillusionment, discontent and greater social problems. But if the individual is thinking of education as a means of sharing and using his reading ability for others' good, as we do when we introduce literacy as a means of access to the Word of God, then literacy for everyone is a good thing. This makes it a matter of personal ethics rather than economics.[12]

Some societies learn better in ways other than through books.[13] Even in communities with a long tradition of literacy, information is disseminated in ways other than writing. The assumption that no one can be a good Christian without reading his Bible every day may impose a heavy burden on young Christians for whom reading has never been a part of their life. We need to use every culturally applicable medium and means and not limit ourselves to traditional methods. Observation and experience indicate however that those limited to a weekly dose of oral Scripture and explanation do not grow to maturity and healthy spiritual independence and reproductivity like those who read the Scriptures for themselves. Certainly the teaching leadership must be literate and have direct, personal access to the Scriptures for an authoritative, sound and fruitful ministry. For the maximum development and ministry of each believer, too, the ability and practice of reading the Word of God for himself is important. For the preservation, multiplication and dissemination of the Scriptures, and for their maximum availability to every individual, the printed page is still the most effective tool.

We accept the fact that God, in his far-seeing omniscience, deliberately chose to make himself and his Son Jesus Christ known by both oral proclamation *and* written document. Since the written is now the only authority for the oral, we believe no man should be without direct access to the basic document. Translation-plus-literacy makes this possible. The biblical commands and precedents for giving attention to reading underlie our commitment not only to translate but to see that in each place a nucleus of readers of the Word is raised up who can not only read themselves, but are reading to others and teaching others to read. If people are illiterate and unable to read the Scriptures for themselves, we feel it should be by their own deliberate choice, not forced upon them by lack of opportunity to learn. Our responsibility under God is to make the Bible available and to offer to teach them to read it.

7

Literacy in the Mother Tongue

WE BELIEVE a person best learns to read in his mother tongue. We are not alone in such belief. Margaret Mead has written: "A basic condition of successful literacy . . . is that it should be attained in the mother tongue. Literacy achieved in any language other than the mother tongue is likely . . . to remain superficial and incomparable with the literacy of people who learned to read in the language in which their mothers sang them to sleep."[1]

Programs teaching people to read and write first in the national or official language of the country are fine for those who speak that language as their mother tongue. When they have been imposed on ethnic minorities native to a country who do not speak the official language they have often created problems and had poor results. Not only have the ethnic minorities remained functionally illiterate, but they have often been embittered because they have been forced to compete in a school system in which they are constantly at a disadvantage because of language and methods of testing.

Advantages

There are several reasons why we believe reading and writing are best taught in the mother tongue. In the first place, the basic reading skill (how to decode written symbols) is learned only once in a person's life. It is best done in a language one understands well and already speaks. For the multilingual person it is best done in the language he under-

110

stands and speaks best. This is usually his mother tongue. If what is read is not clearly understood, if it does not communicate, no matter how loudly it may be shouted or how "fluently" it may be rattled off, it is only nonsensical babbling, not reading in our sense of the term. Faulty habits, negative attitudes and basic insecurities acquired in learning to read in a language a person does not control well may seriously affect his reading ability for the rest of his life.

To teach someone how to read in a language he does not know how to speak, or is expected to learn to speak in the very process of learning how to read, is pedagogically unsound. It is teaching two unknowns at once. Learning to decode and interpret visual symbols on paper and learning to speak and understand a strange language are two quite different tasks. To combine them places extremely heavy psychological and emotional demands on the learner.

Reading and writing (including spelling) in the mother tongue have a definite advantage, especially when the writing is based on a linguistic analysis of the language as currently spoken, with a more or less one-to-one correspondence between sound and symbol. It is not unusual for ethnic minority people who have had no previous schooling to learn to read and write in a matter of weeks. A young Mamainde boy watched a literacy class for men. After two classes he caught on to the idea and disappeared with a copy of the book. Two weeks later he returned. He could read it fluently!

When pronunciation and spelling do not agree, however, as is so often the case in English, reading and writing are more difficult to learn.

Once a person has learned to read well in a language he understands, he can transfer this skill to any other written language with relative ease. His ability to read becomes a tool for learning the other language. Initial literacy in the mother tongue is of value *even if the only purpose of such literacy is transition to a second language.* For minority groups who need to learn another language in order to participate as citizens of a larger national entity, getting their basic training in their own language is not the long way around. It is the most effective route to mastery of the official language.

A Mazatec monolingual who read her own language well picked up and read material in Spanish without further training. Her pronunciation was strongly influenced by her own language but a Spanish-speaking hearer could follow all she read. She herself did not understand a word of it, never having learned Spanish. She needed to learn the meaning of the words she could already read.

Another advantage in mother tongue literacy and education is community support for the program. Pupils can share what they are learning with their parents. This reinforces the children's learning and helps in gaining parent understanding and cooperation. If teachers are members of the community or can speak the language of the community, they can explain to parents and community leaders the plans and purposes of the program and elicit their support.

Culture shock for the pupil is minimized. Children or adults find it a traumatic experience to be faced with a foreign language, foreign culture values, the strangeness of a school environment and a teacher with whom they cannot communicate. Teachers who speak the mother tongue, materials in the mother tongue and recognition of known cultural values and customs limit the cultural shock to the newness of a classroom environment and the novelty of the skills to be learned.

The learner's sense of personal worth and identity is also enhanced. Since the language used and the cultural values taught are already known and recognized as the learner's own, they are presented as worthy of study. The testing of the learner's ability and comprehension is on a standard and scale valid for him. When the language of the classroom is foreign to the learner, he is at a serious disadvantage. He may be penalized for not understanding the teacher, judged unfairly on a basis of foreign standards, alienated and belittled as inherently inferior. This can be disastrous and accounts for much of the resentment minority people often feel, even against well-motivated benefactors.

The learner's mental maturation and capacity to grasp and apply basic concepts develops normally when he learns to read in his mother tongue. Since what is being taught is in terms of his own language and culture, with explanations of new concepts in terms of what he already knows, the potential for understanding is within the learner's reach. New ideas can be applied to real world situations and referents in a meaningful way to verify his understanding of the basic concepts involved. In a foreign language, where learning is often by rote memory and mimicry without understanding, failure to grasp underlying basic concepts and the inability to apply what is taught proves extremely frustrating. Mental development is thus seriously retarded and the dropout rate goes up.

Where there is a wide cultural and economic gap between the minority language group and the national language people, minority children who begin in their own language may actually have an advantage over minority children who start their schooling directly in the national language. This advantage may show up later in superior grades even in the national language. One explanation is that mental development proceeds best in a known language.[2]

When a person learns to read in his mother tongue, his attitude and expectation of progress are positive. He has a sense of accomplishment and confidence that he can learn. He can cope with new situations and apply what has been learned. This is especially needed as he encounters other cultures, learns other languages and begins to participate in the larger world outside his own culture.[3]

The minority language speaker's image of himself, of his people and of his culture is healthier if he learns to read in his own language first. He can read and write his language like others do theirs. His experiences can be written down for others to read. Things from the outside world can be translated and adequately described in his own language. His language and his way of life are intrinsically equal although different from that of others.

Because he has learned to read and write first in his own language, he has the option of continuing to speak and use his mother tongue so long as he chooses and for whatever purposes. He is free to choose to learn another language too.

This flexibility is a liberating thing. He can contribute to, as well as learn from, the carriers of the national culture. He can act independently or cooperate with those of the other culture. Participation in national affairs does not have to mean loss of cultural identity or absorption into the dominant culture if cultural identity and self-determination is first solidly established in one's own language and cultural group.[4]

Use of the mother tongue as a bridge to literacy and competence in the national language can unify rather than divide a country. And the mutual respect engendered by true bilingual instruction can lessen tensions as the linguistic minorities begin to enter the mainstream of political, social and economic life. Where governments have respected minority languages and dignified them by use in education, patriotism has been encouraged and a good attitude created toward the national language and the people who speak it.[5]

Literacy in the mother tongue does not necessarily isolate people from the outside world. It lays a solid basis for later acquisition of other languages as necessary for those who wish further study and involvement in national or international affairs. This is not to say that in a linguistically homogenous population it should ever be obligatory that everyone learn to speak, read and write any language other than their own. Many may never leave their own language area. To insist that they become literate in a language they will in fact never or hardly ever use while remaining illiterate in the language they will use all their lives somehow is not logical.[6]

Mother tongue literacy and education can be a means for the introduction of new ideas to all segments of the mother tongue culture, not just those who are bilingual. This keeps the whole population moving ahead, yet independent of foreign or national government personnel.

Mother tongue literacy and vernacular Scriptures are a powerful combination for the introduction and spread of the Gospel. A Christian in West Africa thanked the translator for giving him the Bible in his own language. He went on to tell of a conversation he had with a pastor whose people had had the Gospel for a hundred years but no vernacular Scriptures.

114

The pastor, although literate in English, was wide of the mark in explaining an English Scripture passage. How great was his surprise when this humble Christian from his mother tongue Bible interpreted the Word more accurately.[7]

The Monolingual Literacy Program

Among the ethnic minorities whose languages have not previously been written, the printed page and the skills of reading and writing are usually considered to belong exclusively to foreign cultures. In pioneer situations, a literacy program begins by explaining the whole idea of reading and writing as a means of receiving and sharing ideas and information with others. The value of being literate may not be self-evident to those whose culture has other methods of education and communication. Until a practical orthography is created and in use for teaching purposes, the possibility that the ethnic language could even be written like other languages may not be granted.

We begin with reading readiness materials to teach those who are unfamiliar with the written page to pay attention to shapes, relate speech to visual symbols, and handle paper and books. Many adults have never held a book in their hands. They do not know which way is up on a page, or how pages are consecutively ordered. They may have to learn to read pictures and illustrations. The Guahibo, for example, did not recognize themselves or their relatives in photographs. Yet they can tell a person by his walk several hundred yards away. People who have lived all their lives in the real world may not recognize familiar objects in miniature on the printed page. Shapes and positions on a line have to be learned. For example, an upside down canoe is still a canoe, but an upside down *u* is no longer a *u* but an *n*.

The traditional orthography of the national or official language is used as far as possible in writing minority languages. Printers have the characters in their fonts of type. Typewriters also have them. Educators and everyone else who has learned to read the language are already familiar with them. And the printed page looks more normal. We prefer to use Roman script but in Moslem areas with a strong tradition of Arabic script we have also used it. In one language we even used the same translation in Roman script for the younger and Arabic of the older generation.

Preliterate languages may have no names for letters of the alphabet. Naming a symbol by its pronunciation is not helpful since many cannot be pronounced in isolation. Our names for them are meaningless in another language. So the Mamaindé invented names for the letters based on what they resemble in their jungle world. *w* is "two-front-teeth." *i* is the "stick-with-the-eye-above-it." "Long-stick-with-nothing" is *l*. "Ball-with-the-tail" is *a*. They describe a series of *w's* as "a whole line of two-front-teeth like birds sitting side by side on the branch of a tree."

After reading readiness, the alphabet is introduced piecemeal, with meaningful practice material at each stage. The primer series should end with the pupil able to read anything written and understand what it says. To develop fluency in reading and interest in what is read, easy reading materials such as stories, letters, newssheets and calendars are prepared.

Readers are taught to write and encouraged to express themselves in original writings on subjects of interest. At one such workshop potential writers visited the zoo, then wrote about the animals seen. Others went to a city market, then explained what went on there for the benefit of the folks back home. When asked to describe something they had seen but which was unknown in their town, one described a telephone receiver as "a handle with a wheel on each end. You talk into one wheel and listen to the other." Given a peanut and five minutes to describe it, a class of writers came up with an unexpected variety of descriptions.

A Totonac who already knew how to write Spanish responded to the translator's invitation to write in his own language. From the very first effort it was evident he wrote with feeling and originality. He filled pages with his experience and the customs of his people. Soon he was helping translate them, translating on his own in beautiful, easy-to-read Totonac. "He must have been born with ink in his veins" the translator said. Bible translation plus original personal writings of such Christians is the beginning of a Christian literature for the indigenous church.

Several people are involved in a pioneer literacy program. It begins with the literacy worker who prepares the first experimental materials and teaches the first individuals to read and write. Indigenous people who help in the analysis of the language and the preparation of reading materials are usually among the first to learn. They may be the first to author original material and teach others. Consultants furnish insights from their experience in similar programs elsewhere. If the program is to continue and reach any sizable number, local community leaders must also be involved in the planning, preferably from the beginning.

The actual program usually begins small. Barriers of suspicion and reticence often must be overcome. Motivating and teaching a few of the bolder ones serves to encourage others to try. Once the program passes the experimental stage, materials have been tested and a few taught to read and teach others, local and national support can often be found that will make the program available to all. This calls for programs for adults as well as each new generation of children. Literacy then becomes one aspect of a broader community development. Once the program is in indigenous hands, we may continue to serve as consultants or as liaisons with national or foreign interests who may help with equipment and funding.

Our experience in northern Ghana is illustrative. Five Bimoba Christians were so anxious to read the Bible that they didn't wait until the Bimoba Scriptures were ready. Without the help of literacy aids, they learned to read the Dagbani language in order to read the Dagbani Scriptures. Then an extremely capable young man came to the Bimoba translator to ask her if she could not start literacy classes in Bimoba. Before long he was the supervisor of a program that trained over twenty teachers and had classes in nine communities. Classes spread to twelve new places, and in each place two or three local men were trained to teach others. Two hundred and fifty new adult pupils were enrolled. Seventy-

117

five from the previous year continued with further studies.

Village chiefs and pastors got behind the program. An annual Literacy Day was inaugurated on which certificates

12. Bimoba literacy class, Ghana.

were given to those who had learned to read well. On the second such day thousands of people gathered at the compound of the paramount chief. The regional commissioner arrived by helicopter. Special drumming and dancing preceded the prize giving. Many of the certificates given out were later framed and proudly displayed in Bimoba homes. The best village literacy group was awarded a gleaming newly varnished table for their class. Each of the sixty-five volunteer teachers, some of whom gave six evenings a week to teach, received a smart document case and a special badge given by the Social Welfare and Community Development Department. New teachers received bright shirts as a mark of their status.

Further west three Tampulma supervisors traveling on bicycles supervised forty-five teachers, many of whom had never been to school but were products of the classes themselves. Soon the number of readers passed five hundred. Many became avid readers of the translated Scriptures.

Still further west among the Vagla, evening literacy classes had a varied reception. One class began well but when the pupils were asked to contribute toward kerosene for the lamp, three of them ran away and never came back. Four more disappeared when they learned they were expected to buy their books. In another village all went well. They finished all the primers and were soon enjoying various storybooks. In another the class disintegrated completely and the teachers were quite depressed.

But classes continued. One well-known chief, with the aid of a very fetching pair of glasses, learned to read. Previous illiterates began sending letters and writing stories. Vagla newspapers were printed and sold. When the Vagla New Testament arrived, there was not only the Book for the readers but there were readers for the Book.

Ongoing literacy programs are the responsibility of the local community and the national government. The Engenni people now have their own Engenni Language Association, formed to promote the reading and writing of Engenni. We restrict our activities to pilot projects in the mother tongue of the ethnic people and to providing transition materials for bilingual programs in which the official language also becomes the vehicle of teaching. Because of our linguistic training and knowledge of the ethnic languages, we are able to help ethnic language pupils learn the national language. But the teaching of the official language can best be done by mother tongue speakers of that language. We are also able to help teachers of the national language understand the nature of the language-related problems encountered by their ethnic language pupils.

Bilingual Literacy Programs

Many ethnic minorities face a difficult situation. Some withdraw further into themselves and their dwindling hinterland to become museum pieces facing ultimate extinction. Some forsake their own ways and are absorbed into the dominant culture around them, but on its terms. In both cases they cease to exist as a people.

We believe there is a better alternative that makes it possible for them to retain their own identity and at the same time relate positively to the larger culture around them. It involves continuing to speak their own language while learning the trade or official language in order to communicate with the world around them.

One way minority people learn the official language of their country is to enter the school system of the dominant culture where only the official language is used. In this case they must learn to speak and read a new language directly, without explanation or help in their own language. This is not impossible, but the social system, the language barrier and the teaching methods combine to put them at a disadvantage. All too often their language, culture and personhood are considered inferior and of little or no value. They end up withdrawing, rebelling or accepting second-class-citizen status for life. With rare exceptions, those who make good do so by disassociating themselves from their own people and culture. Through disuse they may even forget their mother tongue.

Another much less traumatic route to the acquisition of the second language is by way of a grass-roots literacy and literature program in their own language first. Then they are much more ready, often eager, to learn another language, with all the opportunities this brings for further education and participation in the other culture. And they see the advantage of doing so. As an Aguaruna put it, "The man who has a machete is able to do something. The man who has both an axe and a machete is able to do much more. In the same way the person who speaks two languages can do much more than the man who only speaks one language."

A literate person who wants to learn another language for educational or employment purposes finds his ability to read can be a help. Our field workers frequently prepare written materials for bilingual teachers and learners, using the known mother tongue as the basis for learning the second language.

120

Bilingual education may be either of a transfer or simultaneous type. In the transfer type it begins in the mother tongue and culture, then transfers to the official or school language as that language is learned and any further use of the mother tongue is incidental. The mother tongue is used only as an initial help in learning the second language. Transfer bilingual programs are common with adult learners. When used with children of smaller minorities they tend to wean them away from their distinctive cultural identity. If the children still live in a basically mother tongue environment it may be some time before they are really competent in the second language, since they may use it only in school.

In simultaneous bilingual education, learning begins in the mother tongue, then the second language is taught after basic reading and writing skills are learned in the mother tongue. Use of the mother tongue continues. The learner grows in his knowledge of the second language and culture while he continues to learn in his own. Full bilingual programs are almost always with children. For example, the writer's children attended a Mexico City school which had a standard Mexican curriculum in Spanish in the mornings and a standard U.S. school curriculum in English in the afternoons. All children took both. The children were almost one hundred percent from Mexican homes so Spanish was the language on the playground. Extended bilingual education becomes a two-way bridge. Each language and culture is respected. Each contributes something to the other.

A Peruvian educator describes the bilingual schools of his country as "jungle schools with Indian teachers and Indian students where both the Indian language and eventually Spanish are used as the teaching instruments to forge an Indian society conscious of its own value and in possession of the best and most accessible elements of the national culture."[8] In other words, first monolingual then bilingual members of the minority community are trained to teach their own people and provide for them in their own language and environment the basic cultural tools by which they can defend themselves from exploitation. Thus they contribute positively to the utilization of the jungle territories for their own and their nation's benefit.

Our first involvement in bilingual education was in Peru. Following initial literacy in the mother tongue, speakers of the minority languages were sought who knew how to read and write their own language and who had the confidence and backing of their own people and community leaders. Those were selected who knew enough of the official language, Spanish, to understand at least partially the classes which would be given in Spanish by Peruvian instructors. The courses were given in government facilities near our center in the jungle. Our linguists also attended the classes. After the class the concepts and the Spanish vocabulary used were discussed by the speakers of each language in their own language, with the linguist there to help explain what they had not understood. This greatly helped the minority language students since, no matter how simply the Peruvian instructor spoke, the vocabulary used, not to mention many of the concepts taught, was often quite foreign to them. After each day's tutoring in their own language, they were much more able to follow what the lecturer was saying in Spanish. The linguists prepared vernacular textbooks in each ethnic language and the students were taught how to use them.

When the three-month course was over, the students went back to their villages. Those who did well were officially commissioned by the government to establish schools to be taught in the ethnic language of their respective villages. Each sought the cooperation of his people, built a rustic schoolhouse and gathered the children together daily for a first glimpse into the world of reading, writing, arithmetic, hygiene, national heritage, and the privileges and responsibilities of citizenship. Some taught adults in classes in the evenings.

After several months the teachers returned for a second three months of training. Each year new candidates came for the initial course. Year by year as the teachers returned to the center at Yarinacocha more advanced training was added.

The national language, Spanish, was introduced in the

13. *Peruvian educator teaching bilingual school teachers.*

village schools as a foreign language. During the first year the pupils were taught to speak Spanish by oral imitation of their teacher. From the second year on, once they knew how to read and write in their own language, they were taught to read and write in Spanish. Instruction continued in the Indian language all the way through. The Spanish curriculum was increased each year until the students were able to study entirely in Spanish with a minimum of explanation needed in the vernacular.

The Peruvian government supplied the head instructor, financed the budget of the Teacher Training Course and paid a salary to each of the ethnic teachers. Our personnel helped in finding and encouraging potential teachers to come, preparing bilingual materials, tutoring their respective language groups and teaching Vernacular Methods courses when requested to do so. Afterward they visited the teachers in their villages to help and encourage them. The better teachers were promoted by the government to serve as supervisors and inspectors.

14. Bilingual school teachers of eastern Peru.

As year after year more and more teachers were trained, the effect in the jungle villages became more obvious. With poise and confidence former headhunters taught eager students. The faces of the students showed an understanding and rapport that no teacher from the Spanish-speaking cities could obtain, no matter how highly trained. The bilingual school teacher had no language and cultural barriers to bridge before he could guide not only his students but the community into full and effective citizenship. An increasing number of those who graduated from their bilingual village school went on to national schools in the cities, and tertiary education training as doctors, nurses and lawyers, with a view to returning to their own communities to serve them further.

At the closing exercises of one of the Teacher Training Institutes a government official wrote on the blackboard in Spanish for all to read: "The bilingual school teachers of the

124

jungle are the pride of Peru." One of the bilingual teachers typed it on a sheet of paper. Another wrote it in his own language on the blackboard. The original Spanish was erased. Another who had been out of the room was brought back in and asked to translate from the Indian language back into Spanish and write it on the blackboard. He wrote: "Peru is proud of the teachers in the jungle who speak two languages." Educational officials from Lima were duly impressed with the jungle teachers' ability to type their own language as well as Spanish and by the fact that they were able to translate from Spanish to their ethnic language and back with no loss of meaning.

Other countries hearing of the success in Peru have adopted similar bilingual programs for their minority peoples, in several of which we have been privileged to serve as linguistic consultants in the ethnic languages.

Training for Literacy

Literacy has not always had the emphasis in our work that it has today. In the early days of the work it was simply a part of the linguistics-translation-literacy assignment each team was expected to carry out. Many teams, however, discovered that they needed extra personnel specifically assigned to literacy if the program was to succeed.

The idea was also prevalent that literacy work required less skill and ability than linguistics and translation. While it is true that almost anyone who can read can help someone else to read, the master-minding of a total ongoing literacy program calls for much more. We now have members who specialize in literacy. The need for field consultants in literacy, both for our own members and for mission and government programs we are invited to help, has resulted in an increased demand for well-qualified and experienced literacy specialists.

Literacy specialists must learn to speak the language well and have the linguistic ability to recognize orthographic and grammatical problems and propose solutions. The production of textbooks requires insight into the structure of the languages. A linguistic background aids in training mother tongue teachers and authors to utilize the full resources of their languages. Our particular contribution to world literacy is based solidly on linguistics.

Literacy specialists must be perceptive of cultural differences, able to adapt literacy principles and practices to build on ethnic values and ways of teaching and learning. They must be able not only to teach but also to train others to teach. Background studies in anthropology, psychology, education, sociology, and language planning are helpful, but not a formal requirement.

Basic training for the language-assigned member is two semesters of linguistics, plus a third semester which includes field methods in ethnology, principles of translation and principles of literacy. For those expecting to be assigned full time to literacy a fourth semester is required, which includes sociolinguistic aspects of literacy programs and literacy materials, and linguistic aspects of reading theory. For some literacy workers the second semester of linguistics may not be required, which reduces their pre-field preparation to three semesters. A special community development course, dealing with the motivation of communities to develop and change socially of their own choice rather than by pressure from the outside is being developed and is also recommended for those specializing in literacy. Continued upgrading, on the field, during furloughs or on special study programs, builds on this foundation.

Since each ethnic language community is a new testing ground for the validity of literacy principles, members interested in the theoretical aspects of literacy have a field of great potential. Literacy in relation to culture patterns and culture change, the relationship of discourse structure and readability, the psychological link between reading, speaking and creative writing—these are some of the areas of undeveloped theory. In some countries there is more interest in literacy than in linguistics, and literacy specialists are in demand who can not only apply their skills at the grass-roots level but also contribute to the development of literacy theory and the improvement of literacy methodology.

PART TWO
ATTITUDES

While Bible translation, linguistics and literacy are focal activities of the program, a servant attitude (Chapters 8,9), reliance upon God (10,11) and a pioneering spirit (12,13) characterize the way in which these activities are carried on.

8
Serving

A TRUE servant of God also serves his fellow man. As followers of Christ we have his example. He did not come "to be served, but to serve, and to give his life as a ransom for many" (Mk. 10:45). In his service we seek to demonstrate a servant attitude toward all. In addition to the technical services of linguistics, literacy and translation and in keeping with these goals, other types of service are rendered as needs of the community demand and circumstances and our resources permit. These services are performed by request and in partnership with the local people, not imposed on them. They are carried out in cooperation with local host governments, universities, missions and other organizations involved with the ethnic language groups with whom we work.

The Attitude of Servant

Servanthood is taught in the Bible. It is introduced and illustrated in the Old Testament, exemplified in the life and ministry of Jesus Christ and made explicit and normative for his followers in the rest of the New Testament.

In the Old Testment, "servant" means a person at the disposal of another. It is used as an honorary title of people who served God. The patriarchs; Moses; kings, especially David; the prophets; Job; the humble pious in general; the promised Messiah; Israel as a nation; and Nebuchadnezzar are called servants of the Lord (Gen. 26:24; Exod. 14:31; 2

Sam. 3:18; 2 Kings 17:13; Job 1:8; Ps. 135:14; Zech. 3:8; Isa. 41:8).

Joseph, Daniel and Nehemiah are servants of God who faithfully serve foreign governments. In serving God they bore a faithful personal testimony and were instrumental in spreading the knowledge of God and helping his people. We in our work with governments find much in their examples to guide and encourage us.

Rehoboam is a classic example of a ruler who refused to adopt the servant attitude and lost half of his kingdom as a result (1 Kings 12:7ff).

The word "servant" is used of people who for various reasons served human masters. It is used of slaves. Some slaves had menial tasks and hard taskmasters (Exod. 1:11-14). Others held responsible positions and had great freedom (Gen. 15:2, 3; 24:2). Hebrew slaves who served Hebrews had shorter servitude than did non-Hebrew slaves (Exod. 21:2; Lev. 25:40). The Law also makes provision for voluntary, life-time servitude (Ex. 21:5,6).

According to the culture of the day, "servant" is also a term of humble self-designation of self-description used by both kings and commoners when addressing one another (2 Kings 5:17; Neh. 2:5; 1 Sam. 17:34, 36; 2 Kings 16:7).

In the New Testament servanthood is presented as a way of life and ministry pleasing to God. In Greek and Roman society slavery was widespread but the role of slave ranged all the way from abject servitude to virtual independence and respect. Humility was not a virtue but considered despicable. Against this backdrop Christ made voluntary humble service the touchstone of life and character, both to his followers who were vying for position, recognition and power (Mark 10:35-41) and to the world, where privilege and position were used to exploit others (Mark 10:42). When speaking of his own coming to serve, as reported in Mark 10:45, he used his most general title, "Son of Man," making no pretensions, asserting no claims. He identified himself— and Matthew, Peter, and Phillip recognized him—as the "servant of Jehovah" spoken of by Isaiah (Luke 22:27; Matt. 12:18; Acts 3:13; 8:32-35; Isa. 42:1; 52:13).

Christ never became a "slave" in the sense of entering into any servile relationship to anyone else. He did, however, voluntarily assume "the very nature of a servant" in his incarnation (Phil. 2:7). Both in attitude and deed he lived as a servant, even washing his disciples' feet (John 13:4-17). He made it clear his action was a pattern for them to follow. "I have set you an example that you should do as I have done for you" (v. 15). He did not tell them merely to do *what* he had done, but *as* he had done—not a new rite but a new inner attitude—humble, self-negating, loving service to others.

Christ taught that voluntary loving service is to be extended to all people, not just to one's friends. He based this on God's impartiality in sending sun and rain on all alike and on the Old Testament command to love one's neighbors. One's neighbor is anyone in need (Luke 10:25-37), even an avowed enemy (Matt. 5:43-48). He made loving and serving one's neighbor a corollary to loving and serving God.

A true servant works for the honor of the one he serves (John 7:18) and does not seek glory for himself (John 8:50). He does not act independently but does the will of the one who sent him (John 5:30). Faithfulness in the discharge of his master's business is expected (Matt. 24:46; 25:14-30; 1 Cor. 4:21). Further qualifications are that he "must not quarrel; instead, he must be kind to everyone, able to teach, not resentful. Those who oppose him he must gently instruct, in the hope that God will grant them repentance leading them to a knowledge of the truth" (2 Tim. 2:24-25). As a servant, Christ exemplified the qualities he expects of those who serve him.

Servanthood gives no ground for pride. It requires self-abnegation. Christ taught "when you have done everything you were told to do . . . say, 'We are unworthy servants; we have only done our duty'" (Luke 17:10). The servant must decrease, the one served increase, as John the Baptist both said and demonstrated. The final anomaly was Christ's statement to the place-seeking disciples: "Whoever wants to become great among you must be your servant, and whoever wants to be first must be slave of all" (Mark 10:43, 44). He concluded by pointing to himself as the example.

Paul discovered that in Christ he had been set free from the bondage of sin, self, tradition and men. In gratitude and in recognition of Christ's lordship, he voluntarily became his servant (slave in fact) for life. Appointed an Apostle by Christ, he made himself a servant (slave in attitude) to others as part of his obedience to Christ and for the sake of Christ. When his authority was challenged by some at Corinth, he defended himself and insisted on his authority as an Apostle. Yet he did not "lord it" over them (2 Cor. 1:24). To the contrary he said, "For we do not preach ourselves, but Jesus Christ as Lord, and ourselves as your servants for Jesus' sake" (2 Cor. 4:5). He saw himself as unconditionally obligated to serve them and as a joint beneficiary with them of the very Gospel he preached to them (1 Cor. 9:19-23).

In this servant attitude Paul did not restrict himself to fellow believers and friends. While recognizing his rights as an Apostle, Paul made his ministry without charge and himself a servant (slave) to everyone. He deliberately disciplined himself and limited his activities in order to identify with those he sought to win. Without compromising his Lord, his message or his principles, he made concessions to the Jew, the religionist, the atheist and the hypersensitive (1 Cor. 9:18-23). While hating evil he worked to overcome it by doing good to those who practiced it, even to speaking well of those who persecuted him (Rom. 12:9-21). Paul, "the most resolute, in a complicated situation, becomes the most versatile of men."[1] While his policy of becoming all things to all men appeared to some as time-serving and duplicity, he defended it as consistent with his servant role and Gospel stewardship (2 Cor. 1:12; 4:2; 12:16; Gal. 1:10). He did it not as a means justified by the end but as a legitimate expression of his freedom in Christ.

Paul, however, recognized dangers to Christian freedom. Christians who were slaves in the social system of the day, while free in Christ, were still to serve their human masters faithfully. Their Christian freedom included freedom to remain as slaves or to become freemen if opportunity offered. On the other hand, those who were free in the social system who became Christians should be careful not to become enslaved to rules and ceremonies and human leaders. This would deny in fact their freedom and allegiance to Christ. Both Christian slaves and Christian freemen had been bought with a price. They must be careful to let no human influence bring them into servitude again to any other than to Christ (1 Cor. 7:17-24).

In the light of the foregoing we have deliberately chosen to be servants in our relationships with others, from the highest to the lowest with whom we relate.

Service Policies and Practices

This attitude of loving service in the name and after the example of Christ finds expression in certain well-defined field policies and practices of our members.[2]

We recognize the authority of those in charge, from the highest in the land to the humblest local chief. A local pastor was profoundly grateful that our members on entering his village went first to greet the local civic authority. After informing him of their purpose they visited the pastor.[3] By thus showing respect for duly constituted leaders and publicly expressing our desire to serve them, we expedite arrangements for our stay among them. Some civic authorites even offer facilities, make helpful suggestions and provide letters of introduction to others. To avoid or bypass those in authority arouses suspicions, gives rise to misunderstandings, and may prejudice the local people as well as the officials against the work from the very beginning.

We seek to serve the best interests of national and local entities in our host countries. We encourage our members to take the role of servants, without loss of personal or academic integrity, in their relations to local scholars, administrators and citizens. They are the ones who establish policy and set goals for their people. We come to help them, not to compete, duplicate, displace, criticize or overthrow them. We commend what they have already accomplished and do not belittle what they have not. Explaining our interest in studying their minority languages and translating portions of the Bible, we indicate our willingness to serve them and their people in specific ways which they may request and which fall within the field of our competence. We tell them frankly we prefer to work under their guidance rather than independently and ask them how we can best do that. Sometimes they prefer an informal understanding; in other cases a more formal contract. Contracts spell out the long-range goals of the program, the services each party will supply the other, and the particular department, agency or institution with whom we will relate most directly. From the beginning, however, we make it clear that our desire is to serve all, and that any contract is a linking, not a limiting relationship.

In order to serve the host country's long-range interest, we first research what has already been done and what is currently going on in the languages we expect to study. To understand the culture, its values, the people's goals and their way of doing things, we give our members some orientation in the field of anthropology and community development. Some of our members may enroll as students in their national institutions, to learn from them and to become aware of their point of view and of work in progress. The result is an appreciation of their accomplishments, an awareness of where we may contribute without competing, and the development of model projects more in keeping with their situation and needs. We prefer to work things out with our hosts, respecting their point of view. In giving examples from our experience, we find it generally more acceptable and more applicable to cite examples from other developing countries rather than our own or often quite dissimilar countries of origin. Our aim is to supplement, not disrupt what may already be going on. For example, countries with ethnic minority languages need to be reassured that our work with such languages will contribute to and not work against the widest possible use of their official language.

We serve as catalysts for new projects among the ethnic minorities. As soon as possible, local people are involved and the project made self-sustaining. Assured of community interest, national authorities are much more willing to assist such projects from their budgets.

Some of our members teach linguistic courses in host country institutions, orient teachers in the use of ethnic language materials, or serve as consultants for national literacy programs. Such service is upon request and on a temporary basis.

We serve local scholars and other expatriates working in the same or related languages by inviting them to our seminars and workshops. In linguistic workshops local citizens may contribute to us as lecturers or as speakers of the languages studied and others may receive help as researchers. We may help nationals as well as our own members publish the results of their research. Some articles are co-authored.

Non-linguistic technical members also share their skillls. Safety seminars of our Jungle Aviation and Radio Service pilots and mechanics have been held jointly with aviation personnel of host countries working under similar conditions. Sharing experience and lessons learned is mutually beneficial. It also builds tremendous goodwill and opens ways for further service.

Wherever possible dictionaries, primers and literature in the ethnic languages are published under the name of a national sponsor, often a department of government. Mother tongue speakers and national scholars who have contributed materially to the work are recognized. Sponsors and co-laborers are generous in their appreciation and acknowledgement for our share in the work. We believe there is no limit to the amount of good a person can do if he does not care who gets the credit.

We report our activities to the host government through the agency with whom we have been assigned to work. Annual written reports are supplemented by frequent personal visits. Copies of linguistic articles, literacy materials and translated Bible portions are distributed to keep officials and the public informed on the languages being studied and the progress made. We invite leaders, interested people and even those who oppose our work to visit our bases and working locations to see first hand what is going on. We have nothing to hide. Government leaders often participate in special ceremonies, such as the presentation of achievement awards to ethnic language people who have completed special courses of training. One Latin American official wrote a glowing report of a New Testament dedication ceremony he attended in a jungle community.

15. *Kenneth L. Pike, President of the Summer Institute of Linguistics presents a copy of his book* Language *to President Ferdinand E. Marcos of the Philippines.*

The president of another country called a pause in the socializing at a function with all the foreign diplomatic corps and had our director repeat for the benefit of all what he had earlier reported to him concerning the transformation of lives among the ethnic minorities of his country.

We inform our hosts that when our goals are accomplished we plan to withdraw from the area. We have no desire to establish any continuing foreign presence or program. However, we trust our contribution will be long-lasting in the lives of those served. In many cases we expect to give our equipment, buildings and centers as a donation to the government or the community when we leave, trusting they will continue to be used in continuing programs in benefit of the peoples we have served. Equipment considered a national security risk, such as radios and aircraft, may be turned over to the government from the beginning but operated by us on their behalf and under their surveillance in the service of all, including our own members and missions. Our capital investment is part of our total contribution to the country. We have come to give and not get.

Our service is without charge to the host country. We explain that our personal and organizational needs are underwritten by gifts and grants from friends who share our desire to make the Bible available to the minority ethnic groups. We also receive some grants from agencies interested in the scientific and educational aspects of the work. As autonomous, not-for-profit organizations, we serve independent of home government ties or funding. Government agencies and institutions of the host countries often help reduce our costs by providing land for centers, space for offices, exemptions on equipment, and fuel for flights serving them.

The establishment and growth of truly indigenous national programs is our goal. Where churches exist without vernacular Scriptures, we serve them by providing the Bible or by training some of them to translate it. We have encouraged the formation of national Bible translating organizations. National linguistic departments, associations and periodicals that already exist we seek to serve and help by making our data and articles available to them. Where there is no local pattern or precedent, as for example linguistic courses for pioneer linguistics and translation, we may initiate something following our own foreign model, but as soon as possible national staff and leadership is developed which will adapt it to meet the local needs.

We serve the indigenous churches that come into existence as the result of the translation and reading of the Bible in the indigenous languages. Our role is not to dominate or control but to remain in the background, provide the Scriptures and teach them to read and live in obedience to God's Word.

As servants we seek to maintain a low profile. The word "summer" in the name of the Summer Institute of Linguistics, was meant to emphasize the unpretentious and temporary character of the school. Only recently have we begun fall and spring semester sessions and then only in one or two locations.

Special orientation is given our members to help them adapt to humble living and serving in practical ways. Our background and desire for efficiency works against this, however. The use of modern equipment for more efficient living and working is commonplace where we come from. In many cases our supporters want to supply it. The local people may expect or the host governments require that buildings meet standards above that of the people with whom we work. The result is then an outward appearance that seems to belie our servant attitude. Only the use of such equipment and facilities to help others in a genuine spirit of openness and humble service keeps it from becoming an insurmountable barrier in our relations with the people.

To provide essential economical services for teams in isolated areas and train ethnic people without taking them out of their environment, centers are established at strategic points in the hinterland. These beehives of activity tend to become large. The constant movement of people and the use of radio and aircraft in many cases, make them highly visible, especially in a rural setting. Their purpose, however, is still to serve, not only our own members but also the local and outlying ethnic communities.

While recognizing we are guests, we desire to identify with our host country and the ethnic peoples whom we serve. We seek to make our foreignness unabrasive and unobtrusive. Living in their villages, using their language, participating in their activities, recognizing their special days, adopting many of their customs, visiting in their homes and inviting them to ours—these all help. Mexicans appreciate the fact that our headquarters building is adorned with a mural based on a historic Mexican theme and our publications building named after a renowned national leader.

When problems arise we look to local friends and authorities for advice and help. Asking for help from those we serve gives them a good feeling as benefactors and shows we are dependent on them. Asking them for help for the ethnic minorities we serve demonstrates that we are not acting independently but realize their leadership and responsibility. This relaxes feelings of rivalry or threat, and puts us in their debt. As a result, even when our friends have been attacked because they have befriended us, they have responded enthusiastically and have continued to publicly support the work.

Our members serve everyone, as opportunity offers and strength allows, in ways consistent with Christian principles. Not only national officials and members of the ethnic communities, but national and expatriate academic and business personnel, even tourists, are served in the areas where we live and work. Service is not limited to those who are followers of Christ. A special effort is made to find ways of showing loving service to those who oppose the work. After the example and according to the command of Christ we seek to overcome evil with good (Matt. 5:43-48; Rom. 12:17-21). Those who attack us we try to serve in some practical way, to win them as friends. We do not avoid them or attack them as enemies (2 Tim. 2:25).

We serve the whole man. The strength of any nation lies in the moral and spiritual character of its citizens. We are deeply convinced that our greatest service to any ethnic people is in providing the Word of God for their spiritual need. The president of one country, upon being presented with a copy of the New Testament, declared: "This is a forward step for our country." As one Latin American educator expressed it: "We in government do all we can to help our people educationally and economically. We do absolutely nothing to help them spiritually. But your program deals with the whole man. You provide Scripture for his spiritual need. You teach him to read. You help him improve his standard of living. The essential components are all there. No wonder your program succeeds."

Positive effects begin to appear in the lives and communities of those who become readers of the Book and followers of Jesus Christ. They are more eager to learn, obedient to law, respectful of others, free from vice and superstition. In a single generation, many Amazonian people who formerly only met to kill each other in reprisal raids became brothers in Christ who sat down to eat amicably together and settled their traditional rivalries on the soccer field. The still incurable *kuru* disease, which spreads when sorcerers mix brain remains from diseased dead people into the food of unsuspecting victims, was largely eliminated in one part of the Fore area of Papua New Guinea when the people's response to God's Word taught by missionaires in the area resulted in a drastic reduction in the practice of sorcery. The translation of the Bible can thus have far-reaching beneficial effects in the lives of those who receive it. Educational and economic development without spiritual resources to direct it can end in disaster rather than benefit to a community. A three-legged stool with one leg missing cannot stand.

We seek to be loyal to those we serve, of whatever rank, speaking well of them insofar as we honestly can. We do not criticize or seek to demean, but to be friends and serve, earning the right to help remedy what we cannot commend (2 Tim. 2:24). We try not to embarrass those who befriend us by making them responsible for any more of our program than they in good conscience and by conviction choose to endorse.

We serve the ethnic minorities by acting as a liaison, when necessary, with people beyond their borders. We can often put them in touch with government and other officials able to help them. Our members may serve as interpreters. Some have appreciated our help in law cases where language limitations put them at a great disadvantage. We speak and write on behalf of the ethnic people where they are unable to speak for themselves or where their rights are not being defended (Prov. 31:8-9).

We seek to make their culture known and their language appreciated, not only in their own country but internationally. Published research has contributed to the development of linguistic science and given them and their way of life recognition around the world. Today the Mazateco people are widely known by linguists and others through published descriptions of their tonal language and the men's ability to whistle as well as talk the language. Their music is heard weekly on a commercial station in Mexico, along with readings from the Mazatec New Testament.

Our service attitude extends to others at home and abroad whose interest in linguistics, literacy or Bible translation for the ethnic minorities overlaps with ours. Our academic training courses are open to all who stand to profit from them. Frequently we loan personnel to help programs kindred to ours. We have found we are freer to serve all and our service is more acceptable to all if we avoid partisan ties with other organizations.

Within the organizations we serve one another. From the members of the boards of directors and the officers of the corporations on down, those in places of responsibility are expected to serve, not rule. Those in support roles who supply the services and do the necessary jobs to keep those in the ethnic language community work on their jobs, find their satisfaction vicariously in serving those serving the ethnic peoples and giving them the Bible. Language-assigned personnel are expected to be willing to take their turn as necessary to fill supporting roles when no one else is available or assigned. Members are expected to be willing, if elected or appointed, to serve the rest by filling administrative or leadership spots in the organizations.

The servant attitude carries over into our relationships with our supporting constituencies. We see ourselves as serving them in fulfilling their desire to share the Scriptures with the ethnic groups still without them. When visiting or writing our supporters, we find that if we focus on ministering to their needs, on giving rather than on receiving, they are blessed and God takes care of our needs.

There are limits to our service. We believe God has called us to a specific linguistic and translation task. Some types of service are not contributory to our principle objectives. For other kinds of service requested we do not have the skills or personnel. We refer these to agencies set up to meet such needs or we ask God to raise up new agencies to supply the service requested. Broad cross-cultural national programs of community development are the responsibility of national governments. We limit our community service projects to those minority language groups where we have linguistically trained members assigned.

9

Culturally Relevant Service

A FORMER field director wrote "I have never known of a situation where our members just did translation and were not involved in some other way, serving the people to whom the Lord had sent them. This side of the work is not often highlighted. Sometimes it is done informally in 'spare time.'"

Such service usually begins with simple acts of neighborly helpfulness to the people among whom we live. First aid, repair of gadgets, giving people rides to markets—these and many other similar acts of kindness we hope will show that we want to be friendly and helpful. Observing and participating in their activities provides opportunity to hear and use the language and to get acquainted with the people and their ways of doing things.

At first everything seems different from our past experience. The people have a way of doing everything, but it isn't our way, and at first it doesn't make sense to us. But as we ask questions, observe activity around us and learn from our mistakes we discover that their social groupings, values, system of controls and basic world view form an integrated whole that is very meaningful to them.

Until we learn to understand life as they see it and conform our conduct to their way of doing things, our very attempts to be friendly or helpful may prove abortive. It is a bit unnerving to have a mother go screaming down the trail with the baby she brought for medicine and to discover later that our attempt to be friendly by commenting on how cute the baby looked was interpreted as drawing the attention of the evil spirits to it so it would die. But we learn by such experiences. Gradually we begin to feel at home with them and they seem to feel more at ease with us.

Our linguistic, literacy and translation goals require that we learn to understand their culture. We must not only mimic their pronunciation, we must learn when it is appropriate to use each expression. Meanings must be in terms of their cultural situations and usage, not of equivalents in our language. Motivation and methods for teaching people to read must be culturally appropriate if they are to continue teaching others. Bible translation requires that we take a text written to a people of one language and culture and restate it with a minimum of loss or distortion in the words and thought patterns of a totally different language and culture. Everything we say and do involves the culture of the people among whom we live.

Anthropology

The very nature of our work requires us to be diligent students of the social, political, economic and religious, as well as the physical and material, aspects of the life of the people among whom we serve. We therefore stand to profit from the insights and perspectives of anthropology. Thus we seek to give our members an introduction to cultural anthropology before they go to the field, and further anthropology orientation on the field. Our program in anthropology includes classroom courses, readings, workshops, research and technical reporting and publication. Those of our number who have had formal studies in anthropology may be asked to serve as instructors and consultants in the training and field programs.

While few of us are professionals in the field of anthropology, we are constantly encouraged to read what has been written on the cultures of our area and to contribute what we observe in the form of published articles for the help of others. In addition to articles on the languages studied, some of our members have published volumes of folklore,[1] auto-

143

biographies of ethnic people[2], and descriptive analyses of kinship systems[3] and religious practices[4] of the ethnic cultures studied. In addition members have published over 300 purely anthropological articles, plus ethnographic information contained in other publications. What one internationally-known anthropologist said of one of our members is true of many more: "She is motivated by a profound human interest which gives a broader dimension to her understanding of indigenous problems."

To be appreciated and helpful, any service must be relevant to the needs of those served. Our anthropologically-oriented linguistic approach helps us relate to people, discover their areas of need, and then serve them. All cultures are changing, both from forces within and without the community, and there are stresses and strains in the process. Our presence in a minority village creates a new situation which may set further changes in motion. We want those changes to enhance, not destroy, their way of life. Some face the future with a feeling of helplessness and frustration. We want to provide them options that will give hope and restore the will to live.

Our Christian faith recognizes cultural plurality and in no sense requires that a person forsake his ethnic culture to be a Christian. Paul and Peter came to realize that Gentiles had their own law, one that differed from that of the Jews (Rom. 2:14). Both Jews and Gentiles demonstrated the reality of sin and the need of salvation. Imposing foreign cultural ways on those who believe is not part of the Gospel, as Paul strongly argued in his letter to the Galatian church (Gal. 2:14; 5:4; 6:15). Respect for cultural differences within the body of Christ is expected of believers (Acts 15:28, 29). Respect for and obedience to authorities recognized by those belonging to a different cultural tradition is commanded (1 Peter 2:14, 15). Even non-Christian value systems can recognize Christian conduct as good (1 Peter 2:12).

This is not self-evident. A Subanun language helper told the linguist working with him, "A Subanun can't become a Christian."

To which the linguist replied, "It certainly is a fact that a

Subanun can and should remain a Subanun. He can, however, become a Subanun follower of Christ."

After much thought, the Subanun replied, "Yes, that's true." Some time later he chose to follow Christ.

By teaching people to read and write their own language we provide a strong base for cultural continuity, identity and self-expression. The translation of valuable literature from other cultures, such as the Bible, almost always adds to the self-esteem of any linguistic group.

Christian Alternatives

By not imposing our cultural ways upon people but instead offering alternatives which they may choose, we recognize each culture's right to self-determination. How they make their choice will differ. In some cultures the decisions are made by individuals, in others by the chief, in others by the group. We believe God can and does work through any type of political system.

A headhunting chief who chose to follow Christ lost his love for killing. He also dropped his worship of the boa constrictor. As a consequence he also lost the respect and control of the younger men of his tribe. Meeting with other older men one day, the chief spoke out, "God has an answer. We older men must study his Word together so that we can know his answer and teach the younger men the right way to live." The Bible offers an alternate way of life and a new basis for moral conduct. But each culture must apply those principles to its own problems and way of life.

Many minority peoples desire change. They want to improve their way of life. One bilingual school teacher during a conference raised a question that was bothering many. "What do we do about witchcraft out in our villages? Not only are the adults deeply influenced by this but even the children are kept out of school through fear of what the evil spirits are doing."

Another teacher arose and answered, "There are two things we need to fight witchcraft: medicines to show our people that sickness is not really caused by witchdoctors, and the Word of God to show our people that witchcraft is from the devil."

Ethnic people often feel the only way to get ahead is to adopt the ways of the dominant culture. It is precisely at this point however that they need a moral and spiritual base upon which to discern which elements of the national culture are for their good and which are not. All too often the most accessible elements are the less desirable elements. Bilingual Aguaruna teachers showed their people that it was not simply the old versus the new, but that they must choose between the Christian and the non-Christian in the new. This is where the translation of the Bible provides a basis for moral judgment for those facing inevitable changes and the encroachments of civilization.

Historian Arnold Toynbee, after visiting our work in the jungle, wrote: "It has been an unforgettable experience for me. . . . What impressed me most was the spirit of your community. It is not very common for the strong to dedicate themselves to the service of the weak, as you are doing. Thanks to your work for the Indians, the terrific impact of modern civilization upon their life is being eased, so that their encounter with the modern world may perhaps have a happy ending, thanks to you. . . . One can admire man's technological power, but his spiritual power is more admirable."

Changes don't come easily, even for Christians, especially if it involves long-time enemies. The Siriono people use the word "enemy" to refer to their Ayore neighbors. Christian Siriono attending the leadership training course at our center were asked to feed an Ayore Christian who came, but without his wife. They struggled with the old hatred and animosity. What would the people of their village think if they heard they were feeding "the enemy?" Finally they agreed. The Siriono were deeply impressed by the spiritual life of the Ayore man, and he with theirs. Of the twelve different language groups attending the course, the Siriono ended up feeling closest to the Ayore. Now when they write the translator they say, "Send my greetings to 'the enemy' people.'"

146

But even outside, objective observers bear testimony to the difference the Gospel makes. An anthropologist doing research among the Tzeltals noted a new sense of ethnic consciousness and pride among those who had the Scriptures, noticeable economic improvement as a result of freedom from witchcraft and alcoholism, and a new desire for progress with a willingness to choose and take responsibility for directed culture change. With changing work conditions and land tenure patterns among the Manobo, Christians experienced much less traumatic disruption of the social structure than did the rest of the population.

Community Development

Our linguistic, literacy and translation projects and our practical service are only part of the total community activity going on at any one time. To be of lasting benefit they must become a genuine part of the community's ongoing way of life, not just foreign appendages which function while we are around. As soon as possible they must be accepted, planned and guided by the people themselves, with or without help from outside the community. Any such change with a positive result in the lives of the people we refer to as community development.

Community development is helping a community help itself. It requires an attitude on the part of the people and their leaders that together they can improve their lot. To be a catalyst in such programs, we must know and respect the local culture and people, understand the problem from their point of view and help them define it, get some of them involved from the very beginning in solving it, help with advice and training at the level of their need and not go beyond what they can incorporate into their culture and carry on themselves. As Abraham Lincoln said, "You cannot build character and courage by taking away man's initiative and independence. You cannot help men permanently by doing for them what they could and should do for themselves."

Helping a community develop its own resources and lead-

16. *Community development—working together for the benefit of all.*

ership so that it can resolve its own problems is, we believe, an important service we can render. Our service policy embraces the whole community, not simply those who may accept the Gospel, although these are usually the most open and responsive. Because the implications are so vast and far-reaching, and our own service policy is not intended to be all-comprehensive, we have encouraged those trained in community development and anthropology to develop a strategy consonant with our major goals for the guidance of individual teams in the ethnic communities and for the guidance of our field leaders who relate to the government and other development programs of the countries where we work.

The basic principles of our program are:
1. Start where the people are, with the things in which they are already interested;

2. Introduce new ideas only after relationships and confidence have been established and show how these new ideas contribute to the solving of problems the group already has;
3. Keep the program simple and uncomplicated, with only one or two "major thrusts" at a time;
4. Get all activities into hands of local people from the start. Do not plan on doing it yourself first, then "turn it over to the people" because it may never get turned over;
5. Train trainers who can train others. It is the only way to multiply your own efforts;
6. Identify and train local leadership, both existing and emerging;
7. Conduct training in the village or as close to home as possible rather than bringing persons out of their home communities for long periods of time;
8. Train in locally acceptable facilities and formats, using locally acceptable methodologies;
9. Cooperate with local and national governments;
10. Encourage interdependent, rather than dependent or totally independent, relationships.[5]

Types of Service

Our field members perform many different kinds of service for individuals, for the ethnic community, for other organizations and for governments. Services we set up to serve our own members are often extended to others.

The types of service rendered are as varied as the people and the situations. Translators may teach a language helper to read, type, boil drinking water or administer simple medicines. Typing makes the helper more productive in his work with the translator. Boiling water helps his family's health. Administering medicines is a service to the community. In several ethnic groups first aid, simple remedies and medicines for common ailments are now administered entirely by those trained by the translator-nurse. For some it is now a partial means of livelihood.

17. Practical help for felt needs.

Many of our services are in response to requests for help or emergency situations. Scores of times translators personally drive accident or seriously sick cases to the nearest medical facility, or ask for a special flight on one of our planes when that is the only way out. In Peru one monolingual ethnic boy was taught to read his own language in Braille by a pilot's daughter. She learned Braille in order to develop a Braille alphabet for his language. Beginning with marbles and working down to the raised dots on paper she taught him to read. Currently she is putting the Scriptures into Braille for him as it is translated.

Sometimes we are simply the links between the need and those who can meet it. When polio broke out among the Aucas, a physiotherapist from California gave several weeks not only to treat the victims, but to train our members and some of the community to give needed therapy. A crippled Esse Ejja boy was unable to master the use of crutches.

150

Provided a wheelchair by Wycliffe Associates in the States, in two days he learned to operate the wheelchair without help in the jungle. Within a week he was exuding confidence as he rushed here and there, a completely changed person. Such services leave a lasting impression on the entire community, giving new hope and new ideas of what can be done to alleviate their conditions.

Some emergency situations are community wide. When an earthquake devastated central Guatemala, translators returned to find their Quiche village ninety-five percent destroyed, over 500 dead and the rest homeless and starving. Hundreds of pounds of wheat flour had been flown in, but the people, used to corn tortillas, had no idea how to bake bread. Locating two or three usable mudovens, the workers gathered dozens of men and women and through the entire night taught successive groups of them how to make bread for their families. In Brazil, with the aid of the Brazilian Air Force, National Indian Foundation nurses, and herculean day-and-night efforts of our local team, an epidemic that might have wiped out two minority groups in Brazil was checked. In the Philippines, famine followed by rats (by actual count over 6,000 rats per acre) threatened the 400 inhabitants of Caburacanan. Our tribal team's sacrificial sharing, government aid, and additional supplies from many other sources (including effective rat poison) saved the villagers.

Long-range community development projects are carried on in cooperation with government agencies and leaders of the local communities. Our members act as liaisons and help with training until that too is in national hands. In all such projects caution is exercised lest innovations be forced on people that they do not want or that are dependent upon technology which they do not have or skills which they do not control. The development project must be appropriate to the social and economic conditions of the area.

The encroachments of settlers and industry reduces the territory and food supply of many ethnic groups. In Ecuador, we helped get land surveys made so people with whom we were working were able to get title to their property. As we have already mentioned, the desire for education, Bible study and church fellowship may lead to a more localized, sedentary community life. Medicines and sanitation reduce the death rate. Food becomes increasingly scarce for a growing population. A transition to domestic crops and animal husbandry is essential for the survival, health and economic welfare of the community.

In Peru, bilingual school teachers together with local community leaders assess the needs in each ethnic group and choose promising graduates of the village school to get practical training to meet such needs. Some work as apprentices in animal husbandry at our center, learning to take care of domestic cattle. Those in the village clear pasture land. Seed stock to get a herd started are then transported by boat or plane. Others take training in raising poultry, storekeeping, carpentry or fruit tree grafting. Bilingual school teachers and special village sanitation and health officers are taught preventive hygiene. Some communities are really taking the instruction to heart, designating separate successive areas of the river for drinking, bathing and laundry purposes. Cleanliness, garbage disposal, vaccinations, improved diet and more available medicines are producing good results. By charging reasonable rates, some communities now have a self-sustaining health service.

The Workshop in Appropriate Technology conducted at our center in Papua New Guinea brought together forty villagers from all provinces of the country to learn how to make implements and use materials from their own surroundings to improve their standard of living. Courses in nutrition and the preservation of foods, water and sanitation, brickmaking, carpentry and agricultural tool making, charcoal making, sewing and sewing machine maintenance, and weaving were enthusiastically received.

Our technical support personnel often train others in the skills they use in serving the group. In Bolivia, our radio technician and his national helper have trained many to repair radios. In Peru, dozens have been trained in our hangar, radio lab, print and machine shops. Many of them have branched out into business for themselves. Some work in banks and one man runs the two-way radio for a mining company. Another is a pilot-mechanic for the same company. Whole areas of the hinterland where we serve are being opened up, and these workers are playing an important part in the development. Many of them are fine Christians, the fruit of the witness and Bible studies of those who also taught them the practical skills.

Helping ethnic peoples help themselves sometimes involves putting them in touch with those who can help them achieve this goal. Ethnic leaders unfamiliar with city ways and limited in their use of the national language are diffident about approaching people they do not know, especially those in positions of authority. Our members often serve as intermediaries or interpreters. Such help is only temporary. Once the ethnic leaders gain confidence, know their way around and who to contact, they are no longer dependent on us or others.

As the president of one country put it: "When there is someone like this linguistic team living in a village with the know-how and enthusiasm to help personally in improvement projects, that is where the government can put forth special effort with more assurance of adequate returns on its investment."

Our linguistic, literacy and Bible translation programs are also part of our total service and definitely contribute to the long-range development of the community.

Linguistic Service

As already pointed out, the use of the mother tongue provides a much more secure psychological basis for self-determination, community development and participation in the national life.

Our linguistic service also includes alphabets for educational and literary purposes, bilingual dictionaries and bridge materials for those wishing to learn either the minority language or the national language, descriptive and data articles for scholars doing historical and comparative research, and courses in linguistics for both minority and majority language speakers.

Literacy Service

Our literacy program lays a foundation for further education and other kinds of community development. It equips the people with communication skills as authors and teachers. It opens the door for advanced education and professional training and for interaction with both the national and the international communities around them.

Translation Service

Some of us have translated into the languages of the people we live among summaries of the history of their country and laws concerning their rights and obligations as citizens. At the request of a department of government, the national anthem was translated into several of the ethnic languages of Mexico. Translations of booklets prepared by government agencies on how to identify diseased cattle and explain why they had to be killed helped stamp out foot-and-mouth disease in rural Mexico.

The translation of the Bible is also a community service. The presentation of the completed translation is often an occasion for the whole community to celebrate. Community development is really people development and includes a spiritual dimension. The Bible speaks to the moral needs of the community, without which the physical and economic, the educational and social aspects of life are incomplete.[6] Its teachings set a high standard for personal, family and social morality. It teaches respect and obedience for local and national civil authority. People released from the bondage of fear, vice, superstition, ignorance and social degradation become responsible and progressive citizens of their country, an asset to any nation.

We also serve the Christian community by providing the Scriptures for its use and offering to train its members in linguistics, literacy and Bible translation for the fulfillment of their missionary and translation responsibility to still others.

Jungle Aviation and Radio Service (JAARS)

Air transportation and radio communication are essential to our work in the remote areas of several countries. Distance from major population centers, lack of safe overland transportation, and primitive living conditions discourage or render impossible the extended periods of village living necessary for the translators to learn the language, do the translation and help the people in any lasting way. Communication by radio and transportation by plane or helicopter have been the solution.

Planes serve the isolated ethnic groups in several ways. Serious medical cases can be flown out or a doctor flown in. Epidemics can be checked by flying medicines and medical teams in. Whereas traditional surface travel would take weeks or even months, members of the ethnic communities can be flown to centers for special training courses in a very short time. Livestock, reading materials, equipment for new projects and project supervisors are flown out to the ethnic communities.

We do not compete with regular commercial airlines but seek to serve them. Our special performance planes, experienced pilots and radio network serve on search and rescue missions in times of natural disaster and when military or commercial planes go down in remote areas. Weather reports, radioed in from members on location, provide useful weather information for national and international carriers.

The radio network not only keeps the scattered linguistic teams in touch with one another, their director, and the outside world; it also makes communication between ethnic communities possible. In one instance, a revenge raid based on false reports was averted by calling the man who had been reported killed to the radio to assure his people he was alive and well. By means of the radio, doctors have guided members in splinting complicated fractures until the injured person could get to proper facilities.

155

18. *Radio operator maintains contact with workers in remote locations and monitors planes in flight.*

Where there is no commercial air service, our planes and pilots serve everyone on a space available basis. Income from such sources helps make the program self-sustaining. Those who oppose the work are also served. Thus we seek to show them the love of Christ and win them as friends. This attitude of loving service to all is not lost on government officials or local people. Our JAARS technical personnel are known and respected for their Christian character and witness as much as for their professional skill and competence.

JAARS has also been a means of promoting international friendship and good will. Several high performance aircraft have been donated by North American cities to countries where our members are serving the ethnic minorities. Mexico donated a PBY Catalina to Peru in honor of Moises Saenz, Mexico's ambassador to Peru at the time of his death. Public ceremonies involve mayors, ambassadors and even presidents of the countries sending and receiving the planes. These draw attention to the needs of the ethnic minorities and the role of our members in reducing their languages to writing and providing the Scriptures for them. Our Jungle Aviation and Radio Service mechanics and pilots operate and maintain this "Friendship Fleet" on behalf of the governments receiving them in the service of their ethnic peoples.[7]

The Servant's Reward

What has been our reward as servants? A Kiawa wrote the linguist-translator: "I am so happy that I just have to write to you. I am teaching my own people. Why should the civilized people call us 'stupid mules'? This is the first time in my whole life that anyone has entrusted me with any kind of responsibility. Very few are willing to teach without being paid. I just want to do all I can to help my people progress."

19. *Richard S. Pittman receives the Magsaysay Award on behalf of our Philippine Branch members for their service to minority peoples.*

157

Host countries have expressed their appreciation in many different ways. The president of one country, in his final report to the nation, said: "During the (past) six years my government has produced literacy materials in seventeen languages of the Republic. We are deeply indebted to the Summer Institute of Linguistics for its technical help in making this possible."

In 1973 our members in the Philippines received the Ramon Magsaysay Award for International Understanding, the Nobel prize of the Pacific area nations, "for inspired outreach to nonliterate tribespeople, recording and teaching them to read their own languages and enhancing their participation in the larger community of man." In making the award the Foundation recognized the research and service character of the work, the resultant "social and spiritual change" and the "individual and communal stability in the transition from isolation to full citizenship" that resulted.

10

Trusting God

FROM THE beginning we have been dependent upon God for open doors, personnel, finances, policies, public relations and results. Having become Christians by an act of faith in Jesus Christ, we have found that to live as Christians and to achieve our goals we must continually depend on him (Hab. 2:4; Rom. 1:17; Gal. 3:11; Heb. 10:38). Whatever is distinctive about our service and the measure of our success is of God.

This needs to be said. On the surface we are such goal and work-oriented people that our confidence in God may not be obvious to others. All too easily we may find ourselves trusting in our own efforts, and not in God to direct and bless those efforts. While we emphasize the academic nature of our work and the service attitude of our workers, our confidence is not in what we know, the methods we use, the articles we write, the degrees we earn, the people we train, who we know or the institutions we represent, but in the God who uses them. We trust him to do what he has promised and planned. This in no way belies our intense activity nor our striving for excellence. Faith is demonstrated in works, trust in obedience.

What does this mean in terms of our policies and practices?

For Ability to Do the Job

First, we believe that God will enable us to do what he has called us to do. New members are given a good basic, but still limited, training for the field work ahead. With this they tackle linguistic analysis, literacy campaigns, Bible translation and community development projects that stagger the imagination. Each area of activity merits the fulltime effort of highly trained and experienced personnel. Since motivated people with such qualifications are not available in sufficient numbers, we commit ourselves to seemingly impossible goals. To achieve these goals, all workers get further on-the-job help and training. Some go on to advanced studies and degree programs. The promises made to governments are not idle words but serious commitments, possible of fulfillment only by God's help and hard, sustained teamwork.

Take, for example, our Bible translation goal. Our initial feeling of inadequacy is based on ignorance of all that is involved. This rapidly becomes the inadequacy of reality when faced with the demands of faithful exegesis of the text, plus equivalent idiomatic restatement in a language used by people with a totally different world view. The courage to tackle it, the perseverance to see it through, and the effectiveness of the product in the hands of those who use it are evidence of God's faithfulness in response to our trust. Paul the Apostle's "I can do everything through him who gives me strength" (Phil. 4:13) gives us the courage to begin. It is also our testimony when the translation is finished. The steadily increasing number of translations appearing for the first time in previously unwritten languages demonstrates that our trust and industry are not misplaced.

Translators are not supersaints. Not all succeed or survive. Some do much more and better than others. All need help. We are simply doing what it is our duty to do. In the process God does something in us as well as through us. The confidence and poise some members show is not crass self-confidence but the product of experience, further studies, team support and God's faithfulness.

To Use His Word

Second, we believe God will use his Word just as he promised to (Isa. 55:11). We do not worship the Bible or consider it a fetish with magical power. We do not translate

160

merely to have the translation sit on a shelf or add to statistics. But until the translation is available, people cannot know what God has said. Until some are literate, they cannot read it themselves or even hear it read. Unless it is an intelligible translation, they cannot understand it. Even then our confidence is not in the translation itself, nor in the ability of people to read and understand it, but in God to convince readers and hearers that it meets their need.

Linda asked us if she had to be baptized to become a child of God. Did she have to know how to pray? Be able to sing hymns? Read the Scriptures well in her own language? Upon being told that such things were done after acceptance of Christ, not to earn salvation but to express it, she breathed a great sigh of relief. "Oh, then I've been a child of God for a long time." Somewhere during the previous months, as she had helped translate the Scriptures into her language, without any sense of coercion, she had believed Jesus Christ was who he claimed to be and had died and risen for her. Our faith in God to use the translation was strengthened.

We help prepare the seed and the soil, but it is God who mixes it with faith and obedience and implants new life (Heb. 4:2; John 1:12, 13). We may be the ones to point those in need to the appropriate Scripture, but God alone can lead them to act upon it. Many times when we are not present, God uses the translated Scripture in the lives of those who read it. Without coercion but in full recognition of their personal dignity and freedom of choice they commit themselves to Christ and his Word as a way of life.

In a remote area of Asia, the translator's language helper returned each evening to his own village across the valley to report to the men of his village what the passage translated that day said. Then the translator and his family left for several months. During their absence the day came for the annual religious ceremony honoring the village gods. The men of the village decided they would not observe the usual rites since they now worshipped the One of whom the Book spoke. The translator learned of their decision much later when his language helper came to work with him in the city.

The response is by no means automatic or uniform. God never promised it would be (see John 4:35, 36 with Jas. 5:7;

161

Matt. 13:4-9). But transformed communities, a new sense of personal worth and new standards of social concern and morality have been numerous enough to encourage us—yet sparse enough, in spite of our best efforts, to remind us that the results are God's, not ours.

To Build His Church

We trust God to build his church upon the translated Scriptures. Jesus Christ and his Word are the foundation upon which the local church must stand (Matt. 16:18). We are only temporary, to make the translation available, teach some people to read, and train those interested to study and apply the Scriptures. Their faith must be in Christ and the Scriptures which speak of him, not in us or our words.

The Trique New Testament was translated when there was a minimum of interest in it on the part of the people for whom the translators were preparing it. In what was in every sense of the word a pioneer situation, the isolation and unfriendliness of the people more than once brought them to the edge of quitting. No formal organized church was established when the finished translation was publicly presented in the town hall. But the sun was shining as 125 people gathered to hear the mayor, a shy Trique man, give a short introductory speech. He and other prominent men gave their enthusiastic approval to the new book and exhorted the people to buy and read it. Six years later the translators returned and rejoiced with Mennonite colleagues that an infant Trique church was indeed getting under way. People were meeting for Bible study. Young men were going out with the Trique New Testament to witness in surrounding villages. Sales of the New Testament were picking up. God was using his Word as he said he would.

For Indigenous Believers

We trust God to guide the infant church to adopt the rules of conduct and patterns of worship appropriate to them. These should be based on Scriptural principles applied by them to their own culture, not simply the adoption of our

162

foreign ways of doing things. Through the study of the Scriptures, the Holy Spirit can show the church what in its culture is contrary to that Word. We encourage the new Christians to find cultural substitutes for what they now believe is wrong and inconsistent with their faith in Christ. For example, Tzeltal Christian parents, seeking a bride for their son, felt ill at ease offering liquor to the parents of the girl, since they no longer drank themselves. Abundance of meat was also necessary for a good wedding feast, so they substituted gifts of meat, apparently with some success.

Teaching young believers and churches to trust God and obey his Word from day one is necessary if they are to grow to mature independence. The Spirit of God can apply the Word of God to their way of life if they are trained to look to him. We do not make their decisions for them but seek to help them apply the Scriptures in reaching their own decisions. We do not abandon them. We work with them, training them to read and search the Scriptures, encouraging them to trust God and obey his Word.

Charles Taber states it well:

> The only safe procedure is for missionary control and domination not to exist from the start, but for the church to be free under the Spirit and the Scripture from the first day. ... We must rediscover in our missionary ministry the twin powers of the Scriptures and the Spirit of God. To begin with, the sooner the Scriptures are translated, the better; and the more actively involved the young church is in the process of translation the better. ... The dangers inherent in the missionary's indispensable presence are minimized when the Bible early becomes the source of guidance which Christians consult directly and which they understand by the illuminating power of the Holy Spirit. ... It is when a congregation of believers recognizes itself as the people of God subject to the Word of God and the Spirit of God that mission has effectively taken place. ... This can and should be within days of the first conversions.[1]

We have learned that "if a person's spiritual knowledge always has to be mediated through someone else, there are certain things he is unlikely to come across; whereas if he has the Bible in his own language he will get insights that the translator himself never responded to."[2]

To Raise Up Leaders

We do not function as leaders of local congregations. We trust God to raise up persons gifted to preach, teach, pastor and write hymns from among the local believers. Impatience to get things going often results in foreign leadership at the beginning which discourages and delays the development of local talent and leadership. When the Ifugao asked the translator when he was going to build a church, he replied, "No church will be built until you decide to build it." The delay in building the first church was more than compensated for by the rapid growth in numbers and the indigeneity of the work when they later decided to build. They did so during the translator's absence.

For Academic Tasks

The academic side of the work is done in dependence upon Almighty God. While conforming to the academic requirements of the universities where training courses are held, students and faculty customarily include times of special devotion or prayer in their extra-curricular, off-campus activities. Many have testified that God gave renewal for the heavy academic program, provided funds for personal needs, or pointed the direction for future field service. Field workers write friends and churches in their homelands regularly, asking prayer for specific aspects of language learning, analysis and write-up. Dissertations for advanced degrees, monographs and textbooks are undertaken and those involved trust God to see them through. Acknowledgements to professors, colleagues, language resource people, family "and to Almighty God, from whom no secrets of language are hid, and who has graciously answered the prayers of many"[3] are not pious platitudes in dissertations, monographs or textbooks written by our members. Each has its own story of an author trusting God for insights, solutions, strength and perseverance.

164

Early in his field service in Mexico, Kenneth Pike, baffled by the tone system of the Mixtec language, took a day off for prayer and fasting. He dared to ask God for a solution to his problem that would also help his co-workers facing similar problems in other languages. The answer, given that day in a flash of insight, applied the next day at the desk, gave him in a matter of days a solution that had been delayed months. Generalized to apply to other languages, the book that resulted is still a standard text on the analysis of tone languages.

Dependence upon God has never been considered a substitute, however, for painstaking workmanship. Without question many of us would have given up many times had it not been for the confidence that God had called us and he would enable us to see the job through. By the sweat of his brow, man not only eats his food but also finds linguistic solutions and produces Bible translations. Faith keeps us at it and sees us through.

For Personnel Needed

We trust God to supply the personnel needed for the task. When the president of Mexico asked Townsend if other young people would be willing to come and give their lives to help the minority ethnic peoples in practical ways as he was doing, Townsend, confident in God, replied, "Yes, I am sure there are many." And God sent them. In the fall of 1941 Townsend challenged the forty-six workers then in Mexico to pray for fifty new recruits that year. The "Townsend Group" as they were then called, had no office in the homeland, no Board of Directors to assume responsibility, no publications and no public relations personnel. So the members prayed and wrote to friends. The staff of the summer courses at the University of Oklahoma shared the vision with the students. By the end of 1942, God had answered and fifty-one more had joined.

God not only supplies the numbers but the kinds of workers needed. When we needed people with management experience, we appointed a man to be in charge of their recruitment and orientation. Before the need was publicized seven couples turned up the next summer for the linguistic course at Norman, Oklahoma. Each had left a responsible management job in business or industry, believing God was calling them to join us. We, as well as they, were surprised at how quickly and specifically God had answered. Not all personnel needs have been supplied so dramatically or promptly of course. But the pattern is sufficiently well established to enable us to appreciate God's hand at work.

The testimony of many among us is that they were convinced God wanted them to work with us in spite of impossible circumstances, personal footdragging, and the counsel of friends to the contrary. We have never made joining easy nor the job light. Recruits are asked to count the cost: learning an unwritten language; producing linguistic articles, grammars, dictionaries, primers; living under pioneer conditions, and subsistence support with few fringe or terminal benefits. Self-centered, materialistic motives will not suffice.

At the same time, however, in our recruitment we do not minimize the plus factors, which are many. The opportunity and privilege of helping provide the Bible for people who have not had it attracts many. The prospect of ongoing training and supporting teamwork while doing the job encourages others. Step-by-step procedures to achieve the goal makes the job look less impossible. The challenge to trust God in new and exciting ways frightens only the faintest hearted away.

God is not limited. There are enough people for every type of Christian ministry and to reach every culturally distinct group of people. We thank God for the other organizations he is raising up, both at home and abroad, to help complete the task. It is our privilege to help train many of them. While two out of every three we train in linguistics join some other organization, we trust God to provide all the people we need, without drawing any away from other missions.

We also trust God to supply the caliber of people we need both to do the job themselves and to help and teach others. We trust God for wisdom to choose from among those applying those he would have work with us. Some who apply would need more help than the contribution they might

166

make would warrant. These we reject. Some borderline cases are accepted for a trial period to give them every chance to make good. We trust God to overrule where our human judgment would cause us to miss his will. All "common sense" to the contrary, we have accepted stutterers, the legally blind, the physically deformed, the socially immature, wheelchair cases and people who had never won another to Christ. Each had compensating factors that outweighed his handicap and made a good to outstanding contribution to our work. God, we believe, led us to accept them.

To Open Doors

We look to God to open new doors for Bible translation and practical service. We research the need and offer the program to potential host countries. Then we trust God to indicate by providential contracts, evidence of interest and actual invitations where he would have us go. A paper presented at an international scientific congress brought a query, then an invitation to one country. Service to the Bible society and missions in one country, plus lectures to the academic community resulted in an invitation to survey the need of jungle minorities. The result was a government contract. God used a book by Townsend to win strong support for our approach to another country. A casual dinner conversation between a member and a minister of government later brought an unexpected and warm invitation from the president of his country.

Moved by invitations from missions in one country, we approached the government only to find that it was anti-American and anti-religious, and had just created a special department to handle all matters concerning the ethnic minorities. A less propitious moment we could not imagine. The very man with whom we would have had to work most closely outspokenly opposed our overtures. But God overruled. The man's superiors accepted our offer and the man himself became a close personal friend of the member who negotiated the contract.

The beginning in each new country has involved factors beyond our control. Afterward we have marvelled at "all

167

that God had done ... and how he had opened the door of faith" that the ethnic groups might have opportunity to believe in his Son (Acts 14:27). Looked at from the human side only, one could easily say that the spread of the work was due to skillful negotiations, effective salesmanship, well-designed advance and follow-up publicity. But if the whole story were told, our expansion into country after country is not due to our efforts or policies but to the intervention of Almighty God. He disposed those in authority to invite us, accept the validity of our approach and commend us to others. Psalm 44:3 is a classic statement that says it well: "It was not by their sword that they won the land, nor did their arm bring them victory; it was your right hand, your arm, and the light of your face, for you loved them."

For Acceptable Service

We trust God to make our working relationships with governments mutually helpful without, however, compromising our Christian principles. Our contracts spell out what we offer to do for the government and what the government will do for us. When we make these commitments, we do so with faith in God for personnel, equipment and funds. Seldom do we have, or even have promised to us, what we need to fulfill our commitment. We believe God will not only work through friends at home, but also through the host government to help us accomplish what we have promised. One government offered bare land, rent free, for our headquarters on condition we develop it to their specifications within a specified time. We had nowhere near what it would cost but God provided and their specifications and our needs were met. When we prepare literacy materials for an ethnic group, the appropriate government department with which we work publishes them. They may or may not have money in their budget to cover the costs. If not, we look to God to supply through other sources.

Once we offered to print reading material for a famine-stricken minority group whose language we were studying. The government official who prepared the materials had recommended in the book an available but intoxicating beverage. He did so because of the vitamins it contained, which the people desperately needed. It bothered our Christian principles to print something we ourselves could not conscientiously recommend. We felt the moral and physical effects of the resultant drunkenness would more than offset the beverage's nutritional value. So we talked to God and then with the author. He saw the force of our objections from a sociological point of view and quite readily removed the reference from the book.

As guests in a country, we trust God to overrule so that we can be supportive of the incumbent rulers without entering into partisan politics, or furthering programs that will not be for the good of the ethnic peoples. They respect our desire not to get involved in internal politics. When governments change hands, we have to trust God to enable us to establish good relationships with new people in key posts, and at the same time to maintain the friendships developed with their predecessors.

When Under Attack

God is our defense when we are attacked. And attacked we are. When the public press attacks us or charges are presented to authorities against us, we choose to emulate him who "when they hurled their insults at him, ... did not retaliate; when he suffered, he made no threats. Instead, he entrusted himself to him who judges justly" (I Peter 2:23). Rather, we seek to talk to our opponents face to face, to clear up misunderstandings and explain our motives. We look for opportunities to show love instead of hate, to be helpful instead of retaliatory, to "overcome evil with good," according to Romans 12:17-21. Having made our explanations, we commit our cause to God and trust him to defend us (Ps. 37:5, 6). And he has. Friends, including some we did not know we had, without solicitation from us, have publicly gone on record to defend us. On one occasion a university student of the religious persuasion of our attackers wrote a better rebuttal than we ourselves could have done. He had studied under one of us, knew the facts and was incensed at the ignorance and unfairness displayed in the attacks. When criticized by missions who have disagreed with our tactics and threatened with withdrawal of support by churches who did not understand our policies, we have stated our case, committed the matter to God, and trusted him to guide and provide. He has done above and beyond what we expected. In most cases, tensions have been relieved, fellowship restored, and support continued.

For the Completion of the Task

We trust God for the completion of the task. Humanly speaking, when we realize the work still to be done, our mind sometimes boggles. The linguistic, literacy and Bible translation task for well over 2,000 languages has still not even begun. Over one-half the population of the world lives in areas where we as yet do not have permission or invitation to share the Bible with their ethnic minorities. In some of those areas Christians are actually restricted from making any such efforts. If it is to be done, God will have to make it possible. Equally obvious, though we sometimes fail to see it, is that what has been done and is being done is also impossible.

But when we consider who God is and what he has already done, we are optimistic. The ethnic peoples of the world are the object of his love and concern. Jesus Christ his Son died for them too. He commands us to go into all the world, share the Good News with every person, and make disciples of all nations. He committed himself to work with us. He has not abandoned the project nor us. We admit that what we have done so far is the result of his enablement. He has provided everything necessary for its accomplishment. In view of all this, it is easier to believe he will finish the task than to believe he will not!

How God will do it we do not know. He may multiply and expand what is already going on. He may use a whole new approach, in which case we need to be open to innovation and change. He may use someone else. We have never believed we were the only ones God could use. We have encouraged the establishment of other Bible translation organizations. We have been encouraged by the potential of the younger churches to contribute their members and resources to the Bible translation advance. What is important is that it get done, not who does it. So without getting bogged down in the uncertainties of the future we press on, that we may be found faithful when Christ returns. (In chapter 12 we will consider the pioneering attitude that puts feet to our faith that "it shall be done.")

Some critics of our work have deplored the "brain drain" of personnel to translation for the handfuls of small ethnic peoples, especially in view of the desperate need of workers for the millions of unreached people in cities. We press on, however, believing God still wants all the ethnic minorities to have his Word and the supply of workers is not limited. We trust God for workers for the millions in the cities, for task forces to reap the responsive fields, as well as for the personnel to do what is necessary for the small, illiterate and not-yet-responsive groups. We believe God has the resources to do his work and the wisdom to deploy them. He is able to communicate to his listening children where he wants them to work. We rejoice when God blesses other ministries. We make no apology for the many who have joined our ranks but look for many more who are similarly called of God to work with us.

11

Faith and Finances

OUR TRANSLATION push was launched during the Great Depression. People did not have money to contribute. Church mission societies were recalling their overseas workers for lack of funds. The Townsends and those with them had to rely on God for their support, not only on principle but in the face of circumstances. Each person joining the group was expected to look to God for his own needs. As a seal of God's call to go, workers were expected to have enough money to get to Mexico City. No specified amount of continuing support was required. If they were willing to go and trust God to supply, they were accepted. There was no foundation, no general fund, no home organization. The Pioneer Mission Agency in Philadelphia was willing to receive and forward gifts. That was all. But from the very beginning as new people joined and their friends and churches heard, interest and gifts increased.

Once on the field our first members made what they received go farther by taking turns doing things for one another instead of hiring someone to do them. All designated gifts received went as designated, whether to individuals or projects. Gifts not earmarked for particular individuals, families or projects were disbursed to those members receiving the least. Then the group decided to use a "highwater" system. Those receiving the lowest percentage of what was needed were helped first as far as the funds would go. As a basis for this highwater system of disbursing undesignated funds and to be able to answer inquiries concerning need, an estimated monthly support figure pegged to the cost of living was adopted. Children's expenses and special expenses for medical care and travel were added. In order to know each member's needs, the group agreed that each would report total personal income each month, including what was received directly. The field bookkeeper carried personal accounts for each member and made deposits and payments only by authorization granted by the member. Members were expected to thank donors with a personal letter and keep them informed of the progress of the work. Those helped by undesignated gifts were to write personal thank-yous, so donors would have a direct personal relationship to someone on the field.

When money was needed to pay for things that would serve the group as a whole, such as having an office in Mexico City, each member contributed a fixed sum from personal funds to provide for such general overhead expenses. This was five dollars a month at first. In 1942, when home offices in Glendale, California, were first established, this was changed by vote of the members to ten percent of what the new corporations received. This was divided - seven percent for the field office, three percent for the home end. By the members' vote it has been changed from time to time, the most recent division being four percent field, five percent home and one percent international. Thus the basic elements of the financial system that continues to serve us today took shape.

Scriptural Principles and Precedents

From the beginning, in our financial policies as in other matters, we have tried to be consistent with the teachings of the Scriptures we translate.

We believe that as God's children we are to live in dependence upon our Father. We depend upon God in faith to supply all our financial and material needs. By whatever means our needs are met, we believe it is God who has supplied. The Scriptures show God to be the sustainer of all

173

human life (Ps. 145:15, 16). He promises to provide for those who serve him (Matt. 6:33).

He does so in many different ways. For the Levites and especially for the family of Aaron God provided through an assessment (the tithe) and the offerings the Israelites were required to bring to him (Num. 18:8-21, 24). For the prophets who itinerated he provided through the general hospitality of the day (2 Kings 4:8) and voluntary gifts from those they served (1 Sam. 9:7, 8). Some had their own lands and means of livelihood (1 Kings 19:19). Some lived off the ruler's bounty (1 Kings 18:4, 19; Daniel 1:5). Christ and his disciples lived by the hospitality of those they visited (Luke 10:7, 8) and gifts from friends (Luke 8:3).

To meet an unusual, temporary situation created in the early church in Jerusalem by the sudden increase in the numbers of believers, including many who were away from their homes and usual means of support, the Lord provided a mutual, voluntary pooling of resources (Acts 4:32-5:11).

The needs of Paul and those who traveled with him were provided in a variety of ways: through common hospitality offered visitors (Acts 16:34), by their own work and employment as they itinerated (Acts 20:34; 1 Cor. 9:6), and by special gifts from those to whom he had previously ministered (2 Cor. 11:9; Phil. 4:15, 16).[1]

For the poor and those suffering because of famine or calamity, gifts of money (almsgiving) and special collections of food were God's provision (Acts 11:29, 30; 24:17; 2 Cor. 8:4). In other emergency situations, such as the times Israel was in the wilderness and the multitude was by the Sea of Galilee, God provided miraculously.

In his faithfulness and in many different ways, God has supplied our needs. There is biblical precedent for each. By far the principal source of income has been and continues to be donations from groups and individuals who share our faith in Christ and the Bible and our commitment to give the Bible to others in the mother tongue (Phil. 4:10-19). Scholarships and grants have helped many of us on study programs (Dan. 1:3-5). In appreciation for the service rendered, some governments have made facilities available, granted exemptions from fees, and helped in various ways on specific projects (Neh. 2:8, 9). Friends both at home and abroad have often extended hospitality, made gifts in kind, or contributed freely of their own time and skills (Acts 16:15).

Asking God

Members present the needs of the work to God in prayer. Individually and unitedly we ask God to supply the needs of each member and the work as a whole. Our Lord clearly indicated that in the matter of material need, his children are to ask him for help. "Ask and it will be given to you" (Matt. 7:7). James reminded his readers that they lacked because they didn't ask God or because they asked from selfish motives (James 4:2, 3). Whether by command, invitation, promise or precedent, the prophets, Christ, Paul, James and John without exception declare that we are to ask God for what we need (1 Kings 3:5; John 16:23; Eph. 3:20; 1 John 3:22; Matt. 6:11). In keeping with this emphasis, Wycliffe's policy from the beginning has been to ask God, not people, for money. We have always felt free to inform friends and the general public concerning the financial policies of the work, but without presenting specific, personal needs. A current statement to the general Christian public says that we are "dependent on the faithfulness of God and his people for the supply of material needs, including all expenses incurred during the course of the work. Basic personal support and ministry quotas are established for each location and reflect differences in family and assignment situations. Specific information is available on request."

Supplying Information

As indicated in the above statement, we are free to mention specific needs and amounts if asked. Some of our friends and supporters do ask. We have agreed among ourselves that "the needs of the work may also be presented with propriety to those who have indicated that they expect to be informed of such needs."

Requests for information come in different ways. Foundations by their very nature and by-laws are seeking presentations of need that fit the purpose for which they are established. Institutions that advertise scholarships and grants for students who qualify are inviting application. Members of the Wycliffe Associates, an independent lay organization committed to helping us, pay an annual membership fee, and are kept informed of needs. Specific information on selected projects is given them for distribution to their members. Many churches, Sunday school classes and individuals request specific information concerning the needs of individual members or group projects. To them full information is given.

The taking of offerings and "faith promises" and the presentation of needs are recognized to be often in good taste and blessed of God. Such procedures are encouraged when and where they are expected and well received. We do, of course, urge our members and representatives to use discretion and good taste in the presentation of personal and project needs.

We realize that God supplies our needs principally through his people in order that they may share in the spiritual blessing and fruit of the work. Through information God makes his people aware of what he is doing and moves them to become involved, some personally, others financially or by prayer, many in more than one way. We are ready to give such information but seek to do it in ways that do not belie our basic confidence in God.

To keep our giving of information from becoming solicitation we have tried to establish some general guidelines. Lists of needs or specific amounts are not to be included in general letters but may be furnished those who request them. Such specific statements as "Pray that the Lord will supply the remaining twenty-five percent of our support" are to be avoided as too easily interpreted as indirect solicitation.

The Goal of Deputation

The goal of deputation and the motivation of the deputationist is to give, not to get, to be a spiritual blessing to those

176

with whom he shares his burden for the work, not "to raise support." Deputation is carried on as a ministry, with no financial obligation, stated or implied, on the part of those spoken to.

One of our field members hurting for lack of support was rebuked by his home director for his mercenary attitude toward deputation. Chastened, he committed his need to God, dropped his aggressive solicitation of meetings and funds and determined to minister to people and not think only of being ministered to. In the following ten months God brought 165 unsolicited invitations for meetings and provided abundantly for support as the member simply shared what God was doing and what needed to be done. That is the lesson we want all our members to learn.

God has honored this policy by providing for the ever-growing needs of the workers without pleas and campaigns for funds. Each year as new members join us, support increases proportionately. Even with inflation God continues to provide, some years even more than the inflation rate. God loves a cheerful, spontaneous giver and any action or words that would cause people to give unwillingly, or feel pressured to give by suggestion from without rather than conviction from within, works against that ideal.

Payment for Services

Members may accept payment for services rendered (e.g. salary for teaching linguistics at a university) which may supplement or serve in lieu of the usual donor support. But we do not encourage our members to take outside employment to support themselves. The linguistic, literacy and translation work itself is a fulltime job. Sometimes because of low income or unusual expenses, members have taken temporary employment to supplement gifts received. As Paul bent over backward to avoid any appearance of exploiting for personal gain those he served, we seek no remuneration of any kind from the host country or ethnic minorities.

We have authorized our leaders "to write letters to interested pastors on behalf of personal deputationists, stating that they are new members needing support, or that they are members home on furlough lacking full support, with the stated understanding that there will be no plea for funds, and no financial obligation on the part of the church." Precedent for such "letters of commendation" (2 Cor. 3:1) and statement of need may be found in Paul's "third party letters" on behalf of Onesimus (Philemon 1, 2, 10, 17); Phoebe (Rom. 16:1, 2), Timothy (1 Cor. 16:10, 11), Mark (Col. 4:10) and Titus and others (2 Cor. 8:23, 24). Such letters are only written with the consent or at the request of the individual member.

Indebtedness

Members are expected to be good stewards (Luke 16:11), live within the income God supplies and not incur financial obligations they cannot fulfill (Ps. 37:21a). New members must be free of debt before leaving for their first assignment after initial training is completed. We consider a debt "any financial obligation that is not covered by a mortgage or lien or that cannot be cleared readily and directly by sale, insurance benefits or other assets."

As a group we do not go into debt, that is, we do not authorize obligations that exceed our resources or for which we do not have a realistic source of income to make payments.

Finances and God's Will

We believe that the giving and withholding of money is one of many ways God uses to make his will known to us. God may withhold finances to teach us (Phil. 4:12), to test our moral character (Prov. 30:9), to challenge our faith (John 6:6) or to indicate it is not yet his time for a specific step.

Looking ahead to the worldwide ministry of his disciples beyond their own cultural borders, Christ reversed his earlier command to live from hand to mouth (Matt. 10:9, 10) and told them to plan and provide ahead for necessary expenses (Luke 22:35, 36). We have asked those going out

178

for the first time and those returning after furlough to meet certain requirements, including a specific minimum percentage of promised support, as one indication God was sending them. For many the miracle of God's initial provision has been a new and wonderful experience. The continuing supply even for unexpected emergencies while they remained abroad has but underlined God's faithfulness.

Pegged to Needs

Annually each member prepares a statement of his estimated needs to live and carry out his assignment for the coming year. This "quota" figure, as it is called, serves several purposes. It gives the member a specific goal to trust the Lord to supply and the administration a specific figure to use to determine comparative need when distributing emergency funds to those lowest in support. The quota for singles, married couples and family units takes into consideration the current cost of living, ministry expenses, special project needs and home country factors. The Basic Living Factor includes the cost of food, clothing and grooming, normal medical needs, local transportation, vacation and recreation, giving, personal needs, shelter, children's education, taxes, retirement and, assessments for administrative services and contingencies. Children's education amounts do not include advanced education costs. The Ministry Factor covers costs related to one's specific assignment that year, including field travel, equipment, furlough travel, communication with supporters and employment of language helpers. Special Projects may be a vehicle or a house, for example. The Home Country Factor includes costs recommended by the Home Council such as advanced education costs for children, or costs required by the governments of some home countries, such as health insurance and pension.

The quota figure is not a guaranteed salary. It is simply a comprehensive estimate of each member's total need. It is not published and is only given to donors on request.

We are dependent on the gifts God sends through donors. We consider those who donate our partners in the work.

Each member has his own circle of friends who pray, give and follow his work with interest. We believe it is our personal responsibility, in addition to the receipt our office sends, to thank them and share our blessings and concerns with them on a personal level. Even those who give to the work without designating a specific use receive a personal letter of appreciation from the member who received an amount equal to their gift through the distribution of such funds. We hope in this way to establish a personal relationship between the Christian constituency and our member which will be of mutual blessing. We trust God to direct the donor in any expression of interest and we honor that expression in our use of funds. If it is not possible to honor the donor's wishes, he is consulted and given the opportunity to state another preference.

Our entire financial system is built on the support of the individual worker. Each of us looks to God and the circle of friends he has given us and not to an organizational budget. This means we can accept as many qualified workers as the Lord sends. There is no budgetary limitation since we go as God supplies. Since all gifts received without a statement of preference are allocated monthly to meet the needs of members lowest in support, there are no general funds for administrative purposes. For the cost of administration we members have voted a percentage of corporate income to finance our field and home office costs. This limits administrative overhead to member growth and total income. It also guarantees funds for these services in proportion to the number and income of members served. The officers we elect from among our own number to handle our affairs are responsible for the budgeting and use of such funds.

We accept the fact that there is an inequality of income among us. Our projects and needs differ. God does not provide the same amount or even the same percentage of estimated needs for all. We find national and personal differences in standards of living (even at subsistence level) and in the handling of finances. As an expression of their personal Christian stewardship many members give liberally and sacrificially to projects or people both inside and outside the

180

group. New advances and many capital projects have been substantially helped by member gifts. Fellow-members and ethnic neighbors in special need, or ethnic communities suffering catastrophic losses, have received similar help. Since the cost of operations for small branches may be proportionately higher than for larger staffs, small branches often receive member offerings and budget grants from larger ones.

Capital Funding and Projects

Capital funding and group project needs are dependent almost entirely on donations. Linguistic projects are sometimes funded by special research grants. Some governments make grants for literacy and community development projects among minority peoples.

Bible translation and related materials have been paid for or heavily subsidized by agencies such as the World Home Bible League, New York Bible Society, member societies of the United Bible Societies, churches and individuals. Wycliffe Associates from its very beginning has taken on a great variety of projects, both large and small, at home and abroad. Not only funds, equipment and materials have been supplied, but skilled laymen at their own expense have gone to the field to build houses, clinics and hangars and to install water, power and telephone systems.

Whatever the need, the source of supply or the channel that brings them together, we gratefuly acknowledge God as the giver and ourselves, his servants, as recipients and stewards of his bounty.

Finances and the Ethnic People

Those who help us learn their language and translate the Bible on a regular basis must often give up other remunerative employment to do so. Unless local or designated support is forthcoming, we pay our helpers wages out of what we receive. Sometimes whole families brought to workshops for an extended period are supported by the member they are helping. Members also give liberally of their means to provide free or subsidized services to local people, such as literature for new readers and simple medications. Where local people are able to pay a nominal price for medicines, the service can often be self-sustaining. Some nationals have been trained in a skill by the member, and this has provided them a new source of income while rendering valuable service to their community.

Local groups of believers resulting from the work are not controlled nor supported by us. From the very beginning they are expected to do things on a scale they can finance and sustain themselves. This does not prohibit us, as individuals or as a group, from giving to local church projects or sponsoring the training of individuals as a demonstration of fellowship and love. Such non-translation projects as the training of bilingual school teachers, training in crafts, animal husbandry, nursing and community development are often financed by designated gifts or branch funds on an initial experimental basis, but as soon as possible are incorporated into national programs and government financing. Bilingual training schools, teachers' salaries and extensive literacy materials are usually funded by local governments, sometimes with the aid of special grants from abroad.

12

Pioneering

FROM THE beginning a pioneering spirit has characterized the work. We identify with the Apostle Paul's ambition to proclaim the Good News "where Christ was not known, . . . not . . . building on someone else's foundation. Rather, as it is written: 'Those who were not told about him will see, and those who have not heard will understand'" (Rom. 15:20, 21).

Since our way of implementing this pattern is by translating the Bible for people who have never had it in their mother tongue, it involves going not only where the Gospel has never been known, but also sometimes where it is known but where the Scriptures are still available only in a foreign language. In both situations it usually involves learning and writing languages never before written down.

Pioneer Living

In many cases our members live in isolated areas among ethnic minorities where outsiders have never lived before. Only twelve years ago on the borders of the Great Western Desert a nomadic Australian aboriginal people saw white skin for the first time. The translator family they saw now lives in a small house trailer in order to move with them. A family in Asia has a 120-mile, seven-day walking trip from the end of the truck road over an 11,000-foot pass to their home among the people for whom they are translating. If an emergency arises, the nearest telegraph office is a one-hundred-mile run away. In northern Brazil for two dangerous weeks workers inched their way up through the rapids of an angry river and cut their way through the jungle around an impassable waterfall to reach the people among whom they would live during the next nineteen years until the New Testament was delivered to the church which came into existence in the process. And these are not just isolated cases.

20. *An isolated ethnic community of northern Brazil.*

Our members are not the only ones who have to adjust to new situations. People less than a thousand miles south of the United States border rubbed the skin of an American girl "to see if the white stuff would come off and she would look human underneath." Having never seen blond hair before, they insisted she must be the grandmother of her dark-haired, twenty-two-year-old companion in spite of her twenty-one years. Members arriving among stone-age people in the Amazon have been mistaken for spirits from outer

184

space—they arrived by plane. Others thought they were ghosts back from the dead, they were so colorless. One with glasses was a monstrosity with four eyes. The floatplane that brought them was certainly a different kind of bird, huge, noisy, smelly and tasteless—when they licked the fabric. Pioneering has its frightening aspects for some of those to whom we go also.

Not all members work under pioneer living conditions. Many ethnic communities without the Bible have a good standard of living and enjoy the amenities of life. Even some rural minorities have visited and are familiar with modern urban life. Some of our members are assigned to our centers in the hinterlands. Others have responsibilities which require them to be in the capital cities. But all are expected to be pioneers in attitude and, when necessary, in fact.

We emphasize the pioneer aspect of our task, believing that unless we keep our eyes on the total task and the last unreached ethnic group we will lose an important and compelling element of our Lord's commission to us. The world needs to be reminded of people without the Bible, languages that have never been studied, people who cannot read. We cannot acquiesce in "the abandonment of the ultimate few by those interested in the masses." We are not unmindful of the masses, the cities, the millions who speak the major languages of the world. But there are thousands committed to reaching them. The Scriptures already exist in many of their languages. National churches exist, in some cases flourish, in the countries where they live. Our calling from God and therefore our challenge to the Christian public is the need of those for whom nothing of the Bible is available in their own language, those to whom no one has ever gone with the Good News in their mother tongue, those who live beyond the end of the trails and to whom no one else we know of is planning to go. The picture is not overdrawn, for there are still many remote, resistant or hitherto untouched ethnic minorities in the world.

Not all are remote, nor resistant, nor difficult to reach, however. "Hidden people," culturally-distant non-Christians, groups of people who, whether geographically near or far from Christian outreach, are sufficiently different linguistically, socially, economically and culturally that they are simply not realistic candidates for membership in existing Christian churches constitute eighty-four percent of the total non-Christian population of the world.[1] A renewed, non-geographical, cross-cultural pioneer missionary perspective is needed if these social and ethnic enclaves, many of them overlooked among the masses and in the very shadow of existing churches, are to have the opportunity to know of Christ, have his Word, and participate in a vital Christian fellowship representing their own cultural tradition.

Such groups which speak languages still without Scripture are part of our direct concern. Already we are translating for a number of them. Displaced ethnic communities numbering hundreds and thousands now reside in cities and rural communities of America, Europe, the Middle East and Southeast Asia. Members continue translating for over 1,000 Tai Dam in Iowa, refugees from Vietnam. They would much prefer to be among the 250,000 Tai Dam in Vietnam but since that is not possible they are translating here. Through radio now, perhaps some day in print, they hope to reach those in Vietnam with the translated Word.

Hidden groups which speak a language for which Scripture is available may still require cross-cultural methods. Workers may need to learn their language and provide literacy programs to teach them to read their own and the official language of the country where they live. Courses in language learning can be of great help to those called to work among them.

Pioneer Translating

That men should know God in Jesus Christ as presented in the Bible is, we believe, of the highest priority and ultimate value. So long as there are people who do not have the Bible, someone should provide it for them. If no one else is planning to provide it, then to the limit of our resources we will seek to recruit, train and send those who will. Even if they have heard the Gospel and believed in Christ, if no one of them is able, available or called to translate the Scriptures for them, we believe someone should. Where there are expatriate or mother tongue translators planning to translate, we thank God, offer any help they desire which we can provide, and press on to still others for whom no one else is doing anything. There is no place for competition, duplication or overlap in effort while so much remains completely untouched.

Our special training makes us all the more responsible. Our experience in reducing languages to writing, analyzing languages starting with the raw spoken data, preparing reading readiness and literacy materials, motivating mother tongue speakers to write original material, and working through the initial linguistic and cultural problems to find ways of expressing biblical truth add to our reponsibility. This training and experience should be used to the fullest and in the most difficult and needy situations.

Not that no one else has ever done this before. Not at all. In no way are we the first or only pioneers. But we began with a pioneer vision and our whole operation is geared to pioneering. Until every ethnic language group has its own translation of the Word of God, pioneering is required. And no ethnic language group is unimportant.

First-time Bible translation is also needed in many languages where the conditions are much less primitive, indeed may be quite highly developed and modern. The people who speak these languages may be generally well-educated, some even to university level. General education, even Bible schools and seminaries, in an official or trade language still foreign to most of the people is not enough. Churches may also exist in such communities, but with no Scripture in the mother tongue of the pastor or his people.

The writer has attended churches where the pastor had to prepare his message and read the Scripture from an English Bible, then deliver the sermon in his mother tongue. In one such situation, since those who taught him always spoke in English and used an interpreter, the pastor also spoke in English and had one of his elders interpret for him, to his own people in his own mother tongue! The fact that he spoke in English gave me the opportunity however to follow his explanation of the text for the day. Neither his seminary training nor his knowledge of Greek saved him from an unfamiliar nuance of English grammar in the English Bible he was speaking from, and the main point of his message came out exactly the reverse of what Paul had written! That man and his people needed a translation in their mother tongue.

Some realize their limitations in the English language and jump at the opportunity to help produce a translation for their people. It is enlightening to hear their gasps of amazement as they carefully work through the Scriptures with an expatriate co-translator. Time after time they remark, "I never knew that's what it meant!" Ambiguous English was a subtle trap to the Kwakiutl who explained "the Lord is my shepherd" as "The Lord is the one who takes care of my sheep!" Extended meanings can likewise play havoc with a message. The person to whom the word "flesh" always means "meat" is in trouble with "All flesh is as grass!"

If the Bible has never been translated into a language before, whether the language itself is already written or not, it is a pioneer task. The standard of living, level of education, degree of social or political sophistication or geographical location are not the only or even crucial issues in pioneer Bible translation.

Mother tongue speakers of Bibleless languages who catch the vision of translating for their own people are also pioneer translators. They do not have to learn another language, since they already speak the language into which they will translate. They do not have to leave home, unless to get further Bible training or work at a translation center. But they do face the problem of how to write their own language if it has never been reduced to written form before. They also face the problem every translator faces of understanding what the text to be translated means and how to express it clearly and faithfully in the translation.

An Engenni pastor, superintendent of some thirty churches, attempting to translate for his own people gave up when neither English nor Ibo alphabets seemed to fit the sounds of his language. He needed help in analyzing and writing his own language. Hearing of a linguistic course we were offering in his local university, he attended. Classes in linguistic principles underlying alphabet decisions and sample solutions of Bible translation problems revived his hopes. With the help of a translation-literacy team assigned to work with him, one Gospel was soon finished. Later, during his long vacation while on advanced studies in America, he used our workshop facilities in Mexico and was helped by our consultants. Several more books were translated that summer. Now the Engenni New Testament is published and in use among his people. He too is a pioneer Bible translator, joining the ranks of Wycliffe and Luther who likewise provided it for their people in the mother tongue.

But to wait until after the church is established and able to translate for itself is to condemn the first generation of Christians to living without the Scriptures in their own language. This can contribute to the all-too-prevalent attitude that a person can be a good Christian without the Spirit-given means of knowing what his Lord's will is. We cannot consider it more than second-best to be laying the foundation of Scripture in the vernacular *after* church government and teaching becomes established without it. We believe people need the Scriptures not some time but as soon as possible. This again pushes us to pioneer. Pioneer translations for initial evangelism and teaching can be followed by church-sponsored revisions and further translation by those raised up and nurtured on the former.

With our emphasis on pioneer work we constantly need workers for *new* translation projects. The most recent figures indicate we are beginning work in another language on an average of every ten and a half days. With few exceptions these are pioneer translation projects. At the same time we also have calls to help others engaged in translation and literacy work. As new fields and projects are undertaken more support personnel are needed to provide essential services.

Not all new workers pioneer. Some language projects

have been left unfinished by workers called to other urgent needs or who have left the work. New teams must pick up the work and carry it through to completion. Other language projects require an additional team if literacy and community development are going to be adequately cared for.

Pioneer Qualifications and Training

Our candidate qualifications reflect our pioneer emphasis. Pioneer work takes us away from the comforts of home, family and country, and makes us strangers in foreign environments. No longer are we part of a well-established Christian fellowship. Our personal convictions and cultural habits are no longer understood or accepted as normal. Interpersonal communication puts us at the disadvantage of an unknown or only partially mastered foreign language. Candidates, therefore, must demonstrate maturity of character, an ability to take care of themselves physically and spiritually under pioneer circumstances, a willingness and ability to learn new things from others, and a personal drive and self-discipline to get on with the job with limited supervision.

Independence, self-sufficiency and deep convictions are necessary to survive in pioneer situations. Yet these very characteristics may create problems in a team effort and make one difficult to live with under close quarters. Our approach maximizes the independent elements in the individual location and project, yet requires cooperation, teachability and compatibility in the workshop, consultant, and team aspects of the program. "Frontier" life forces people to live in close proximity with all types, without space to avoid those one might not like or choose as friends. Candidates then must be prepared to love all, even their enemies, to "eat with publicans and sinners" as their Lord did and to be non-sectarian in their service to others.

Our training program after a candidate has been accepted has been developed with pioneer situations in mind. Jungle camps and field orientation courses in Mexico, West Africa and Papua New Guinea emphasize improvisation, use of local materials and resources, learning to do unfamiliar

190

things, survival techniques, calmness and resourcefulness in new situations, self-discipline, trust in the Lord, and compatibility in working with teammates.

21. *Training for simpler living comes at jungle camp and field orientation.*

One couple wrote at the end of their eighteen-week Jungle Camp experience:

It's been a tremendous time for us both. We've picked up a lot of new skills and techniques. Nancy's baking in a cast iron skillet on a mud stove is as good as in our electric range at home. We've beheaded poultry, cut up and canned quartered beef, cooked and planned for 100 hungry people; we've gone on a fifty-mile hike, learned how to find and get found in the jungle, been on a dugout canoe trip, done battle with ticks and army ants, studied Tzeltal firsthand, memorized, categorized, sterilized, and on and on. We've helped Tzeltal folk prepare a cornfield using the ancient slash-and-burn technique. Nancy

191

has observed what happens to corn from the storage house to the stomach. The people grind it, drink it, feed it to their animals, and eat in in a number of ways, especially as tortillas.

I helped eighteen-year-old Antonio learn to read and taught his little brother to separate a sheet of stamps and put them right-side-up in the top right corner of the front of an envelope. We've gained a lot of valuable training studying the Tzeltal language and culture. We've picked up positive attitudes (and discarded negative ones) through a heap of brand new experiences. We just returned from our four days and four nights of survival hike: a minimum of equipment, no food for the first two days and almost none the next two. That left us psychologically naked and pulled up the shades on some diffcult areas of our lives. The added burden of hundreds of distracting tick bites made me cry "uncle" to God.

We found out more about togetherness, both with fellow-campers and the Tzeltal. We gained a new awareness: What constitutes modesty to a Tzeltal? And how do they feel about wealth, spirituality, hospitality, punctuality? What is funny to them? This is hard on me—after all, isn't our way of doing things always best?

We've strengthened our marriage. We've worked together hauling and boiling water, starting and maintaining fires, splitting firewood, cooking, doing laundry at the river laundromat. So, at every moment, under every circumstance, no matter what happens, or who caused it to happen, we've found God is there. And that he helps us. And even makes us *happy*. And we've loved it!

Physical fitness is another benefit of Field Orientation. As one camper put it, "Thirty pounds of me liked Jungle Camp so well they just stayed there."

And the readiness to improvise pays off. One translator far from the nearest large letter typewriter, cut stencils for his trial primers with a bent pin and the light tap of a hammer, and the primers were soon in use.

Pioneering in Linguistics

Our linguistic training stresses a step-by-step, how-to-do-it approach to language learning and language analysis. To

192

tackle any language anywhere in the world, students are exposed to some 500 speech sounds and scores of grammatical devices with actual language samples. Even so, one team came up with a whole series of sounds that we had not taught or even knew existed in actual languages, sounds made with heavy friction at various points in the mouth. The air for these sounds didn't come from the lungs but from the plunger-like action of the closed vocal cords pushing air out through the mouth.

Students learn discovery procedures for analyzing hitherto undescribed languages from scratch.[2] Before leaving the course, they apply the procedures in a simulated pioneer language learning situation, working on a language they have never studied before, without traditional helps such as grammars and dictionaries. Beginning students are trained in one approach. Advanced courses present them with other ways of handling the language data. The pioneer often needs alternate sets of tools when facing new types of problems. He needs to know one approach well and how to use it in getting started. He also needs to know where to go for help when he bogs down.

Included in each student's training is a demonstration of how to learn a language by gesture, without the aid of any intermediate or common language. Situations still exist where this is the only or preferable way to get started.[3] Of the first eleven languages studied in Brazil, seven had to be learned this way. No speaker of the ethnic languages knew enough Portuguese to act as an interpreter.

From a linguistic point of view, pioneering in new and often radically different languages calls for an ability to apply various linguistic methods, an understanding of principles and a flexibility to experiment with different approaches until solutions are found and progress made. The assumption is that more will be accomplished by each one pushing as far as he can on his own, then seeking help from others working on similar problems or with more experience. Our field workshop and consultant service arose to keep our frontline linguists moving ahead.

Not all language workers pioneer. Some are assigned

where the linguistic pioneering has been done and they will be using materials prepared by others. In such cases, however, new teams are encouraged to go beyond what others have done and make their own unique contribution.

Pushing the frontiers of knowledge and theory further is a type of pioneering and adds excitement to the task. With data from languages currently spoken in the Americas and using already well-developed comparative historical methods, a number of our members have reconstructed the Otomanguean family of languages of the New World in a manner similar to what scholars had previously done for the Indo-European languages of the Old World.[4] Our theoreticians, working with our members on a broad spectrum of languages, have also been making noteworthy contributions in the recent field of discourse analysis. Findings are being applied to the analysis of biblical languages and the text of Scripture and to translations in process in the ethnic languages.[5]

Our published research in previously undescribed languages enables us to make a genuine contribution to the knowledge of the world's languages. Articles in scientific journals or on microfiche make the information available to the academic world. To assess and improve our own competence in the language we encourage our members to publish. Members who complete advanced degree programs in linguistics or anthropology help fellow workers keep somewhat abreast of the latest developments in linguistics by sharing through field seminars. Such studies help keep a sharper edge on the axe for clearing still other virgin forests!

Assignments

Our pioneering drive affects our assignment of workers. Other things being equal, open doors to new fields have often been given priority over assignments to further languages in already open fields. We act upon invitations to work in new areas as soon as possible, while interest is high and the invitation fresh. This puts a strain on personnel and resources, but we trust God to supply both for new advances and further work in already existing fields.

Many new members are assigned to pioneer language projects. In the case of new fields or countries, some experienced leadership is necessary but often this is a minimum. The challenge of a pioneer situation brings the best out in some people. Having to fit into the mold of an older team's work often stifles initiative.

In allocating teams we seek to avoid duplication of effort and any appearance of competition with other organizations in the same language area. Thus we may choose to work beyond where others have gone, beyond work in progress to where no one is working, beyond villages with churches to villages with no believers. By doing this, we make friends and share the Good News with yet another village rather than just increase personnel where work is already in progress. For linguistic reasons we may pass up a more prestigious bilingual community for a more monolingual village. On the other hand, once the language is learned, we may withdraw to major centers or workshop facilities to get away from local interruptions and complete the analysis or the translation.

The vigor of our pioneering emphasis may be evident from the fact that the movement was eight years old and almost one hundred workers strong when we first organized formally. In one country workers were allocated and busily at work in seven remote language groups *before* centers were built for them to come back to, let alone go out from! Many rules and procedures were matters of precedent, passed on by oral instruction. Only later were they systematized, officially adopted and written down.

In some cases national languages are learned *after* the worker is proficient in the ethnic language of his assignment. This keeps our emphasis on the language group where we live and for whom we translate and lessens the likelihood of our becoming involved in activities in a national language in which the Scriptures are already available. Knowledge of the national language is needed, of course, to relate properly with officials or others outside the ethnic language community. In fact, in some fields national language study comes first, but seldom is it given the same time as the ethnic language. Our major emphasis is still on adequate control of the ethnic language as soon as possible.

Moving On

Upon completion of the pioneer task in one language, many are encouraged to move on to another language. One team has completed three New Testaments consecutively, another three simultaneously. A growing number are now on their second language project. Others have become consultants or have moved into administration.

Our pioneering emphasis keeps us from becoming involved in many good but institutional or continuing type ministries. We expect these to be handled by others, either governmental or private organizations established with such goals in mind. Programs we initiate are as soon as possible phased over into the hands of those we train. Churches resulting from our witness are never organizationally part of us.

Once the Bible translation is done and our linguistic and other commitments to the government and universities are fulfilled, we expect to move on. This is made clear to officials and the people in general as well as to other organizations whom we may serve in one way or another. Our operation is not deemed permanent in any country. We insist on terminal goals for completion of our work in each country. In some cases terminal dates have already been set and phaseout plans drawn up. Buildings and other improvements on property loaned to us will be turned over to the proper authorities when we leave. This commitment to move on relieves a lot of nationalistic fears. Having deadlines pushes us to complete our pioneer part of the work and train local people without delay for the ongoing aspects of the program.

An example of institutions that are expendable to our organization once they have served their purpose is the medical clinic among the Tzeltal of Mexico. A doctor and some nurses trained some Tzeltal medical workers. Left to the local Christians, the training center deteriorated and was finally abandoned. By that time, however, experienced Tzeltal trainees had trained others and fifty-five village clinics are now scattered over the entire area. The abandoned training center is a symbol of success, not of failure.[6]

Innovation

Our pioneering emphasis has kept us innovative and open to new ways of involving more people both in home and field operations. Some people remonstrated when single women were sent to remote tribes. When Townsend told the first two of the objections to their going, they replied, "but can't the Lord take care of us too?" Unable to answer except in the affirmative, he let them go. Today there are more women than men in pioneer posts. In some ways and in certain situations the women have been able to pioneer where men might not have succeeded. One head-hunting chief said that if men had come to his area he would have killed them on sight and taken their wives. But when two women came he considered them no threat and let them stay.

The pioneering spirit is not limited to the young. When a fifty-five-year-old woman who had already learned Navajo applied for membership, any idea of an age limit on applicants for membership was forgotten. She not only completed a translation of the New Testament in Navajo but nine years later had completed the New Testament in Apache. Then in her seventies, she went to Alaska to give help to some of the younger workers there.[7] When retired people anxious to help and with skills we needed asked about pioneering a second career, we found places for them. At one time as high as eighty-six such people were filling essential spots, most of them abroad.

At the home end, when a former used-car salesman caught the vision and wanted to help, he was encouraged, and the Wycliffe Associates was formed to build friendships, raise funds and channel skilled help to urgent field projects. Experts in education, management, biblical languages and public relations have been thrilled to serve on special projects both at home and abroad where their expertise could be used in training our members for greater effectiveness in these fields.

22. *JAARS helicopter arrives in mountaintop village of Papua New Guinea.*

We have pioneered in the use of the very latest technological advances to speed up the work. Use of radio and aircraft, including helicopters, makes resident linguist-translation projects feasible for every language group, no matter how remote. The use of computers for business, dictionary making, matching of lexicons to chapter and verse of Bible translation passages, text-editing, typesetting and proofreading has speeded up the linguistic analysis and translation processes. As this is written, our technical staff are field-testing a battery-pack suitcase-size computer for use in linguistic research and text-editing right in the village where the translator lives. Our Printing Arts Department has pioneered in making special fonts of type for phototypesetting text in any language, eliminating many of the delays in commercial printing.

Enough has been said to indicate that for us pioneering is a way of life, not for its own sake but with the goal of completing the task of Bible translation for all earth's ethnic minorities.

13

Finishing the Task

WE ARE committed to pioneering until at least a minimum Bible translation job is completed for all the languages of the world. To find out the dimensions of the unfinished task, specialists gather information from published studies, personal interviews and correspondence with knowledgeable people.[1] In areas in which we are working or expect to work, members conduct surveys to find out where the language groups are, what research and translation has been done, and what is in process or planned by others. We direct our major effort toward those ethnic groups in which nothing has as yet been done.

Interviews provide information on how many different languages may actually exist and people's attitudes about them. But such information varies greatly in reliability and is seldom complete. So linguistically trained workers visit different communities to transcribe and record lists of words as spoken by the local people. By comparing lists and plotting significant differences on a map, they can roughly determine the boundaries between languages. To determine how well people of related dialects understand each other's speech, they may also carry out dialect intelligibility surveys, using recorded samples of each dialect to test a listener's comprehension.[2] They may also make surveys to determine how many people in a given language community are bilingual, how bilingual they are, and whether the language in which they are bilingual is one in which the Scriptures are already available. Further along in the program, tests may be conducted to determine if written material in one dialect can be read and understood by those who speak other dialects. Such surveys and tests provide a basis for deciding how many different translations will be needed. When we began, the best information available listed less than fifty languages in Mexico. Today we know that 150 languages or dialects need separate translations.

Survey reports not only contribute to linguistic knowledge; they also serve national institutions and other organizations in determining language policy with respect to minority groups. When the boundaries, relationships and social attitudes of language communities are recognized, planning can proceed on a more realistic and socially sensitive basis.

Because we have gathered this information, however, it does not mean we expect to do all the remaining work ourselves. To the limits of our ability we are ready to help both mother tongue speakers and other expatriate workers get training and on-the-job help. We have no desire to compete with or overlap the efforts of others, but where no one else seems ready to do it we are committed to doing everything in our power to see that it gets done.

Possessing the linguistic tools to learn languages, initiate literacy and translate the Scriptures, we believe we are responsible to continue to break new ground. Only in this way will the job ever get done. If we become anchored to our successes and do not move on, our drive will lose its momentum and our contribution its distinctiveness. Others are called to ministries of nurturing believers, organizing churches and training leadership. Our concern is those who still have nothing of God's Word in their own language.

Our emphasis on pioneering until the job is done is based on three things—the worldwide nature of the program of God, the example and command of Christ and the pioneering ministry of the Apostle Paul.

The Worldwide Task

God's purpose has always included the whole human race. Even when he chose Abraham, Isaac, Jacob and the people of

Israel, God made it clear that through them all the nations of the world would be blessed (Gen. 12:3). The Psalmist clearly recognized the missionary obligation of Israel (Ps. 67). The prophet Isaiah extended the invitation, "Turn to me and be saved, all you ends of the earth; for I am God, and there is no other"(Is. 45:22). But Israel was reluctant, like Jonah, and did little to make him known. Later, Judaism became more aggressive and gained some followers among the Greeks (Matt. 23:15).

But with the advent of Christ, God's purpose for all mankind was again in view. Simeon called Christ "a light for revelation to the Gentiles" (Luke 2:32). John the Baptist announced that in Christ "all mankind will see God's salvation" (Luke 3:6).

The Example and Command of Christ

Although Christ restricted his own ministry largely to Israel, he also ministered to Romans, Syrophoenicians, Gergesenes and Samaritans (Matt. 8:5-11; Mark 7:24-26; Matt. 8:28; John 4). In response to a Roman centurion's faith, Christ told his followers ". . . many will come from the east and the west, and will take their places at the feast with Abraham, Isaac and Jacob in the kingdom of heaven" (Matt. 8:11). He presented a picture of worldwide dispersion and witness, "the field . . . the world" and "the good seed . . . the sons of the kingdom" (Matt. 13:38). He had "other sheep" than Israel which he must bring (John 10:16). He reminded the religious leaders of Jerusalem that in the plan of God the temple was to be "a house of prayer for all nations" (Mark 11:17).

Christ not only said the task was worldwide; it was also urgent. The goal of completing his part of the task set the priorities of his life and ministry. There was an unavoidable "must" about his actions. He must be about his Father's business (Luke 2:49). He must fulfill Scripture (Luke 24:44). He must "preach the good news of the kingdom of God to other towns also" (Luke 4:43). He must go through Samaria (John 4:4). He must go to Jerusalem and suffer

(Matt. 16:21). He "must keep going today and tomorrow and the next day" (Luke 13:33). Not just a sense of obligation or constraint based on personal commitment, but necessity in the very nature of the case, urged him on.

It was not enough to be doing the will of God; he must finish it (John 4:34). Finally, he was able to triumphantly announce to his Father, "I have brought you glory on earth by completing the work you gave me to do" (John 17:4).

Christ's training of his disciples increasingly had the same urgent and worldwide emphasis. In a Samaritan setting to disciples whose thinking was "four months more and then the harvest" he said, "Open your eyes and look at the fields! They are ripe for harvest . . . now . . . now" (John 4:35, 36). When he sent out the seventy, he again emphasized the urgency of the task and the smallness of their numbers (Luke 10:2-4). Later, when his disciples questioned him about the future and his coming again, he answered, "This gospel of the kingdom will be preached in the whole world as a testimony to all nations, and then the end will come" (Matt. 24:14).

With his departure imminent, Christ's statements to his disciples became clear and direct. They heard him say to the Father, "As you sent me into the world, I have sent them into the world" (John 17:18). After his ressurection he spoke directly to them. "As the Father has sent me, I am sending you" (John 20:21). "Repentance and forgiveness of sins will be preached in his name to all nations . . . . You are witnesses of these things" (Luke 24:47, 48). "Go into all the world and preach the good news to all creation" (Mark 16:15). When the disciples asked concerning the timing of his kingdom, his answer was to stress again the priority of their worldwide witness, "Jerusalem . . . all Judea . . . Samaria, and to the ends of the earth" (Acts 1:8). With the promised presence and enabling of the Holy Spirit, all signs were "Go." Without question he had made them and their followers responsible to make him known by delivering the message he had given them.

The worldwide purpose of God and the Great Commission given by Christ are binding upon each generation of his followers until the job is done. It includes making him known to every ethnic group and teaching those who choose to follow him to obey everything he has commanded (Matt. 28:19). Unless his commands are available in a language they understand, how can this be done? The Bible, the record of all he said and did must be made available to all. The translation of the Bible for all the remaining languages in the world is implicit in the commission.

The Book of Acts highlights both the urgency and the expanding horizons of the movement. First, there is a crowd in Jerusalem "from every nation under heaven" (2:5). Next, a persecution that scattered the Jerusalem church throughout Judea and Samaria (8:1). Then in rapid succession an Ethiopian statesman, a Jewish religious leader and a Roman army officer become followers of Christ (Acts 8, 9, 10). The Good News hurries across Syria, Asia Minor, Macedonia and Greece to Italy. Acts begins in Jerusalem and ends with a man in Rome hoping to go to Spain. John in the Book of Revelation leaps far beyond to the ultimate triumphant completion, "A great multitude that no one could count, from every nation, tribe, people and language, standing before the throne" (Rev. 7:9).

The Pioneering Ministry of Paul

To get the program off the ground God did not choose one of the twelve. Even Peter, the most forward of them, proved reluctant and vacillating in contacts with people of other nations. Instead, Christ chose the ringleader of the opposition, suddenly and soundly turned him about-face and three days later declared him "my chosen instrument to carry my name before the Gentiles and their kings and before the people of Israel" (Acts 9:15). Thus Saul of Tarsus became Paul the pioneer, Apostle to the nations.

Tempted to linger with believers at Damascus, then in Jerusalem, Saul was kept moving by threats to his life in each place. After eight years ministering in Cilicia and Syria, working out from his hometown, Tarsus, he was brought by Barnabas to Antioch, the base-to-be of the Gentile advance.

Back in Jerusalem on a famine relief ministry, the warm reception tempted Saul to stay but the Lord appeared to him saying: "Go. I will send you far away to the Gentiles" (Acts 22:21). God had called him to pioneer, and he did not want him settling down in Jerusalem, Tarsus, nor even Antioch.

No sooner was Saul back in Antioch than the Holy Spirit said to the church: "Set apart for me Barnabas and Saul for the work to which I have called them" (Acts 13:2). Beginning in Cyprus Saul dropped his Hebrew name and assumed his Gentile name, Paul. Sergius Paulus became his first recorded Gentile convert. Rejected by the Jews in Pisidian Antioch he turned to the Gentiles, many believed, and the first thoroughly Gentile congregation, separate from the synagogue, was established there. Paul's stirring report at Antioch in Syria of how God had opened the door to the Gentiles came into conflict with the convictions of die-hard Judaizers, since he had not required the Gentile believers to be circumcised. The Jerusalem conference declared that salvation was by faith alone and Paul resumed his pioneering.

On his second missionary journey Paul chose Silas, a Roman citizen, as companion, revisited the cities evangelized on the first journey, then pushed on to new territory. The Lord kept them moving, prohibiting them from preaching in the province of Asia, although they were allowed to cross it from southeast to northwest. He even stopped them from setting foot in Bithynia, although it certainly needed the Gospel and hurried them across Mysia, not even letting them stop to preach. They finally by-passed populous Ephesus and crossed into Macedonia, the next great Roman province westward. In Corinth Paul met Priscilla and Aquila, recently from Rome, and what he learned set his heart on fire and his sights on the farthest regions of the western Roman empire.

On his third journey, he wrote ahead from Ephesus to Corinth to get their problems settled before he arrived, as he did not want to be delayed there. "Our hope is that, as your faith continues to grow, our area of activity among you will greatly expand, so that we can preach the Gospel in the regions beyond you" (2 Cor. 10:15, 16). What lay beyond Corinth and Greece? Italy, Rome, and far beyond, Spain, the "uttermost part" of the then-known world. Later from Corinth he wrote to Rome that "from Jerusalem all the way round to Illyricum (present day Albania and Yugoslavia) I have fully proclaimed the Gospel of Christ" (Rom 15:19). His pioneer task of introducing the Gospel, he said, left "no more place for me to work in these regions . . . I hope to visit you while passing through (en route to Spain) and to have you assist me on my journey there" (Rom. 15:23, 24).

Antioch, Corinth, even Rome—not ends, but simply bases from which further advance could be launched. En route to Jerusalem he told the elders of Ephesus that pioneering was his task, nurturing the flock was theirs (Acts 20:24-28). The last we hear of Paul he is in Rome, in prison, not facing east as the Jews faced Jerusalem, not looking to retirement in Tarsus, but facing west, where the sun had not risen yet, pioneering to the very end. On the way he had said, "I consider my life worth nothing to me, if only I may . . . complete the task the Lord Jesus has given me" (Acts 20:24). Finally, like his Master before him, Paul sensed his personal part of the job was done. Shortly before the end he said, "But the Lord stood at my side and gave me strength, so that through me the message might be fully proclaimed and all the Gentiles might hear it" (2 Tim. 4:17).

Paul's ambition to pioneer has been a constant inspiration to us to translate the Bible where Christ was not known, not to build on someone else's foundation, to the same end that "those who were not told about him will see, and those who have not heard will understand" (Rom. 15:20, 21).

Pioneering Principles

God's guidance of our Bible translation movement in pioneering principles and methods parallels in several ways his guidance of Paul. Paul went to culturally strategic centers. We go to culturally strategic entities—language communities.

Paul recognized that Jews and God-fearing Gentiles had legitimate spiritual needs, but he did not let this keep him from giving top priority to those who had never heard. We believe churches both at home and abroad have many spiritual needs, but this should not sidetrack us from our top

205

priority—to provide the Word of God for those with no light at all.

Paul considered his job was to introduce the message and lay foundations on which others would then build. We too are laying foundations by providing the basic document for evangelism, teaching and discipline by others.

Paul did not work where others had already laid a foundation. We do not translate where translations are already available, in progress or planned by others.

Paul was not called to a settled pastoral ministry, although he helped churches get started and appointed others to lead them. We do not take positions of leadership in local churches, although many have resulted from our witness and work. Others perform the ecclesiastical functions.

Paul did not give his name to any church or bring any church under the control of his sending or supporting churches. We do not place our name on or claim control over any church.

Like Paul, we emphasize the training of believers in the Scriptures, committing to them the responsibility of local ministry and extension.

Paul considered areas reached and his work finished once his phase of the work was done. He then moved on to pioneer again. We consider our work done once the Scriptures are available and there are those who have been taught to read and use them. Members are encouraged to go on to other fields and pioneer again.

Paul's written ministry was far more extensive than his oral ministry, in his own lifetime and beyond. What we translate goes far beyond our oral witness, and will continue to do so for generations to come.

Under the Holy Spirit's guidance Paul wrote autographs of Scripture. He was not called to translate. In contrast, we are called to translate what he and others wrote.

Church History

History also provides the Bible translation movement with important principles that highlight the urgency of the task if we are to pioneer to a finish. Until A.D. 1800 the great majority of pioneer translations were done by bilingual believers translating into their mother tongue for already existent churches among their own people. Martin Luther, for example, translated for the Germans and John Wycliffe for the English, each into his mother tongue. Until such translations were made, the Scriptures were read only by those who knew Latin or some other foreign language, and who were fortunate enough to have access to a copy in that language. The Bible was essentially a book for the leaders of the church.

With the advent of the modern missionary era, expatriate missionaries undertook translation as a part of their task. It was often done very early, in some cases before the establishing of churches and as a means to it. When Bible translation became the pioneer missionary's task, it literally swept around the world with the rapid expansion of missions in the nineteenth century.

Not all missions, however, provided the Scriptures for those they served. Many churches are still without vernacular Bibles for either the pew or pulpit. Wycliffes and Luthers who will translate the Bible for the first time into their own language for their own people are still urgently needed. Since they already speak the language, they should do this without further delay. Training in Bible knowledge, linguistics and translation, as well as consultant help, is available. The Nigeria Bible Translation Trust, for example, is an organization of Nigerians training Nigerians to translate into their own and other Nigerian languages.

On the other hand, there are still many churches without vernacular Bibles, and hundreds of ethnic groups to which the Gospel has never yet been preached for which the initiative to produce a translation in their mother tongue must be taken by an expatriate translator. In both cases the translator will still be dependent on local speakers of the language to teach him the language and make sure the translation is natural. The wise translator will, as quickly as possible, train those who help him to carry more and more of the responsibility. Some, in fact, have become co-translators and translators in their own right as the work has progressed and their training has continued.

Not all expatriate translators are American or European. Translators with the Wycliffe Bible Translators and Summer Institute of Linguistics come from twenty-four nationalities, including Japanese, Chinese, Mexican, Peruvian and Ghanaian. Christians from churches around the world which already have the Bible are catching the vision of translating for others, either in their own countries or abroad. This involves learning languages foreign to them (even if spoken in their own country) and requires similar training and ability as for any expatriate worker. A Mexican whose mother tongue is Spanish is translating for the Otomi of her country, a Filipino for the Isneg of his. The full resources of the church around the world must be utilized to get the pioneer translation job done. Whether in one's own mother tongue or in a language one must learn, those producing first translations are pioneering. Both mother tongue and expatriate translators are needed until the job is completed for all. We may be late, centuries late, in providing God's Word for some. But by God's grace we won't be later.

Completion of the Task

What constitutes the completion of the task? This depends on the task assigned. Christ's part was finished with his death and resurrection (Luke 24:46; John 17:3,4; 19:30). Paul's when he had proclaimed the Gospel in the major centers of the different provinces of the Empire.

Our calling from God is to translate the Bible for people who do not have it. We consider our pioneer task in a given language completed when we have fulfilled our linguistic commitments to the government; translated the New Testament and, at least in summary form, some Old Testament portions; taught some to read and to teach others to read with some assurance of an ongoing literacy program; and trained a nucleus of believers to use the Scriptures. When this is true for each viable ethnic minority language group, the pioneering aspect of Bible translation will be done.

Some people have been called by God to mass evangelism, church planting and theological training ministries. We have not. The very difference of our tasks enables us to serve and complement each other. Their ministries will be better with the Bible in the language of the people than without it. Their ministries supplement ours and thus leave us freer to move on.

Some years ago the translator among the Piro had completed the New Testament, and our founder, William Cameron ("Cam") Townsend, was urging her to go to another group without Scriptures. She remonstrated that the believers needed more teaching and no one else was available to do it. Finally on the promise that they would trust God to provide the training needed, and the willingness of the people themselves "to give her up" since "we who are full owe a debt to those who are hungry," she moved on. Within a year an organization specializing in Bible school training for the ethnic minority peoples moved into the area.

Not all transitions work out so well. But the pioneer must move on or the task will never be started, let alone completed, for the millions without the witness of the Word.

When will the worldwide pioneer translating task be done? Over the five year period 1979-1983 an average of twenty-five languages per year received published portions of the Bible for the first time, according to United Bible Societies figures, the most complete available. At this rate it could take a hundred more years!

There are indications however that the pace is quickening. More people are becoming involved in Bible translation. Nationals in many countries are catching the vision both to translate into their mother tongues and for other languages. New Bible translation organizations are coming into existence both in America and abroad. In our own case the pace of published translations has gradually been accelerating. Currently a whole New Testament manuscript is being sent in for typesetting every eleven days. Most of these have already had lesser portions published, used and revised before inclusion in the complete New Testament.

The need for a translation has already been clearly established for several hundred languages. Surveys to assess pioneer translation needs have been completed in some countries, are underway or planned in others. Relevant linguistic, social, political, religious and other information is being gathered and studied to determine the need in each language. Personnel and resources must be found. Detailed realistic plans for each project must be made and a timetable set for completion of the various stages of the project.

Completion of the task is furthest along in the Americas. Translation projects are completed in fifty-eight languages, 300 are in progress and 100 are still to begin. In some countries we expect to finish in the 1980s. Some areas of Africa and the Pacific may finish in the '90s. A few more translations are being made for communities of displaced peoples but the closed areas of Asia are not yet on the prediction charts. Townsend, our founder, still pioneering at 83, is, however, actively exploring possibilities even there.

What will it take to get the job done? Two things: people and permission. God has promised to provide all our needs, but he commanded us to pray for workers and for rulers (Matt. 9:38; 1 Tim. 2:1-7).

Several years ago a Piro believer wrote a message to people in the United States in which he said, "We have heard that you and your ancestors learned about salvation before we did. We just recently found it. Our ancestors did not know Jesus. Other tribes who live around us still lack the Word of God and do not yet know their Creator. For that reason, I remind you who know our Lord very well: What are you waiting for?"

PART THREE
RELATIONSHIPS

Significant are not only activities and attitudes but relationships, both organizational (Chapter 14) and personal, among ourselves as members (15) and with others (16).

14

Organization

SOON AFTER we began in Guatemala, one of our members attended a gathering of missionaries to discuss mutual concerns in the work among the language groups of that country. He was there representing the head of the government Department of Indian Affairs, who had been invited but was unable to attend. At an Interamerican Indian Institute meeting (in Panama) some years ago the head of the American government delegation was surprised to find Cam Townsend part of the official delegation from Peru. One of a group of experts called together by UNESCO to discuss language problems in West Africa was Kenneth Pike, professor of linguistics at the University of Michigan, also president of our Summer Institute of Linguistics. These types of situations are only explainable in terms of our rather unique working relationship with governments and universities.

The Summer Institute of Linguistics

From the very beginning Cam Townsend envisioned working in close cooperation with governments and academic institutions. Working with governments would facilitate permissions to live in their countries, and our linguistic work would be of service to them and their minority people. By working closely with academic institutions, our research would profit from and contribute to linguistic science.

Since governments and universities do not usually sponsor religious enterprises, the work is done on a non-ecclesiastical

213

basis distinct from traditional missionary work so as not to compromise or embarrass those under whose auspices we work. Our Christian motivation and desire to translate the Bible and the Christian motivation of those who support the work financially is not hidden from them. Bible translation, however, is not a part of their sponsorship, except as they may be willing to include it as literature of high moral value.

When Mexican officials, knowing our Bible translation goals, were asked on what basis we should apply for papers to enter their country, they suggested as "investigators of Indian languages." When the University of Oklahoma invited us to offer our linguistic courses on its campus, it was prohibited by state law from official sponsorship of any religious organization. By incorporating the educational and scientific aspects of the work separately as the Summer Institute of Linguistics we solved their problem. The University still recognized the Christian dedication of our members, however, and annually asked us to take responsibility for one of the Sunday evening religious services on campus.

As the Summer Institute of Linguistics, Inc., we have agreements with governments and universities outlining the services we offer and the services they will provide. As members of the Summer Institute of Linguistics we agree to work under the terms of such agreements. This means our reporting relationship is primarily to governments and academic communities rather than religious institutions. A number of our more competent linguists hold teaching positions at universities at home and abroad, under arrangements that divide their time between lectures at the university and field work with us. This gives our work quite a different orientation from the conventional mission but one not inconsistent with biblical teaching.

Biblical Basis for Service to Governments

The Bible states that the governments of this world operate by God's authority and are answerable to him. We who profess to be his also operate under his authority and are responsible to him. Ideally we should be mutually supportive, not in conflict. As citizens of this world God has placed us under civil authorities, our own and those of foreign countries where we may live temporarily (Dan. 4:32; Rom. 13:1-7).

According to the Old Testament, God uses men and nations as his agents to punish evil but he holds those so used responsible for their actions (Isa. 10:5, 6, 12, 13; Jer. 25:9, 12). Nations and rulers also serve God in carrying out his beneficent purposes (Ezra 7:11-26). In the providence of God, though not by their own choice, Joseph, Daniel, Shadrach, Meshach, Abednego, Esther, Mordecai and Nehemiah served under foreign governments (Gen. 50:20; Dan. 1-3; Esther 2:5-7; 4:14; 8:1,2; Neh. 2:1-3). All were God-fearing persons. They faithfully served the best interests of their sovereign and his people. Under the sometimes critical or even antagonistic eyes of government officials, they lived exemplary lives of faith in God without compromise (Dan. 6:5,10). Each made bold to ask the authorities to help, protect and further the work of God and his people. In the Old Testament period, God's people were subject to governments, actively participated in and furthered the purpose of governments, and in turn were helped by governments.

As a man, Christ came under the law of God ordaining human government for all mankind, and specifically under the Roman law of his day. He taught and exemplified obedience to civil authority, local Jewish authorities and the law of Moses. He paid taxes and never advocated revolt in attitude or act against imperial or local authorities, even when pressed to do so by radicals. He did not disregard the jurisdiction of or advocate disobedience to the findings of courts. Yet he was not overawed by officials nor unaware of their true moral characters. By his statement, "Give to Caesar what is Caesar's and to God what is God's," Christ distinguished the secular from the sacred without rejecting either (Mk. 12:13-17). Both have legitimate rights.

Rome looked upon the first generation of Christians as a variety of Jew and included them under the imperial protection given Judaism as a recognized religion. In both his Gospel and Acts, Luke shows that even local Roman authorities recognized Christians as law-abiding people and those who opposed them as the troublemakers. While the officials in no sense approved of the Christians' witness they did recognize its legitimacy under the freedoms they provided (Acts 18:12-16; 19:37-40).

The early church understood that obedience to God did not exclude obedience to the state, as long as the state operated as established by God and within its proper sphere and jurisdiction. But when authorities asked for what was properly God's, then Christians reacted, out of the very same conscience before God that in all other respects caused them to obey (Acts 4:19; 5:29; 1 Pet. 2:13-17; 3:13-16).

Paul also recognized the God-given authority and role of civil government and the Christian's duty voluntarily and continually to submit to those in positions of authority over him, of whatever rank or character (Rom. 13:1-7). He urges as a matter of first importance that "requests, prayers, intercession and thanksgiving be made for everyone—for kings and all those in authority," that is, from the emperor down to local administrators. The purpose of such praying was that the authorities might fulfill their God-given role of keeping law and order, upon which the spread of the Gospel and the completion of his task depended (1 Tim. 2:1-7).

Later, when Christianity became distinct from Judaism and lost its legal protection, persecution arose. But even when they suffered for being Christians, and doing good, they were exhorted to show respect to the emperor and not retaliate (1 Pet. 2:11-23). Under Domitian, emperor worship was demanded and the government itself became the persecutor of all who refused to worship Caesar. While John on Patmos could find not one good word to describe the rulers of his day he still maintained, "God has put it into their hearts to accomplish his purpose . . . until God's words are fulfilled" and "This calls for patient endurance and faithfulness on the part of the saints (Rev. 17:17; 13:10). Thus in the face of gross provocation, Christians sought to maintain their proper loyalty to the government.

Roman government provided a general social stability in Palestine and throughout the Empire that was an important factor in the rise and spread of the Christian faith. Christ and his followers saw in the government of their day God's agent for their good and the carrying out of his purpose. They strengthened the hands of the authorities, including them in their witness and in their prayers. They did not acquiesce in the evil deeds or characters of those authorities but chose to overcome evil with good, by moral rather than political force.

God has continued to use governments during the centuries since. When Constantine made Christianity the religion of the Empire, it hastened its spread, although it had its unfortunate effects too. "The conversion of the peoples of Western Europe was ... largely by mass movements of entire tribes or people, led by their chieftans or kings."[1] The teaching that followed was usually carried on by Christians of real piety and faith. Among the masses thus exposed to the Word of God many came to Christ, and genuine Christian movements began. In the sixteenth, seventeenth and first half of the eighteenth centuries, European Catholic, Protestant and Orthodox missionaries scattered in all directions under the auspices of ostensibly Christian governments. The Reformation survived in Europe only in those countries where it had government support and protection. In the rapid expansion of missionary work in the nineteenth and twentieth centuries, government sponsorship became increasingly less. Without a doubt movements for political independence have had an influence in the recent rise of vigorous independent national churches and a whole new day in missions.

In the relatively short span of our work we can see how God is still using human governments to accomplish his purposes. The maintenance of law and order, the guarantees of religious liberty and the protection of the rights of minority peoples are positive results of government that we can applaud. Insistence on nationalization of foreign enterprises has helped national Christians see their own importance in helping complete the translation task both for their own and other peoples. It has underlined for us the importance of training more of them to carry more responsibility sooner in all aspects of the work.

God has delivered his Word into the hands of his people

217

to share with people of every language in the world. God is the one who makes access to these peoples possible (Rev. 3:7). He has ordained that governments should be his door-keepers and maintain the liberties and conditions necessary. We who bear the Book should support them in the fulfillment of their responsibilities, without making them responsible for our actions.

Our policy, then, is active cooperation with host governments. We seek to keep them informed about what we are doing and make our work serve their highest goals and the good of their peoples. God has used them to help and protect us. Yet we have never so bound ourselves to any government that we were forced to assume its tactics or be dependent on its political continuance. As foreigners we do not take sides in internal politics. As Christians we do put our efforts and influence on the side of morality and justice.

The Wycliffe Bible Translators

I sat one day in the office of the head of the Department of Indian Affairs of a Latin American government. She was telling me of her problems in getting funds for programs and finding staff who would be willing to live in the ethnic areas long enough to see a project through. "No one is willing to give up the comforts of the city long enough to get anything more than data for a report," she said. "They would quit rather than take an assignment that required them to live in an isolated village."

She was personally acquainted with most of our workers, had visited some on location and knew their enthusiasm to get to their ethnic locations. Our problem was often the reverse of hers, how to get them back to the city periodically for a rest and change for their own good. "They seem so happy," she said. "How do you do it?" So again I explained to her how our motivation to translate the Bible, analyze the language, teach people to read, serve her department and the ethnic people, pioneer in remote areas and live without financial gain came as a result of our faith in God, obedience to Christ's command and gratefulness for what the Holy Spirit had done in our lives as we read the Bible.

218

"Where does the money come from?" was her next question.

I went on to explain that friends of the workers and churches with the same motivation voluntarily, regularly and often sacrificially, sent gifts of money so the work could go on.

To relate to such a constituency, both to get recruits to do the work and to gain and retain the confidence and support of donors, we incorporated as the Wycliffe Bible Translators, a parallel sister organization to the Summer Institute of Linguistics. The primary purpose of the Wycliffe Bible Translators is the translation of the Bible and its statement of faith is biblical and evangelical.

Links

The Wycliffe Bible Translators and its constituency accept the academic emphasis and the non-ecclesiastical, linguistically-oriented and government-related approach of the Summer Institute of Linguistics as a way to achieve its goal of giving all the peoples of the world an opporunity to have the Scriptures in their mother tongue. Members accepted by the Wycliffe Bible Translators must also be acceptable to and accepted by the Summer Institute of Linguistics as members of that organization and be in accord with its policies and restrictions.

Members assigned to language or field-related training and projects serve under the Summer Institute of Linguistics. Those serving primarily in constituency-related programs are assigned to the Wycliffe Bible Translators. Membership is in both organizations, assignment is in one or the other.

Funds received by the Wycliffe Bible Translators for support of the field programs are transferred to the Summer Institute of Linguistics for that purpose. The Summer Institute of Linguistics also receives some grants and gifts from other sources.

Close cooperation between the two organizations was intended from the beginning. The purposes of the Wycliffe Bible Translators include, in addition to the translation of the Bible, linguistic training, literacy and Bible study, medical and other practical assistance to ethnic groups, as well as cooperation with and assistance to scientific and educational institutions engaged in these tasks. The Board of the Wycliffe Bible Translators entered into an agreement with the Board of the Summer Institute of Linguistics that the people who serve as their directors, the chief executive officer of each organization and the quorum for doing business would be the same. For practical reasons the two organizations are structured along parallel lines in their international administration. International meetings of both groups are held at the same time and place.

Differences

Yet the two organizations differ in several ways. They have different presidents and vice-presidents of the Board. They keep separate minutes and accounts.

Honorary members of the Wycliffe Bible Translators are Christian leaders who have served on its Board or headquarters staff in the past. The Summer Institute of Linguistics recognizes academic and government leaders and others who have been outstanding in their furtherance and support of our work in their respective countries.

The two organizations issue different publications. The Wycliffe Bible Translators issues a series of books for the Christian and general reader. The Summer Institute of Linguistics produces technical articles for publication in scientific journals around the world. It also publishes books, including textbooks on linguistic and related subjects, for the scientific and academic public. By far the greatest volume of publications are literacy materials and literature in the ethnic languages studied. These are usually published in cooperation with the local educational authorities. Most of the Bible translations are submitted to outside agencies which specialize in the publication of biblical materials.

The two organizations report to different constituencies. The Summer Institute of Linguistics reports to governments and academic institutions, the Wycliffe Bible Translators to the Christian public.

At the local level the two organizations are organized

quite differently. The activities of the Wycliffe Bible Translators are organized into home divisions by the country of origin of the members. Members who originate or whose support comes from a specific country are members of the division in that country. Divisions have a director and a home council, which includes non-members from the constituency. The activities of the Summer Institute of Linguistics are organized into field branches by the country of assignment. Members working in a specific country or geographical area are members of the branch in that country or area. Branches have a director and a field executive committee consisting entirely of field members. The home division administrative functions and personnel are quite different from the field branch administrative functions and personnel. Where there are too few members involved to form either a division or branch, members generally relate directly to an international area director.

The mix or distribution of members in branches and divisions is totally different. For example, the British Division's 208 members are with a few exceptions British, but are serving in seventeen countries and branches abroad. In contrast the Brazil Branch's 247 members include Canadian, American, British, South African, Swiss, Dutch, German, Australian and Brazilian citizens. Forty-one British members are common to both lists. While all of us are members of both organizations, our associates and our responsibilities in each are quite different.

The countries in which each organization operates are on the whole quite different. The Wycliffe Bible Translators function principally in the twenty-four countries from which its members come and receive their support. The Summer Institute of Linguistics conducts training schools in five of these countries. The Summer Institute of Linguistics has members in field programs in thirty-one countries. Eight of these are countries from which we also have members.

In countries where both a Wycliffe Bible Translators division and a Summer Institute of Linguistics branch work, the headquarters, personnel, work locations and type of activities are in sharp contrast. For example, in Australia the Wycliffe Bible Translators division headquarters is located near Melbourne with branch offices in six different states. The division headquarters receives and receipts gifts, publishes literature in English that will keep the Christian public informed about Bible translation needs and progress around the world, and generally keeps in touch with other types of sending agencies. Assigned Australian members and non-member employees carry on the office work necessary and arrange meetings and conduct educational seminars in churches and student groups.

The Summer Institute of Linguistics branch headquarters is located near Darwin, with projects in twenty different aboriginal areas. The sixty-nine members of the branch from Australia, New Zealand, the British Isles, Canada, Germany and the United States are engaged in linguistic, literacy, translation and community development work in the aboriginal areas and in routine office, accounting and printing work at the headquarters. The literature consists mainly of reading materials in aboriginal languages plus technical articles and news sheets to friends of the members in English. Officers and members of the branch keep in constant touch with government and university people involved with the aborigines.

Subsidiaries

The two organizations have different subsidiaries. The Jungle Aviation and Radio Service (JAARS) is a subsidiary of the Summer Institute of Linguistics. It provides communication and transportation services for our field operations. JAARS handles the technical screening and training of pilots, mechanics and radio personnel who otherwise qualify for membership; procures, modifies and maintains the equipment needed; sets the standards and monitors the technical aspects of the communication and transportation service in each country; and coordinates the worldwide computer research, construction and maintenance. The technical personnel and equipment in each branch are under the direction of the field administration and serve in accord with their policies.

The International Linguistic Center, Inc. is a subsidiary of the Summer Institute of Linguistics. The Board of the International Linguistic Center is composed primarily of business people from our constituency of friends and supporters, plus some of our members. Its purpose is to develop a center in Dallas, Texas for the year-round training of personnel.

Wycliffe Associates, Inc. is not a subsidiary but a separately incorporated organization of laymen in the United States wholly committed to furthering the work of the Wycliffe Bible Translators.[2]

Relationships with Other Organizations

The relationship of the Wycliffe Bible Translators with the Summer Institute of Linguistics takes priority over other relationships. By conviction, and to facilitate the above relationship, the Wycliffe Bible Translators is non-sectarian and non-ecclesiastical.

The Wycliffe Bible Translators, except for its British and Australian divisions, does not hold membership in associations of churches or missions. Individual members may occasionally attend as observers; enjoy Christian fellowship and share information as technical consultants. We believe our call from God to translate the Scriptures requires our full attention. Any other involvements that might detract from this are strictly limited. Specific service to individuals, missions, churches or associations is given when it contributes to the ultimate goal of giving the Scriptures to every ethnic group as soon as possible. But in many instances we can best serve by being organizationally separate.

The Wycliffe Bible Translators serves as a channel for churches to send people and funds to further the work of Bible translation. We assure them that those we accept are sound in their faith and motivated and qualified for the task for which they are applying. Members must have one or more churches or groups of believers committed to praying for them and sharing in their support before they leave for their fields of service. The Wycliffe Bible Translators sends financial support to the Summer Institute of Linguistics on the field and receives reports of the work and items for prayer from the field for the supporters at home. The main responsibility for maintaining the links with the supporting constituency, however, lies with the members themselves. Each member is expected to personally thank those who support the project in which he or she is engaged, and to keep them informed of the progress of the work. This is done through correspondence while on the field and personal visits during furlough.

As members of a pioneer agency majoring in linguistics and Bible translation, we have fellowship with and can be of service to many missionaries. Most missionaries must learn to speak another language. Many are involved in linguistic, literacy or translation tasks. The Summer Institute of Linguistics training is of special help to those in pioneer language work. Of the more than 12,000 students who have taken our courses to date, two-thirds are serving or have served with other organizations. Our consultants and workshops have been a help to many missionaries. They and especially the ethnic churches that have resulted from their work have used the translations we have produced. A few of our members have been loaned for longer or shorter periods to missions or Bible agencies for linguistic and translation assignments.

While our members come from many different denominational backgrounds and agree to work with us on a non-denominational, non-ecclesiastical basis, we recognize that the job is bigger than any one organization. Many people share our vision for Bible translation but prefer to work in an organization that recognizes their denominational distinctives. We have therefore welcomed the formation of the Lutheran Bible Translators, the Evangel Bible Translators, the Pioneer Bible Translators and the Logos Bible Translators and have encouraged them to get linguistic training and field consultation service for their members.

We believe that those among the ethnic peoples who respond to the translated Scriptures should form their own churches, indigenous from the beginning. Many countries already have strong national language churches. Both ethnic minority and national churches have the potential for furthering the Bible translation task. Our field members encourage nationals to train for linguistic and translation work, to form their own national Bible translating organizations and to challenge their own churches to support such work. So as not to compromise our non-ecclesiastical relationships with the government, we do not enter into formal agreements with national churches unless requested to do so by the government itself. We give linguistic training and technical assistance to them as to all others without distinction of race, color or creed, often through courses in their own universities.

23. *An Asaro prints the first book of the Bible in his own language (Papua New Guinea)*

We are a Bible *translating* group. Publication and distribution is normally handled by others. The World Home Bible League for several years has underwritten the greater part of our Scripture publication costs. The New York Bible Society International, member societies of the United Bible Societies, and several other organizations have also published portions we have translated. Since commercial printers are seldom set up to handle texts in exotic languages, we have through the years served as printers for these publishing agencies, doing the typesetting and printing in our printshops on the fields where the languages are spoken. This has the advantage that the expatriate and national translators can edit and proofread the text, supervise the delivery and participate in the public dedication and initial distribution of the finished product. Recently we have also developed text editing, typesetting and printing facilities at some of our centers in England and the United States.

The people who run the presses abroad are often from the ethnic groups for whom we translate. An Asaro man failed his school exams and came to our center in Papua New Guinea, looking for work. Under the supervision of our printer he soon learned to run the offset press. Imagine his thrill three months later to print the translation of Genesis, the first book in his own language. Although he speaks Kate, Pidgin and English, he insisted that his own language was the easiest to understand when you read it.

15
Membership

IN THE beginning our movement had no organization and no formal membership. Anyone who shared Cam Townsend's burden for ethnic peoples without the Bible and believed linguistics was the key to translating it into their language was welcome to participate with him. Applications, formal interviews, letters of acceptance were not required. "The Townsend Group" was a highly motivated group of individuals with a common leader, a common commitment, and little or no structure. The entire group lived, planned, made decisions and acted together. When Townsend visited government officials everyone went along.

Yet certain things were very individual. Funds and praying friends were God's provision for the individual and the individual was personally responsible to maintain the lines of communication. The place of assignment, the language work, each was different and very much one's own. This respect for the individual still begins early. One timid candidate later described her experience: "The very first people I met were staff members. They treated me as if I were their equal. They even insisted on being called by their first names. . . . They cared enough to learn to say my name right . . . It seemed like the closest thing to a classless society I'd ever seen . . . They evaluated me on the basis of what I demonstrated I could do, not on what I didn't know. My self-esteem was given a boost."

As numbers grew, it obviously became increasingly difficult for the whole group to participate in everything. Tasks had to be delegated. Some were asked to perform services for the group as a whole. Rules of procedure evolved. Organization came grudgingly, however, only sufficient to meet urgent needs. Individual rights bent to necessary group controls but were never completely given up.

Then "one of the greatest moral decisions in missionary history was made, when our founder, William Cameron Townsend, insisted that the executive committee, composed of younger and less experienced men than he, have authority over him."[1] This distinctive, that ultimate authority rests in the members, explains our unusual esprit de corps. We are not working for an organization. We are the organizations. This is why membership means so much to each of us.

In spite of our growth in numbers, geographical scatter and cultural diversity, a feeling of "family" is still strong throughout the group. Our common commitment to Christ and his Word, our varied gifts and mutual interdependence, shared-under-pressure experiences in linguistic courses and jungle training—these account for some of the feeling. Long periods of isolation on the field, then face-to-face encounters in workshops and conferences, each one with his or her own unique allocation, language, ethnic friends, or support job to talk about—these enrich it. Then to discover that your fellow member is a British mathematician, a Japanese student, an American veterinarian, a German glassblower, an Australian sheep farmer or a Canadian doctor, and to hear the variety of means God used to bring you both to himself and then together—this makes you thank God for the sheer diversity in the special family that is ours.

Membership

The training courses began small. They are still the door to membership. Seminary students, pastors, Bible school graduates and university language majors came to Arkansas to learn to translate the Bible. Those from other professions, less sure if they qualified, found themselves hooked on linguistics after three months of exposure. A flying instructor at a Canadian airport, when he found languages were not his forte, was thrilled to discover his technical skills were needed, and joined. Year by year screening procedures developed and membership standards were evolved.

No one applies for a job with us. Membership is a calling from God. We are a group of students, technicians and scholars who acknowledge Jesus Christ as Lord and Savior and believe he has called us to serve in any way we can to provide the Bible for those in the world who still do not have it.

Reading about our goals, one university student wrote, "I want to be part of a group that has those kinds of commitments." We expect applicants to be unreservedly committed to the task, the methods and the policies of the group. They must have a good working knowledge of the Bible, accept its authority and inerrancy, and have a personal vital relationship with the Jesus Christ of whom it speaks.

Because of the pioneer conditions under which we often work, applicants must be mature and disciplined in character with sufficiently good health to survive and get the job done. We accept members for language related tasks, not because they are already qualified but because they have the basic academic ability and are the kind of people who can be trained to do the work. Support people must meet general standards and have some special skill we can use. All must be mutually compatible, flexible and willing to learn. Acceptance is based on all the relevant factors. Borderline qualification in one area may, of course, be balanced by higher qualifications in another. There are no age limits, although some may be accepted with age or health restrictions. Present membership includes people from many different denominations, several races and twenty-one different nationalities.

We like interested people to get in touch with us early in their careers. Skills lacking may be acquired. Areas of weakness can be strengthened. Disqualifying factors can be pointed out sooner. Through mistaken ideas of what the job requires and ignorance of our ongoing in-process training, some disqualify themselves by not applying. Many who have taken our introductory course as an exploratory step have been confirmed in their interest and discovered aptitudes they did not know they had.

As increasingly we have an opportunity to train nationals, host governments are requiring that more of our members have advanced degrees. We therefore encourage some of our members to get them before going to the field. Others do so after time on the field, after they have language material already gathered for their research projects.

Like all organizations, of course, we need typists, printers, artists, accountants, managers, doctors, nurses, pilots, mechanics, radio and computer technicians, teachers for our members' children, builders, children's home parents, shippers, buyers and people of many other abilities. While not themselves translating, they help keep the language-assigned members at their jobs and thus play an essential part in achieving our goals.

We accept applicants as members-in-training. Our Member-In-Training Department guides them in a program specially designed to prepare them for their future assignments on the field. This includes linguistic, literacy, translation or community development studies, general orientation to our practices and policies, and training for living under field conditions. We keep members-in-training informed of worldwide translation needs as periodically updated and of overall priorities. We ask them to pray about these needs and priorities. The member's own sense of call and guidance to a specific field or type of work is given primary consideration in making assignments. Members without such specific guidance are assigned where most needed. After all reports from the training program are in hand and the member has been interviewed, field assignments are made by a committee of the international administration. Before going to the field, the "MITs" strengthen their links with family, friends and supporting churches, informing them of their assignment and trusting God to provide the prayer and financial support that is so necessary to this kind of work.

When they arrive at their field of service, members-in-training become junior members. They then begin orientation specific to that country and national language studies. The local directorate then consults with the junior member about specific assignment to an ethnic language or a supporting job. Junior members report regularly on their progress and discuss any changes in their assignment with their field leaders. Those who supervise their work are expected to review and discuss their programs with them periodically and make appropriate recommendations to the directorate for any changes in assignment.

After two years of satisfactory service, junior members become eligible for senior membership by recommendation of their director and vote of their fellow-members who serve on the field executive committee. Once they become senior members they have full voting privileges, are eligible for election to any office and will have representation at the international conferences, the highest policy-making meetings of the members.

In most allocations to an ethnic group the minimum team is a married couple, two single women or two single men. Where the program warrants, additional workers may be assigned to some specialized part of the task, such as literacy or community development.

Partners, whether singles or married couple, are encouraged to undertake different aspects of the work, to supplement rather than compete with each other. This allows each to proceed at his or her own pace and make a unique contribution. At the dinner table, each has something to contribute to the conversation. A mother is expected to learn the language but any other assignments are adjusted to allow for family responsibilities.

Privileges and Responsibilities

Our organizations are democratic and membership brings privileges and responsibilities. We elect our own leaders and determine our own policies at both local and international levels. We share in group plans for life, baggage and car insurance, and have mutual aid plans for hospital and surgery expenses. The home office staff provides many services for all members. For example, it mails receipts for donations and keeps friends informed about the work. Staff members on the field handle host government contacts and provide a myriad of other services for those at or beyond the end of the supply lines.

Membership also involves obligations. With minimum supervision the member is expected to show initiative, discipline and perseverance in completing his assignment, whether he is analyzing a language, translating the Bible or maintaining facilities at a center. Each of us is expected to carry his share of the load. We may be asked to take time from our own work to help others as consultants. This may involve taking even more time for further training. Members on the field are expected to help maintain good public relations with the village authorities and, as occasion offers, with people at higher levels. If we are appointed or elected to some office, we contribute our time and talents to serve the entire group. Each of us also shares responsibility for the spiritual welfare and testimony of the group as a whole.

One in Spirit

While our common task unites us in our everyday activities, a common spiritual life and fellowship knits us together as a family. We come from many different backgrounds. Individually we are quite different, and the pioneering attitude and experience can accentuate our idiosyncrasies. Yet our interdependence and mutual esteem for each other produces a bond that is very valued and supportive. Our common allegiance to Jesus Christ, nurtured by times of group Bible study and prayer, more than compensates for our differences.

Members of our organizations speak more than fifteen different languages as their mother tongues. On one field alone, members speak five different mother tongues and come from eight different countries. If all of us are to share in a common fellowship and group decision-making, some common language is necessary, so English is used, not because it is a superior language but because most of our members already know it. It is also the principal second language of those whose mother tongue is not English. Then, too, more linguistic and translation aids are available in English than in any other language. And legally our official records must be kept in it.

A knowledge of English is not required for acceptance into membership, however. The initial linguistic training required for membership is now offered in English, German, French, Japanese, Spanish, and Portuguese. But advanced courses are only available in English yet. For senior membership, proficiency in English is required. We try to ease tensions between members of different cultural backgrounds in our orientation programs. The education of children whose parents do not speak English is a special problem, since most of them will take advanced education in their parents' homeland.

All of us profess belief in the essential core doctrines of the Christian faith: the divine inspiration and consequent authority of the canonical Scriptures; the doctrine of the Trinity; the fall of man, his consequent moral depravity and need for regeneration; atonement through the substitutionary death of Christ; justification by faith; the resurrection of the body of both the just and the unjust; and the eternal life of the saved and the eternal punishment of the lost. We reaffirm our adherence to these periodically.

We do not require uniformity of belief on other matters. In the translation of the Bible we expect translators and consultants to stay within the range of interpretation of generally accepted historic evangelical Christian scholarship. We keep Christian fellowship strong by emphasizing what we agree on and practicing patience and tolerance on things we do not agree on, according to Philippians 3:12-16. Within the "family," we are largely unconscious of denominational backgrounds. Any member who insists on a divisive promotion of his own convictions, in fact, provides grounds for his dismissal from the membership.

Without legislating conduct, we have adopted the strong traditions of predominantly evangelical Christian practice. A member may be disciplined for actions contrary to our constitution and by-laws; for gross insubordination to those in authority over him; for conduct that disturbs the harmony, impairs the good name or endangers the welfare of the organization; or for inadequate performance in his assignment. Discipline ranges from a reprimand to a recommendation for dismissal. Members, however, have a constitutional right to appeal to their fellow members.

All members are entitled to an annual vacation and a one-year furlough every four or five years (or a shorter one more often). The director to whom a member is responsible may, at his discretion, grant sick leaves. He may also grant leaves of absence to those who are temporarily out of the program but who expect to return to service later. Age and health may modify assignments, but there is no mandatory age for retirement.

Support Roles and Terms

About half of our members are not in language assignments but instead serve in essential support roles at the centers. A Dutch Canadian went to Papua New Guinea to build houses. His wife worked in the center post office. Eight years and several houses later, the husband was building a cultural center, native style, with thatched grass roofs and woven bamboo wall coverings. Then we asked him to coordinate the training of Papuaniuguineans in skills which would help their communities. He went to Paupa New Guinea simply to support translators, but eventually assumed both a practical and a spiritual ministry to many of the ethnic minority people themselves.

People qualified to meet specific needs of the organization or over sixty years of age may apply as Short-Term Assistants (STAs). Terms vary from six months to three or more years. They are not eligible to vote or hold office and must have their own financial support. On an average, three to four hundred STAs serve us each year. Many of them are teachers on sabbatical who teach our children at schools at our centers.

Branches report that a good percentage of those who serve as STAs later take the linguistic course and apply for full membership. Here are the reasons one gave:

234

The normal pattern for big organizations is to become impersonal. The people on the lower rungs of the ladder are unknown or even forgotten by those at the top . . . .The idea of a ladder is virtually non-existent here. Several times those in positions of leadership have shown personal interest in what I am doing. I have seen leaders becoming servants to those for whom they are responsible. I was made to feel part—not of an organization—but of a big, wonderful family. Then one day a boy picked up a book with Bible verses in his language. Pointing to a verse he grinned and said, "I came across this book a couple of weeks ago and began reading it. When I read this verse, I stopped and asked Christ to be my Savior." That helped me realize the importance of getting God's Word into written form for those speaking minority languages. So I'm going back.

The character of our organizations, as members view them, is a special blend of six operating principles which give a six-dimensional view of our way of doing things.

1. The members control the organization.

Members soon sense that they are important, so important they in fact control the organizations. The extensive amount of time and effort devoted to orientation is not merely to prepare new members to do their jobs, but also to help them fulfill their responsibilities as members. Senior members have a vote in the setting of policies, the choice of directors, and the establishing of standards for membership. Junior members normally have a voice at branch or division meetings. The entire membership is too large and scattered to meet together, but the biennial international conference, at which every senior member has an elected representative delegate, is the final authority in matters of policy. The newest senior member's vote counts the same as that of the highest ranking officer. Leadership is by persuasion, not decree. When decisions are made we expect members to accept the will of the majority and carry them out. Despite all the shortcomings of democracy that lead many organizations to severely modify it, we have rejected every temptation to take ultimate control from the membership itself.

24. *International Biennial Conference delegates in business session in Mexico City.*

We have even built in safeguards to strengthen control by the members. Senior member representative delegates must always be a majority at the international conference. No elected or appointed office is for more than a two-year term. Only one of the committee that nominates for positions on the board of directors can be a board member. Conference delegates may override decisions of the administrators and board by vote or referendum.

We try to protect a member's rights, including the rights of a minority to be heard on a given issue. Such an "exhaust system" has held us together when tensions have built up. All meetings are open to any member, except personal matters which the members themselves agree should not be common knowledge. Members have access to the minutes of the meetings. We keep "confidential" minutes and correspondence to an absolute minimum. Members have the right to appeal any decision affecting them to a higher officer or body and ultimately to their fellow members.

The result is that members feel they own and operate the organizations. Operational budgets depend primarily on the percentage they vote for that purpose. To make group services largely self-sustaining, members set and pay rates for such things as room and board in group housing, plane flights to their locations and use of group cars. Many capital development projects, such as headquarters buildings, for which we must look to the Lord for substantial gifts, have often gotten started by gifts from members. We are not in the work for what we can get out of it but for what we can put into it.

2. Initiative is encouraged and control kept to a minimum.

Every effort is made to maximize each member's contribution. The general idea is never to do for a member what he ought to do for himself, but provide help for the things he cannot do for himself or would take him from a higher priority task. For example, members-in-training are expected to make their own travel arrangements. (We do, of course, provide helpful instructions.) At jungle camp and field orientation, members are taught to improvise, make do with what is available, and not depend on others or outside sources. On the field we are expected to make plans and goals within general guidelines provided and in consultation with our supervisors, then discipline ourselves to do as much as possible on our own. We are encouraged to ask for help when we need it and not reject it when others feel we need it. But the responsibility is ours to push through to completion.

We encourage the autonomy and initiative of branches and divisions. Where a sufficiently large group of members is working to be able to provide its own leadership and handle its own affairs, charters are granted. The international administration is a coordinating agency which can give suggestions and guidance but is largely dependent on the personnel and facilities of branches and divisions.

In summary, we look for the maximum development and contribution of every person, do what we can to develop it, but control the individual as little as possible.

In new fields, until specialized personnel becomes available, members of necessity may have to do many jobs for which they are not trained. In highly technical jobs, of course, we must have competent people. God has given us many who have technical skills. They have performed routine duties but often have seen new applications in our work for standard procedures and adapted the latest technological equipment to serve our needs. What has already been said about the use of aircraft and computers is an example. With each new venture God has sent along the specialists needed to operate, maintain and adapt the equipment according to our needs.

The type of specialist we need must be not only able to do his own job well, but also innovative in using his skill to help in other ways, especially in training local people to do what he is doing. Equipment must be such that local people can ultimately learn to use and maintain it. Our radio men, printers, typists, carpenters, mechanics, and other technically gifted members have trained local people as apprentices in their respective skills. One Isneg from the Philippines has already qualified as a JAARS pilot.

Our rapid expansion has been largely due to the initiative allowed members to follow up providential openings. On a plane flight, Cam Townsend once found himself the seatmate of a high-ranking official in a South American government and accepted his invitation to visit him. It opened up another country to our work. Another member was given a roving assignment to search out displaced groups from countries not open to us. In an amazingly short time she had linguistic and translation projects underway in seven or eight more quite diverse languages. Many projects are already moving ahead vigorously even before they are brought into the framework of the overall administration. The boards have encouraged our area directors to be flexible in situations that do not lend themselves to our traditional approach.

Fundamental to this balancing of initiative and control is a mutual trust in each other, a confidence that God will guide our fellow members too, and the assurance that we are all committed to the group's policies and goals. In financial matters we trust each other to report all funds received directly, be responsible stewards of what God has given, and follow policy and precedent in allocating charges. In matters of policy, while our elected officers are expected to monitor our activities, we members, having a hand in determining policy, are also responsible for keeping each other in line. While discipline and control are on the whole informal, procedures are available for the guidance of administrators and the protection of the rights of members.

We are on record as believing in the importance of being free to express our opinions and judgments. Delegates who represent their fellow members at the international conference have as much right to the floor as any board member. Though they represent the opinions of other members, delegates are not bound by their instructions as to how to vote but are to follow their own best judgment in deciding issues.

While the linguistic theory developed by Dr. Kenneth L. Pike is taught, our schools have considerable liberty in what they emphasize. All, however, are expected to cover a certain common ground in preparing new members for field work. Normal academic debate and disagreement are not frowned on but welcomed. Differing viewpoints do complicate the consultants' work since those they are helping may come from quite diverse linguistic traditions, but a flexibility of approach that allows individual initiative is prized more than any uniformity of linguistic model or theory.

Though we encourage initiative, there are controls. Everyone from the administrative officer to the newest member has someone to whom he reports. The international vice presidents plan and promote programs to achieve the goals of the organizations but must get the approval of the boards. The boards are subject to the international conference of the membership. Branch directors answer to field executive committees and the membership of the branch which elected them. Translations of Scripture, technical linguistic articles, and published material from duplicated prayer letters to full-size books, are first submitted to someone else for comment and approval before they are published. The purpose is not to restrict but to help and protect the author, the group and friends who may be involved or mentioned. With the number of highly motivated people among us, this is the best way we have found to maximize strengths, encourage initiative and safeguard results.

3. Leadership is from the ranks.

Our leaders, with the exception of a few specified board and council members, are elected by and from the very people they are to lead. Any senior member is eligible for any position. People over sixty-five, however, may not fill certain specified international administrative posts.

We do not see leadership as a status to be sought but a duty to be performed. Leaders are normally elected or appointed for two-year terms, subject to renewal, up to a maximum of six to eight years. Like all other members, leaders receive no stated salary but are dependent on what God supplies each month.

After their term of duty, leaders may resume their previous work. For example, they may complete their language analysis and translation. Or, if that is done, they may take up some other task assigned by the new administration. We feel that leaders lose their field perspective if they have spent too long a time out of personal participation in field programs. We therefore prefer that experienced executives be recycled back into the field. This mobility and reversibility of rank-and-file membership and leadership welds us together in a bond of mutual esteem and support.

Since leaders come from the ranks, they learn to lead primarily by leading. Some have had experience on field committees or in administration, but in general they are largely untrained for the management responsibilities of their positions. As our centers were established and special departments grew, we have therefore asked the administration to recruit members with management training and experience who would not only fill key positions but also give management training to others.

Academically, we have developed our own corps of teachers and consultants. Students who do well are asked back the following year to serve as section leaders for groups of students. Briefed ahead of time by more experienced instructors they now teach what they themselves have only recently learned. Those who go on to field research on actual languages and graduate linguistic studies constitute the backbone of our teaching staff and field consultant services. New consultants learn by observing senior consultants, then by serving as apprentices under them to help others find solutions to their problems. Branches are strongly urged to train more of their members for such service both to speed up their own work and to build up a potential for helping others.

According to Scripture, the one who leads is a servant of all (Matt. 20:27, 28). That we justify leadership in terms of service is an attractive and powerful bond that unites us. A student arriving at one of our linguistic schools was impressed when he later discovered that the one who had carried his baggage in was the director of the summer courses! Some have been surprised to find that it was a board member's wife who made up the beds for transient arrivals. I have never heard a member say anything that implied he was working for board members. I have heard them say board members were working for them.

4. Decisions are made at the grassroots.

As far as possible, decisions are made where the action is, with input by the members most directly involved. Parents decide when their children go away to school. The area director, branch director and field members made the decision to remain in South Vietnam after the Tet offensive and the destruction of our center at Kontum. Our field personnel in Peru made the decisions and handled the negotiations during recent times of crisis there. Time after time our confidence in our local leaders and members to make the right decision has been vindicated. Field branches, home divisions, linguistic schools, administrative departments—in each case, decisions are made by those administrators and members closest to the situation. Decisions affecting other entities, however, are to be made in consultation with them or referred up the line of command.

Certain operating groups may even be granted autonomy within the system. For example, once there are ten members on a field, they may draw up a tentative constitution, elect an advisory field committee and nominate a director to be appointed by the SIL board. From then on, to all intents and purposes they run their own affairs. The board seldom has to use its veto power and control through the appointed director. After five years of experience and evidence that the members have made good progress, followed policies, made sound decisions, maintained good public relations and have sufficient depth of leadership to handle any crisis that may come, they are granted a charter. This means they elect their own director who answers to their elected field committee rather than to the board. The international board and administrative officers serve a consultative role but are no longer responsible for running the branch.

Members are granted senior membership by fellow members of the branch or division where they serve, who are best able to evaluate their performance and readiness. This field decision automatically gives them senior membership rights at the international level. Members assigned to one branch or division who are temporarily in another are under the jurisdiction of the latter. Discipline, including the recommendation of dismissal, can only originate where the member is at the time the misdemeanor occurred, and be initiated by the leaders nearest the scene. A board cannot bypass local leadership to initiate discipline.

5. The field point of view dominates.

Field work began and a field organization developed before there was any home organization. All decisions were made by members on the field and with their interests solely in view.

Even when friends at home have not understood or agreed with our field policies and have threatened to withdraw support, we have placed field needs ahead of home attitudes.

When home divisions were established, people with field experience were usually asked to lead them, even though it might be painful for them to be recalled from their field assignment. We encourage other home division administrators to visit a field or get actual field experience. We have always considered it important that a sizable number of home council members be those with field experience.

Divisions see themselves as existing to meet the needs of the field members and to have a ministry to the churches and Christian constituency at home that will keep their field interest growing.

Of the eighteen members on the current international boards seven are field assigned, seven had field service, and only four have never served on the field. The delegate system for biennial international conferences guarantees that delegates representing current field interests outnumber all others.

Our linguistic training program is geared for practical field work. A high percentage of the staff and department heads for the linguistic courses are members brought directly back from the field. Other faculty are members on furlough or study programs. Members presenting papers at scientific congresses are recognized as field linguists, their conclusions based on data gained and verified in talking the language conversationally with the people.

Once assigned to a branch, a member works out his program with his field director. Division directors and school directors may request field members for staff service but the granting of such requests comes from the field administration. The member's furlough year at home will be worked out with the field director and often includes further study in preparation for field and group service on returning to the field.

The percentage of all income voted by the members for

operations is so divided among the field, home and international administrations that finances are kept in balance and cannot be distributed in ways that would be prejudicial to the work abroad. Donor interest is overwhelmingly in field projects. This is good but does not do away with the fact that the needs at home for programs to recruit and train new members, maintain prayer interest and provide funds for the work abroad are equally worthy and essential.

6. Institutions are expendable and are only developed when needed.

Townsend's leadership was "by cloud and pillar of fire" (Numbers 9:15-23), strongly influenced by providential contacts and provisions. Opportunities were seized while hot. Often we "lengthened the cords" and later got around to "strengthening the stakes" that anchored them (Isaiah 54:2). The result was rapid growth and considerable output with very limited resources and facilities.

The work in Mexico was in its eighth year, and over ninety workers were on the field or on their way before a home office was established and the work officially organized. Members assigned to language projects in new areas, because of the lack of specialized support personnel, often had to help build hangars, install plumbing and keep the books before they got started! At the beginning of the work in South America, one worker was in a remote location and out of touch with fellow members and the director for fourteen months. Our Jungle Aviation and Radio Service was the solution. It is now part of the planning in all new allocations in remote or otherwise largely inaccessible regions.

We often rent housing. We buy or build in countries abroad. In some cases, we have built headquarters or workshop facilities on land put at our disposal by the host government or the national university.

Linguistic courses began in an abandoned farm house with nailkegs for seats. Then we moved to rented campsites. Summer courses are now offered in several locations under the auspices of other organizations and on their premises. This pattern frees us from having to maintain and utilize buildings the rest of the year. More recently, however, with the need for year-round training in addition to summer courses, we are finally developing facilities of our own in the United States, Europe and Australia. Linguistic research is constantly feeding back into the training program and textbooks. One summer, individual pages of a written-in-process textbook were given out each day, then collected again for binding when the summer was over.

Home division needs tend to get taken care of last of all. At first the Pioneer Mission Agency in Pennsylvania handled home office needs for us. Then a room over retired businessman William G. Nyman's garage in California became headquarters. Next came a rented office, then an old church building, and finally an efficient office built on donated land. We have seldom had more than needed, and most of the time it seemed woefully inadequate for the job being done. The story in Australia, Great Britain, Germany, Switzerland and the Netherlands has been the same.

When we began, our members spoke to meetings arranged by others. Then friends at the home end donated time to arrange meetings for us, especially for members home from the field. But as we have grown, a more permanent type of home representation has been necessary. We now assign some members to home office duties upon request of the divisions or the members. Others help in their home country programs while on furlough from their field assignments. More recently lay people have greatly strengthened our outreach to the home constituencies, in the United States, Canada and Australia.

16

Others Also

WE ARE a group of specialists motivated by God's love for us and the world. The minority peoples of the world are made of the same human stuff we are. They weep, they laugh, they love, they hate. We are basically no different from them. Our apparent differences are cultural, acquired, often superficial. "Christ's love compels us, because we are convinced that one died for all . . . that those who live should no longer live for themselves but for him who died for them and was raised again" (2 Cor. 5:14, 15). We find ourselves in the same human predicaments they do, incapable of solving life's problems ourselves, knowing we have sinned and come short of what God expects of us (Rom 3:23). But we have found in Jesus Christ, as described in the Bible, the one who "is the atoning sacrifice for our sins, and not only for ours but also for the sins of the whole world" (1 John 2:2).

Personal Sharing

We get to know people of all walks of life in our work. We find they have the same sense of spiritual need. We simply share with them the one who meets our need and the Book that tells of him. Many of them find he meets their need, too. A little Mazatec mother lay on a thin palm mat on the dirt floor, shivering under a threadbare blanket. A few days before she had given birth to a baby girl, only to see it die a few hours later. She looked up and plaintively asked our workers: "Do you have any medicine for sadness?"

Knowing themselves the "encouragement of the Scriptures" (Rom. 15:4; 2 Cor. 1:4), they shared with her Bible verses they had translated into her language. She thanked them as they left. The "medicine" seemed to help, for on subsequent visits she welcomed them into her home and wanted to hear more.

A public school teacher in the Philippines, well educated, trilingual and linguistically sharp was teaching one of our teams her language. But she had a hunger in her heart to know God. True, once she had opposed the Gospel and openly despised those who said they believed it. But now she could hardly wait for the language learning time to conclude so she could talk about the Word of God and ask questions about spiritual matters. After discussion and searching the Scriptures she concluded that "if I am going to know God I will have to come to him on his own terms." She bowed her head and asked Christ into her life as Savior and Lord.

A powerful headhunter who worshipped the boa constrictor was helping the translator put John 1:12 into his language. Suddenly he paused in his staccato, rapid-fire talking, then blurted out: "How does a man receive Jesus Christ?"

Patiently the translator explained, then asked, "Do you want to receive Jesus Christ?"

Back came the abrupt answer, "Yes. I want him very much."

"Just tell God what you just told me, that you want Jesus very much," she replied.

And he did. Shortly after, as he stepped into his own hut nearby she overheard his booming voice calling his wives and children to attention, as he explained to them that he was now a child of God, "because that verse said so." He proceeded to quote what he had just helped translate, "Yet to all who received him . . . he gave the right to become children of God" (John 1:12).

Not all find it easy to believe. Two of us were in the office of the head of an inter-government organization on a business errand. After concluding official matters, for two hours the official plied us with questions about what the Bible said about sickness, poverty, the inequities of life and the character of God. Philosophy and his religion, he said, had not provided answers. Driving him home one evening from our headquarters, I heard him say, "I wish I could believe as you people do."

It is because we are specialists that we have such opportunities. We are specialists in linguistics, majoring in the minority languages that have not been previously analyzed or written. We are also specialists in Bible translation, basing our spiritual service and sharing on the Scriptures. The people with whom we relate—linguists, government personnel, church people, villagers—soon realize that we are people of the Book, that we read it ourselves and share it with them and others. The head of one Department of Indian Affairs with whom we worked told me one day that she loved to get away from her office and visit one of our translator families. Their times of Bible reading and prayer around the table after meals with their children and language associates, she said, did something for her that she desperately needed in the hectic pressures of political life.

Although our cooperation with others may be on the strictly professional level of linguistics or literacy, they know of our preoccupation with Bible translating and are fascinated by it. Dr. Kenneth L. Pike and I were sitting one day sipping tea and talking linguistics in the garden of an internationally-known linguist in Europe. Soon our host's wife turned the conversation to a book included in the last batch of reprints of linguistic articles Pike had sent her husband. It was written by Pike's sister, Eunice, describing her life as a pioneer Bible translator and the interesting problem which arose as she explained the Gospel to the Mazatec people.[1] When the conversation between Pike and her husband went back to linguistics, the wife continued asking me many more questions about the spiritual side of our life with the people.

The Bible translator has many opportunities like this to share his faith.

Specialization

Specialization, one of the characteristics of our work, has scriptural precedent. Christ limited himself to "the lost sheep of Israel" (Matt. 15:24). God called Paul to major in Gentile missions, Peter in Jewish missions (Gal. 2:8, 9). Paul restricted his ecclesiastical activity lest his basic ministry suffer, "for Christ did not send me to baptize, but to preach the gospel" (1 Cor. 1:17). Paul's preaching was even restricted by the Holy Spirit (Acts 16:6). Paul's call to pioneer meant he could not stay with the church in Jerusalem (Acts 22:18, 21) or Ephesus (Acts 20:32) or Corinth (2 Cor. 10:15, 16). That was for others to do. Even in the body of Christ God has specialized by giving people differing gifts or ministries (Rom. 12:3-8; 1 Cor. 12).

God has led us as the Summer Institute of Linguistics to specialize in linguistic work in the minority languages, in cooperation with universities and governments. We therefore restrict ourselves from missionary and ecclesiastical activities or religious affiliations that would alienate or embarrass those institutions. Many of our Christian friends in the countries where we work who want us to formally or organizationally link ourselves with them in their work have found this position difficult to understand and accept. Since we specialize in minority languages, we also limit our activities, even of a personal and informal kind, in the national language, lest we get sidetracked from our tasks.

For us to fill leadership roles at meetings of nationals is contrary to our own indigenous principles. We are sometimes embarrassed by the number of foreigners who attend New Testament dedication services, since they seem to draw attention out of all proportion to their numbers.

This does not mean we avoid or disassociate ourselves from other Christians. Where there are national churches, members are encouraged to attend—but without taking leadership positions. In our group facilities we entertain hundreds of missionaries. Our planes fly them. Fellowship meetings of our members are open to them. Often we have been able to help them establish contacts with government agencies. Thousands of those who have followed Christ as a result of our translation and verbal witness have been added to the national and mission churches.

Christ deliberately delayed his public presentation of himself until the appropriate time (Matt. 16:20; John 7:3-6).

Because early involvement in religious activity would frighten many of our sponsors or cause them to question the genuineness of our linguistic commitment, we limit our Christian witness until we are able to express ourselves in the ethnic language. In one country the official with whom we were in contact asked us to research one of the smallest language groups first. We assigned one of our Ph.D.s to the task for six months and the results more than pleased him. Later he told us he had made the request deliberately, to test the sincerity of our offer to do linguistics. Once assured of our linguistic productivity, he was more ready to listen to our Christian witness.

We find it better to push vigorously ahead in learning to speak the language first, then, as soon as possible, to tentative translations of portions of Scripture. Until a translator is able to speak the local language, attempts at kindness, overtures of friendliness, foreign patterns of Christian conduct and personal witness concerning Christ may be misunderstood. Once we have passages of the Bible translated, informal one-to-one or small group Bible studies give opportunity for introducing people to the Scriptures, to Christ as presented there and to biblical principles of living.

Sharing While Translating

But it is in the actual translating and checking process that we have the greatest opportunity to share the Gospel. The translation of the Bible, when carried on with language helpers who do not know Christ, is evangelism of a most powerful and fruitful kind. The Scriptures themselves "are able to make ... wise for salvation through faith in Christ Jesus" (2 Tim. 3:15). In the process of discussing the meaning of the text and how to express it in his mother tongue, the translation helper is brought face to face with the truth. The open nature of the discussion as we together explore all the nuances of meaning minimizes personal pressure but maximizes understanding and application. Many find Christ at the translation desk.

A Mazatec was helping me revise the translation of Paul's

letter to the Romans. He was quick to grasp many of the truths stated there. I reminded him that the book had not been written just for the Romans, but was equally relevant to his need today.

"Yes," he agreed, "but I think I'll wait until after I'm married before I deliver myself into the hands of Christ."

Intrigued by his answer, I asked how he had come to that decision.

"Didn't Paul tell the Corinthians that a believer should not get married to an unbeliever?" he replied.

"Why, yes," I said, "that's one application of that passage."

"Well," he want on, "the girl I want to marry isn't a believer, so if I believed now, I couldn't marry her, could I?"

I admired his honesty and was pleased he was applying the Scriptures to his own situation, but assured him that if he accepted Christ first, then he would have Christ's help in finding the best girl for him. Some days later, as we finished the book of Romans, he put his faith in the Savior. Later he married the girl of his choice.

In the course of checking a translation many different people are exposed to the text of Scripture, individually or in groups. In the course of literacy work, translated portions of the Scriptures are part of the literature available to read. Helping people improve their reading skills involves checking their comprehension of what they have read. This results in many questions and open, uninhibited discussion of what the Bible says and means. As a result, Philip's experience with the Ethiopian is often repeated (Acts 8:30-35).

I was a pastor and in youth work before going to the field as a translator. I had more opportunity to talk to people about Christ as a translator than I ever had as a Christian worker at home. My wife and I agreed that if any person came into our home long enough to sit down and visit, we would seek to share the Gospel with him using the passages we had already translated. Over several months we averaged five people a day, most of whom had never heard the Gospel before.

Much teaching goes on while members are translating the Bible. Words in context, parallel passages and illustrations are all used carefully and intensively to an extent seldom achieved other than by the most thorough of expository preachers. No seminary or Bible school today requires that the student not only read but understand and in his own words state to the satisfaction of his instructor the meaning of every book, chapter, verse and phrase of the text of Scripture. Yet this is normal procedure for the translator and co-worker.

Sharing our Good News must be done with genuine love for and identification with the people, not just professionally. An old, Miniafia sorcerer became our translator's language helper. One day at a workshop in the highlands, he complained of being cold and asked for the translator's portable kerosene heater. At first the translator refused, saying his children needed it. But he felt he'd done the wrong thing. Others he told of the sorcerer's request loaned heaters they were not using and soon the old man had one.

A couple of weeks later the sorcerer came into the translator's living room. "David, I will speak and you will listen. Long ago some missionaries came to my village. They held a black book in their hands and said that it was God's words. They were not loving, and I did not believe them. Then two years ago, you came to my village. You held that book in your hands and said that it was God's words. I've been watching you. Now you have brought me to this cold place where there are many people like you. You are all holding that book and saying that it is God's words. I look at you and see that you are loving me, and now I am believing." A little old kerosene heater had brought warmth to more than just his body.

Support personnel also have opportunities for witness. Highly respected for their technical expertise, our pilots often have the opportunity to give a personal word of testimony and a portion of Scripture to those they fly, whether government officials, anthropologists, businessmen, religious leaders, bilingual school teachers or tourists. One tourist, an elder in an American church, found Christ as Savior while talking to the pilot on the landing ramp after the flight. A lad from a nearby frontier town who worked in the hangar accepted Christ through studying the Bible with one of the mechanics.

Support people do not work directly with the Word as translators do. Like any person in the homeland doing comparable work, they have to find opportunities for personal witness and ministry with local people with whom they work, in whose neighborhood they live, or whom they meet when they come to the center as visitors. Members are encouraged to visit and develop personal friendships that will provide oppportunities for sharing Christ with others.

Church Planting and Growth

Our specialization as linguists in the mother tongue and as Christian workers in Bible translation contributes to the numerical growth and strengthening of churches among the ethnic peoples.

We translate where there are no believers in Christ and for believers who have no Scriptures. We are not a church planting organization, but God nevertheless uses the translated Word as the seed that produces believers and as the food that causes them to grow in numbers and in spiritual maturity for service (Isa. 55:11).

We encourage believers to gather for Bible study. We meet with them and help train them in the use of the Scriptures. We do not claim them as belonging in any way to us. Groups that begin as a result of our witness and the translated Word are indigenous from the beginning, with the Scriptures in their own language, leaders of their own choice and services conducted according to their own cultural ways. Many of them link up with national churches of their choice in the area and may take on the characteristics of those with whom they identify.

We do not consider our members' work in a language complete until some of the local group are capable of reading the printed Word and there is a nucleus of believers to carry on themselves or with another evangelical group which

253

has taken responsibility for establishing such a nucleus.

Some of our translators have seen immediate results, others have lived and witnessed for many years with little or no fruit. Christ prepared us for the fact that not all soils respond in the same way, even though the same quality of seed is sown. Even the "good soil" produced different yields, a hundred, sixty or thirty times what was sown (Matt. 13:1-9).

The Chuj first heard the Gospel through a neighboring people. But they had no Chuj Scriptures and few knew how to read. Twelve years after a team began, one thousand Christians attended two dedication services for the New Testament. Five years later the translators revisited the area to find nearly half the tribe gathering in three large congregations with three Indian pastors. Several lay workers were holding services in villages every day throughout the area. Volunteers taught literacy classes and seven Chuj were teaching in a Bible institute. Two Chuj believers had gone to other language groups as missionaries.

When a translation team was first assigned to the Higi, the church was already several thousand strong. Soon an alphabet was devised and a tentative grammatical analysis made. Then one of the Higi pastors with theological college training, responsible for a dozen congregations, was freed by the district council for three years to work on the translation. He drafted the translation in his combination workroom and granary, using commentaries and various helps. Our co-translator went over the draft, then typed copies for Higi men to take to the villages to try out with the people. As portions came out they were put in use in the weekly church services all over the area. When the Gospel of Mark first came out, it sold out in a few days. A three-day course for evangelists and church leaders on how to conduct literacy classes for their people met with enthusiastic response. Ten thousand hours of hard work, sweat and perseverance by the two co-translators went into the finished New Testament for the 100,000 Higi speakers.

After six years as a "son of the Higi," our member was given a roaring send-off by two thousand people. Traditional music and dancing interspersed with prayers and speeches

254

continued for four hours. When it was all over, the chief, tall and erect in his full dignity, took off the co-translator's Higi cap, placed his right hand on his head and invoked God's blessing on his white son who had helped give them the Word.

Among the Balangao, things began to happen after the translator had a head-on confrontation with a powerful shaman working over a six-year-old boy in convulsions. Through prayer, the reading of Scripture and daily visits to reassure the family that God could be trusted, the family was finally released from the paralyzing fear of spirit reprisals. How thankful the translator was for the passages already translated that explained who Christ was and how he had power over evil spirits.

Later the shaman herself was delivered from "the spirits who," she said, "made me do it."

Such evidence of the power of Christ, reinforced by the Scriptures, brought a new sense of hope to the village. Believers increased. Churches grew. Already a third annual Bible conference has been held with two hundred Balangao hosting sixty guests from other ethnic language groups. They have been a great inspiration to believers in neighboring languages and have their first missionary family in service.

Recent research into church growth as the result of our work in the Philippines[2] showed thirty-seven churches in twelve language groups after eight years, plus seven smaller groups in six other languages. Protestant missions have planted churches in thirteen other language groups. In ten tribes where we are working there are as yet no functioning churches.

Changing Cultures

Language is the key to culture. The Bible provides a moral basis for recognizing that man's true worth and dignity is based on the fact he is made in the image of God. Linguistics and Bible translation enable us to be of practical help in changing cultures with a minimum of cultural disturbance. By working in the language of the culture, training and leaving control in the hands of members of the ethnic group, and offering the Bible in their language, we respect and strengthen their own culture, respect their right of self-determination, and offset many of the disadvantages they otherwise have in their encounter with other cultures. "There is indeed in the teachings of Christ great innovation. But Christianity, with very few exceptions is compatible with the customs and lifestyles of any people. It is much more compatible, we would say, than any of the philosophies created by the West, such as existentialism or Marxism."[3]

Language, which symbolizes cultural differences, thus becomes a vehicle for enhancing each culture's worth and ethnic uniqueness. The Bible gets to the heart of cultural differences, including tribal disrespect and animosity. Those who choose to believe and obey the Word of God are transformed in character and attitudes. They are free to accept others, even former enemies, as equals and as fellow recipients of the grace of God.

Cultures also change from within. The Bible can direct those changes positively. Among the Tzeltal, heads of families and other able-bodied men are required by local custom to help on village projects at the call of their own ethnic authorities. Often men tried to evade such work. To enforce attendance local police take some object of value from each home which can only be reclaimed by the head of the home showing up for work. After Romans 13:1-8 was translated and in the hands of the believers, the men turned out en masse in response to the call of their non-believing leaders. It was no longer necessary to send police to take things out of their homes to force them to come. An announcement sent to the pastor, read in the church service, was all that was necessary. Obedience to civil authority became for them a natural part of their obedience to God. The traditional authorities who opposed the Gospel were non-plussed.

Cultures also have to contend with forces from the outside. The Ticunas live in northeastern Peru. For centuries Spanish conquerors and their descendants had claimed their land. Over the years other ethnic groups in the region had lost their identity, been absorbed into the dominant culture or died off. The Ticuna people and the land they occupied were the property of the Spanish patron. They were told they must sell their produce to the Spanish overlord. The enthusiasm of the people as they built their first church building impressed a visiting government official. Through his efforts the government surveyed the area and deeded the land to the Ticuna. They no longer have to hire themselves out to work. They can sell to anyone they choose. When merchants offered them free alcoholic drinks to "soften them up" for exploitive deals, they refused. They planned and rebuilt their whole village, including a school, and sent some of their finest young men to train as teachers.

Their medical clinic has changed the health situation, and a community store has put an end to exploitation by plantation owners. More impressive than their material progress is the spirit of the community, their individual commitment to work for progress, and the new set of values that guides and motivates their lives. Today Cusillococha is a village that Peru is proud of and the rumrunners pass by.[4]

A Ticuna bilingual school teacher, speaking to government officials from Lima who had come to the inaugurate a new powerplant in his Ticuna village, said:

You are today in the land inhabited for centuries by my Ticuna ancestors. From being lords of the jungle, they became those dominated by others with the advantages of civilization and education. They lost their nobility to become slaves of the rubber hunters. The years passed from our fathers to us. Our inheritance was uncertainty. We were without any real initiative. Then the government offered us bilingual education and the security of our lands. We have worked with pride in the development of our village. Before, we sought a life of individual convenience, but in recent years we have been privileged to know God and his commandments through his holy Word. We have put our faith and complete confidence in him, and he, besides having given us eternal life, has blessed us much more in this world than a simple village of Indians could have hoped. Day after day he has given us new light in our spirits, and now, a new light for our village also. We cannot do less than give him all our thanks. We hope that the Light which has been put in Cushillocoha will be extended until it includes the last savage, to show him the way out of darkness.

257

Epilogue

SOME YEARS ago in Mexico my wife, Florrie, and I, part of the Mazatec New Testament team, moved to an isolated ranch to be free from the frequent interruptions in the Mazatec village. Old Aniceta and her family graciously shared their home with us during the months of intensive revision work. Aniceta was like a mother to us.

When we left the Mazatecs for our annual teaching assignment at the Wycliffe Language Course in England, we often thought of Aniceta and prayed for her. One day we wrote her a letter to let her know we hadn't forgotten her and that we still loved her and were looking forward to returning soon. What a thrill it would be for the old woman to receive a letter for the first time in her life! We could just picture the excitement. She would talk about it for the rest of her days.

But the problem of how to get a letter to her arose. She lived away out in the mountains. The man in the town post office would not know who she was. After having lived almost seventy years without ever receiving a letter, there was little likelihood she would ask for one now.

But one of her sons, a close friend of ours, worked in the mail town. The man in the post office would know him. Because of our close friendship, we knew the son would consider it a privilege to deliver our letter to his mother.

Three months later when we arrived in the village, we visited our old friend. She was overjoyed to see us but didn't mention the letter, much to our surprise. Finally we asked if she had received it.

"Letter? What letter?" No, she hadn't received it.

Later we saw the son. Had he received our letter from England, written to his mother?

"Oh, yes. Several weeks ago."

"But we've just been to the ranch, and your mother said she didn't receive it," we said.

Chagrined, the son confessed he had forgotten to deliver the letter—it must still be in his town house. He emptied table drawers, looked under sacks of coffee berries, and moved mounds of corn in the search. He never found the letter.

Something deep down in our hearts hurt. We had counted on the son, but he had failed us—not maliciously, but through failing to give it immediate attention.

Then we remembered that almost 2,000 years before, God had written a love letter to let people know he had not forgotten them. God faced a problem of delivery, too. So he sent it in care of us who know and love him. But we've failed to deliver it—not maliciously, but by doing nothing about it.

Because of our neglect, over 3,000 language groups still have not received the message of God's love that he sent to them.

That is why we as members of the Wycliffe Bible Translators and the Summer Institute of Linguistics do what we do the way we do. May God give us the personnel and the means to deliver God's letter to all those who still have not received it.

Notes

Chapter 1

1. Lest the figures given be misunderstood, at the end of 1983 the whole Bible had been published in 283 languages, an entire Testament in 572 additional languages, and one complete book or more of the Bible in 930 more, for a total of 1,785 languages. For a summary of Bible translation through the centuries, with examples, see *The Book of a Thousand Tongues,* rev. ed. (London: United Bible Societies, 1972).

2. See Barbara F. Grimes, ed., *Ethnologue* (10th ed.; Dallas, Texas: Wycliffe Bible Translators, 1984), which lists 5,445 languages by countries, with further details on language affiliation, number of speakers and Bible translation need.

3. For a fuller account of the foregoing as well as later developments the reader is referred to E. E. Wallis and M. A. Bennett, *Two Thousand Tongues To Go* (New York: Harper and Brothers, 1959); James and Marti Hefley, *Uncle Cam* (Waco, Texas: Word Books, 1974); and Ruth M. Brend and Kenneth L. Pike, eds., *The Summer Institute of Linguistics: Its Works and Contributions* (The Hague: Mouton, 1977).

1. David B. Barrett, *Schism and Renewal in Africa* (Nairobi: Oxford University Press, 1968), p. 133.
2. In James Boswell, *Life of Samuel Johnson LL.D.,* Great Books of the Western World (Encyclopedia Britannica, 1952) p. 151.

3. D. J. V. Lane, "Tradition," *The New Bible Dictionary,* ed. J. D. Douglas (Grand Rapids: Eerdmans, 1962).

4. *Ibid.*

5. *Ibid.*

6. K. A. Kitchen, *Ancient Orient and Old Testament* (Chicago: Inter Varsity Press, 1966), p. 136.

7. Morton, *Penguin Science News,* no. 43 (London, 1957), p. 26, says it has been estimated that in New Testament times "a gospel represents in papyrus alone a year's wages and a New Testament about eight years' pay of a skilled workman."

8. Sherwood Wirt, *You Can Tell the World* (Los Angeles: Augsburg, 1975), p. 55.

9. Written translations also involve interpretation and may be slanted too. See chapter 3, "At What Standard of Translation Do We Aim?" for steps taken to safeguard this in our own work.

Chapter 3

1. See Thomas Dolaghan and David Scates. *The Navajos are Coming to Jesus* (South Pasadena: William Carey Library, 1978), pp. 41-44.

2. Those desiring to know more of what is involved in making a translation both faithful and intelligible should see John Beekman and John Callow, *Translating the Word of God* (Grand Rapids: Zondervan, 1974); Eugene A. Nida, *Bible Translating* (London: United Bible Societies, 1961), and Eugene A. Nida and Charles R. Taber, *The Theory and Practice of Translation* (London: E. J. Brill, 1969).

Chapter 4

1. This and the following figures are based on Grimes, *Ethnologue* (See note 2, chapter 1). Exhaustive surveys have not been completed yet for many areas. More languages may still be found. Some linguists would set the figure at 6,000. All such figures are subject to fluctuation as better information becomes available. Language situations are also

constantly changing. The United Bible Societies figure of 1,785 languages in which one or more books of the Bible have already been published is a cumulative figure and includes languages no longer spoken or in which translations made are no longer available or usable.

2. For example, ethnic language communities for which we are currently translating range in size from 47,000 down to 180 in Papua New Guinea; 3,000 to 120 in Australia; 7,000 to 7 in Brazil, and 300,000 to 4,800 in Ghana. Displaced language projects are being carried on for populations not now accessible, which number in the millions.

3. The term "expatriate" as used throughout this book indicates a person working in a country other than his own, "national" a person working in his own country.

4. For a helpful discussion of some of the most commonly used terms in the field of language learning and use, see Paul Christophersen, *Second-Language Learning* (Penguin Modern Lingusitics Texts, 1973), pp. 29ff.

5. From K. L. Pike, "What's on My Mind (A Preview)" in *Stir-Change-Create,* (Grand Rapids: Eerdmans, 1967), pp. 14-15.

6. See Gleason Archer Jr., *A Survey of Old Testament Introduction* (Chicago: Moody Press, 1962), p. 400.

7. Mithridates of Pontus (120-63 B.C.) was reported to be able to converse with his subjects in more than twenty different languages. *Noctes Atticae* 17.17.2 in H. S. Gehman, *The Interpreters of Foreign Languages Among the Ancients,* (Lancaster, Pa., 1914), quoted in R. H. Robins, *A Short History of Linguistics* (London: Longmans, 1967), p. 47.

8. Ralph P. Martin, *Epistle of Paul to the Philippians,* Tyndale N. T. Commentaries (London: Tyndale Press, 1959), p. 142.

9. See his commentary on the *Acts of the Apostles,* ch. 8.

10. From S. Pearce Carey, *William Carey* (New York: George H. Doran Company, 1923), p. 407.

11. R. S. Pittman, private communication.

Chapter 5

1. For a detailed description, see Ruth M. Brend and Kenneth L. Pike, eds., *The Summer Institute of Linguistics: Its*

Works and Contributions (The Hague: Mouton, 1977).

2. See Calvin R. Rensch, "Training Programs for Those Involved with SIL in Language Projects," *Notes on Linguistics* no. 1 (Dallas: Summer Institute of Linguistics, January 1977), pp. 7-12.

3. From *Summer Institute of Linguistics Catalogue,* 1976 ed. (Dallas: Summer Institute of Linguistics).

4. For full details of courses in all the locations mentioned, see the current *Summer Institute of Linguistics Catalogue,* available from 7500 W. Camp Wisdom Road, Dallas, TX 75236, U.S.A.

5. Charles F. Hockett in *A Manual of Phonology* (Indiana University Publications in Anthropology and Linguistics, Memoir II, 1955), pp. 1-2, for example, said: "A number of factors have contributed to this widening of our empiric base, but one above all others deserves mention here: the far-flung field research of missionaries trained by the Summer Institute of Linguistics. Their brief factual reports are perhaps rarely exciting but show on the average a high reliability; . . . . a few years ago Pike and Pike prepared and published an IC analysis of Mazateco phonology . . . .in my opinion it is one of the really germinal contributions to linguistics in the last few decades."

For the most recent summary of the scholarly output of our total membership the reader is referred to the *Bibliography of the Summer Institute of Linguistics,* Alan C. Wares, compiler, (Dallas: Summer Institute of Linguistics, 1974). The *Bibliography of the Wycliffe Bible Translators* (Huntington Beach, California: Wycliffe Bible Translators, Inc., 1970) lists member translators, languages and Scripture portions translated.

6. Historically, of course, there is ample precedent for missionaries, while pursuing spiritual goals, being scholars and contributing to linguistic science and general knowledge. For a survey, see "Linguistics and Christian Missions," by William L. Wonderly and Eugene A. Nida in *Anthropological Linguistics,* January 1963, reprinted in *The Bible Translator,* Vol. 15 (1964). For one man's statement, see Kenneth L. Pike, *With Heart and Mind: A Personal Synthesis of Scholarship and Devotion* (Grand Rapids: Eerdmans, 1962).

7. For the story, see E. E. Wallis, *The Dayuma Story* (New York: Harper and Row, 1960).

Chapter 6

1. From an unpublished letter of Edward P. Torjesen, missionary, the Evangelical Alliance Mission, April 8, 1965.

2. See Martha Duff, "Contrastive Features of Written and Oral Texts in Amuesha (Arawakan)," in *Lenguaje y Ciencias,* Vol. 14 (1974), pp. 168-180.

3. See Morris Watkins, *Literacy, Bible Reading, and Church Growth* (South Pasadena: William Carey Library, 1978), pp. 163-164.

4. From an unpublished letter of John Duitsman of the Lutheran Bible Translators, July, 1978.

5. The *Linguistic Reporter* of October, 1972, pointed out that this continued until the time of Augustine (A.D. 397), who in one of his *Confessions* (Bk VI) records his amazement on finding his teacher, Ambrose, reading silently, apparently to save his voice, which was quite weak.

6. E. C. Richardson, "Writing," "Book," *International Standard Bible Encyclopaedia,* ed. James Orr, 5 vols. (Grand Rapids: Eerdmans, 1930).

7. Watkins, pp. 11-12.

8. *Ibid.,* p. 21.

9. *Ibid.,* p. 34.

10. *Ibid.,* p. 52.

11. *Ibid.,* p. 170.

12. See Jan Knoppert, "The State of our Knowledge of African Languages," *Linguistics,* (March 15, 1974), pp. 72-90.

13. See Marvin Mayers, address to Evangelical Literature Overseas, February 1970, "Culture Stress and Reader Motivation"—reported in *Lit-Tec,* Vol. 3, no. 2, (Spring-Summer 1970), pp. 1-6.

Chapter 7

1. Quoted in *Ethno-Pedagogy* by Henry Borger, p. 69.

2. For evidence from the Philippines, see "The Iloilo

Experiment in Education Through the Vernacular" by Pedro T. Orta in *The Use of Vernacular Languages in Education,* (Paris, UNESCO, 1953); from Mexico, see "Bilingual Education for Children of Linguistic Minorities," by Nancy Modiano in *America Indigena,* Vol. XXVIII, no. 2, (1968); from Peru, see "Indian Education in Indian Languages," by B. F. Elson in *America Indigena,* Vol. XXV, no. 2, (April 1965), p. 242; and from the U.S.A., see Sarah Gudschinsky in *A Manual of Literacy for Preliterate Peoples* (Dallas: Summer Institute of Linguistics, 1973), p. 7, and *Language Policy in Indian Education* (Arlington, Virginia: Center for Applied Linguistics, 1973).

3. See S. G. Harris, "A Local Government Council Sponsored Vernacular Literacy Program," Papua New Guinea *Journal of Education,* Vol. 7, No. 3 (Oct. 1971), pp. 42-48.
4. Elson, pp. 239-44.
5. Harris, p. 47
6. See chapter 6, note 12.
7. From *Floodtide* (Spring 1964), p. 9.
8. This and much of the following is based on a report by J. Wroughton in 1963 at a public convocation of the Summer Institute of Linguistics at the University of North Dakota.

Chapter 8

1. G. G. Findlay in *Expositors Greek New Testament* on 1 Cor. 9 (5 vols.; Grand Rapids: Eerdmans, 1952), 3:855.
2. For an independent statement of similar principles, see Joseph C. Shenk, "Missionary Identity and Servanthood," in *Missiology,* Vol. 1, no. 4 (October 1973), pp. 505-515. 515.
3. W. C. Townsend and R. S. Pittman, *Remember All The Way* (Huntington Beach, California: Wycliffe Bible Translators, 1975), pp. 111-112.

Chapter 9

1. Examples: Mary Shaw, ed., *According to Our Ancestors: Folktexts from Guatemala and Honduras* (Norman, Oklahoma:

Summer Institute of Linguistics of the University of Oklahoma, 1971), and Walter Miller, *Cuentos Mixes,* Biblioteca de Folklore Indigena (Mexico: Instituto Nacional Indigenista, 1956).

2. For example, Ethel Wallis, *Tariri, My Story* (New York: Harper and Row, 1965).

3. For example, R. D. Shaw, ed., *Kinship Studies in Papua New Guinea* (Papua New Guinea: Summer Institute of Linguistics, 1974).

4. For example: R. G. Wasson, G. and F. Cowan and W. Rhodes, *Maria Sabina and Her Mazatec Mushroom Velada* (New York: Harcourt Brace Jovanovich, 1975).

5. From Larry Yost, "A Strategy for Community Development in the Summer Institute of Linguistics," mimeographed manuscript (1978).

6. Cf. A. F. Glasser in "Timeless Lessons from the Western Missionary Penetration of China," *Missiology,* Vol. 1, No. 4 (October 1973), pp. 458-461: "It is not enough that the Christian be socially compassionate. God would have him socially creative as well." He distinguishes "redemption" and "lift." "Redemption has to do with Christ's saving activity in the human heart . . . . Lift has to do with benefits or improvements that the convert begins to reach for following his conversion. They embrace his personal, educational, economic and social development."

7. For more on the Jungle Aviation and Radio Service, see Jamie Buckingham *Into the Glory* (Plainfield, N.J.: Logos International, 1974).

Chapter 10

1. From "What is Mission All About?", an address given April 7, 1974.

2. From an unpublished manuscript of Joe Grimes.

3. From David Bendor-Samuel, *Hierarchical Structures in Guajajara,* a doctoral thesis at the University of London, 1966, Summer Institute of Linguistics Publications in Linguistics and Related Fields, Publication Number 37, Irvine Davis, ed. (Norman, Oklahoma: Summer Institute of Linguistics of the University of Oklahoma, 1972).

Chapter 11

1. William M. Ramsay in *St. Paul, the Traveller and Roman Citizen* (Grand Rapids, Michigan: Baker Book House, 1962), pp. 310-312, suggests Paul may have been helped by a private inheritance at the end of his ministry.

Chapter 12

1. See Ralph D. Winter, *Penetrating the Last Frontier* (Pasadena, California: U. S. Center for World Mission, 1978), pp. 11-12.

2. R. Longacre, *Grammar Discovery Procedures: A Field Manual* (The Hague: Mouton, 1964) is one such text written by a member for use in our courses.

3. Helpful suggestions on language learning by gesture are given in the appendix to *Language Learner's Field Guide* by Alan Healey, ed., (Papua New Guinea: Summer Institute of Linguistics). This was prepared especially for linguistic field workers studying unwritten languages.

4. For the technical data, see C. R. Rensch *Comparative Otomanguean Phonology,* Indiana University Publications, Language Science Monographs, Vol. 14 (Bloomington: Indiana University, 1976).

5. For some of the concepts being applied, see J. Grimes, *The Thread of Discourse,* No. 1, National Science Foundation Grant GS-3180 (Ithaca: Cornell University, 1972), and C. Callow, *Discourse Considerations in Translating the Word of God* (Grand Rapids, Michigan: Zondervan, 1974).

6. See J. Samuel Hofman, "The Story of a White Elephant" in *Missionary Monthly, A Reformed Mission Magazine,* (August 1977).

7. For the life story of this remarkable woman see Ethel M. Wallis, *God Speaks Navajo* (New York: Harper and Row, 1968).

Chapter 13

1. For example, field teams from Gospel Recordings, Inc., pacesetters in pioneering the Gospel message in lan-

guages that have never heard it, have often furnished us information and spurred us on to translate. Our work in the Pacific began as a response to their presentation of the language situation and translation need in the Philippines. For our latest cumulative listing of languages needing translation, see Chapter 1, note 2.

2. See Eugene H. Casad, *Dialect Intelligibility Testing,* Summer Institute of Linguistics Publications in Linguistics and Related Fields (Dallas: Summer Institute of Linguistics, 1974).

Chapter 14

1. K. S. Latourette, *A History of Christianity* (New York: Harper and Row, 1953), p. 351.

2. For a fuller description of the activities of the Wycliffe Associates, see James C. Hefley, *God's Free Lancers* (Orange, California: Wycliffe Associates, Inc., 1978).

Chapter 15

1. Statement by Dr. Kenneth L. Pike.

Chapter 16

1. See Eunice V. Pike, *Words Wanted* (Chicago: Moody Press, 1958).

2. Based on an unpublished thesis by Tom Headland, "Wycliffe Bible Translators and Church Growth in the Philippines."

3. From "Language and Man's Dignity" by Francisco Miro Quesada in *Gente,* Lima, March 17, 1978. Translated from the Spanish.

4. For fuller accounts, see Sanna Barlow Rossi, *God's City in the Jungle* (Huntington Beach, Califonia: Wycliffe Bible Translators, 1975), and Albert J. Solnit, *Bilingual Education and Community Development in the Amazon* (Peru: Ministry of Public Education, 1966).

INDEX